Culture Wise
AMERICA

The Essential Guide to Culture, Customs & Business Etiquette

David Hampshire & Anthony Poulton-Smith

Survival Books • London • England

First published 2009

Survival Books Limited
26 York Street, London W1U 6PZ, United Kingdom
☎ +44 (0)20-7788 7644, 📄 +44 (0)870-762 3212
✉ info@survivalbooks.net
🖥 www.survivalbooks.net

British Library Cataloguing in Publication Data.
A CIP record for this book is available
from the British Library.
ISBN: 978 -1-905303-20-5

Printed and bound in India by Ajanta Offset

ACKNOWLEDGEMENTS

The authors would like to thank their many friends, family members and colleagues – unfortunately too many to mention – who provided information for this book. We would particularly like to thank Robbi Forrester Atilgan for her research and editing, without whom this book would never have seen the light of day, Peter Read for additional editing, Rachel Wright for final checks, Lilac Johnson for proof-reading, Di Tolland for DTP and photo selection, and Jim Watson for the cover design, maps and cartoons.

Finally, a special thank you to all the photographers (listed on page 270) – the unsung heroes – whose beautiful images add colour and bring America to life.

THE AUTHORS

David Hampshire: David was born in England and after serving in the Royal Air Force, was employed for many years in the computer industry. His work has taken him around the world and he has lived and worked in many countries, including Australia, France, Germany, Malaysia, the Netherlands, Panama, Singapore, Spain, Switzerland and the USA. David has been a full-time author since 1990 and is the author, co-author or editor of over 20 titles, including *Buying a Home in Florida* and *Living and Working in America*. David lives with his partner in England and Panama, and is a frequent visitor to the USA.

Anthony Poulton-Smith: After a few years grammar school, Anthony shunned further education in the pursuit of 'real' knowledge – not to mention a little spending money! After almost 20 years in light engineering, he began writing full-time in 1991 and since then has had over 450 articles and eight books published (mostly on the origin of place names), together with innumerable crosswords and puzzles. In his 'spare' time he has educated his two children at home, dabbles in professional landscape gardening to maintain his fitness, and gives talks in person and on radio around the subject of place-name origins.

When in the UK, Anthony's home is in Tamworth in Staffordshire, where locals are know as 'Tammies', while in his home across the pond in Detroit (Michigan) he becomes a 'Wolverine' (despite the fact that there hasn't been a single sighting of this animal in the state for over 120 years!).

What readers & reviewers have said about Survival Books:

'If you need to find out how France works then this book is indispensable. Native French people probably have a less thorough understanding of how their country functions.'

Living France

'It's everything you always wanted to ask but didn't for fear of the contemptuous put down. The best English-language guide. Its pages are stuffed with practical information on everyday subjects and are designed to compliment the traditional guidebook.'

Swiss News

'Rarely has a 'survival guide' contained such useful advice – This book dispels doubts for first-time travellers, yet is also useful for seasoned globetrotters – In a word, if you're planning to move to the US or go there for a long-term stay, then buy this book both for general reading and as a ready-reference.'

American Citizens Abroad

'Let's say it at once. David Hampshire's Living and Working in France is the best handbook ever produced for visitors and foreign residents in this country; indeed, my discussion with locals showed that it has much to teach even those born and bred in l'Hexagone – It is Hampshire's meticulous detail which lifts his work way beyond the range of other books with similar titles. Often you think of a supplementary question and search for the answer in vain. With Hampshire this is rarely the case. – He writes with great clarity (and gives French equivalents of all key terms), a touch of humour and a ready eye for the odd (and often illuminating) fact. – This book is absolutely indispensable.'

The Riviera Reporter

'A must for all future expats. I invested in several books but this is the only one you need. Every issue and concern is covered, every daft question you have but are frightened to ask is answered honestly without pulling any punches. Highly recommended.'

Reader

'In answer to the desert island question about the one how-to book on France, this book would be it.'

The Recorder

'The ultimate reference book. Every subject imaginable is exhaustively explained in simple terms. An excellent introduction to fully enjoy all that this fine country has to offer and save time and money in the process.'

American Club of Zurich

'The amount of information covered is not short of incredible. I thought I knew enough about my birth country. This book has proved me wrong. Don't go to France without it. Big mistake if you do. Absolutely priceless!'

Reader

'When you buy a model plane for your child, a video recorder, or some new computer gizmo, you get with it a leaflet or booklet pleading 'Read Me First', or bearing large friendly letters or bold type saying 'IMPORTANT - follow the instructions carefully'. This book should be similarly supplied to all those entering France with anything more durable than a 5-day return ticket. – It is worth reading even if you are just visiting briefly, or if you have lived here for years and feel totally knowledgeable and secure. But if you need to find out how France works then it is indispensable. Native French people probably have a less thorough understanding of how their country functions. – Where it is most essential, the book is most up to the minute.

Living France

A comprehensive guide to all things French, written in a highly readable and amusing style, for anyone planning to live, work or retire in France.

The Times

Covers every conceivable question that might be asked concerning everyday life – I know of no other book that could take the place of this one.

France in Print

A concise, thorough account of the Do's and DONT's for a foreigner in Switzerland – Crammed with useful information and lightened with humorous quips which make the facts more readable.

American Citizens Abroad

'I found this a wonderful book crammed with facts and figures, with a straightforward approach to the problems and pitfalls you are likely to encounter. The whole laced with humour and a thorough understanding of what's involved. Gets my vote!'

Reader

'A vital tool in the war against real estate sharks; don't even think of buying without reading this book first!'

Everything Spain

'We would like to congratulate you on this work: it is really super! We hand it out to our expatriates and they read it with great interest and pleasure.'

ICI (Switzerland) AG

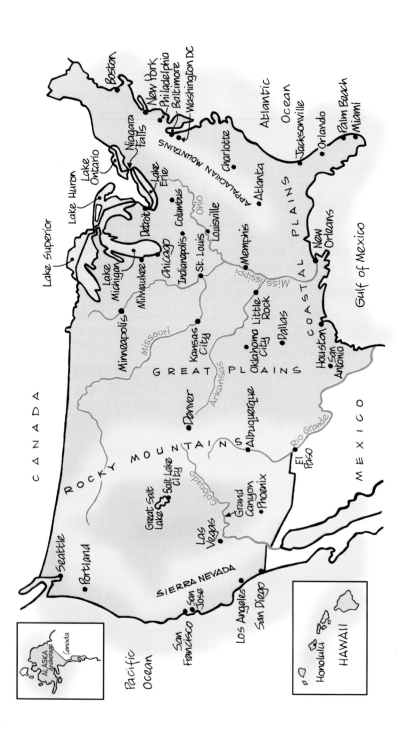

CONTENTS

1. A CHANGE OF CULTURE — **13**

America is different	13
Culture shock	15
Families in America	22
A multicultural society	23
A new life	23

2. WHO ARE THE AMERICANS? — **27**

A potted history	28
The people	35
Sense of humour	38
Children	40
The class system	41
Attitudes to foreigners	42
Icons	43

3. GETTING STARTED — **65**

Immigration	65
Bureaucracy	67
Accommodation	68
Buying or hiring a car	71
Emergency services	73
Health services	74
Insurance	78
Education	79
Council services	83
Utilities	84
Staying informed	87
Banking	90
Taxes	92
Cost of living	93

4. BREAKING THE ICE — **97**

Community life	97
Sexual attitudes	98
Meeting people	101
Invitations	105

Respecting privacy 107
Taboos 108
Expat community 110
Confrontation 111
Dealing with officials 112

5. THE LANGUAGE BARRIER **115**

Learning American English 115
The English language 117
Other languages 119
Slang & swearing 123
Body & sign language 124
Forms of address 126
Greetings 128
Telephone, letters & email 129

6. THE AMERICANS AT WORK **133**

Work ethic 133
Permits & paperwork 134
Finding a job 135
Contracts 140
Starting or buying a business 140
Black economy 144
Working women 144
Business etiquette 145
Employing people 148
Trade unions 149
Working week 149

7. ON THE MOVE **155**

Driving 155
Public transport 162
Hitchhiking 168
Cycling 168
Accommodation 169

8. THE AMERICANS AT PLAY **171**

Dress code 171
Eating 173
Drinking 179
Cafes, restaurants & diners 181

Nightlife   183
Family occasions   184
Clubs   190
Popular culture   190

9. RETAIL THERAPY   **199**

Customer service   199
Opening hours   200
Black market   201
Queuing   201
Sales & discounts   201
Types of shop   203
Markets   204
Paying   205
Food & wine   206
Clothes   208
Collectables   210
Mail-order shopping   211
Returning goods   212

10. ODDS & ENDS   **215**

Geography   215
Climate   216
Crime   219
Flag & anthem   220
Government   222
International relations   225
Religion   227
Military service   227
Pets   228
Time difference   228
Tipping   229
Toilets   230

APPENDICES   **233**

Appendix A: Embassies & Consulates   233
Appendix B: Further Reading   235
Appendix C: Useful Websites   239
Appendix D: American Idioms   247
Appendix E: Map of States   254

INDEX   **257**

Statue of Liberty, NY

INTRODUCTION

I f you're planning a trip to America or just want to learn more about the country, you'll find the information contained in *Culture Wise America* invaluable. Whether you're travelling on business or pleasure, visiting for a few days or planning to stay for a lifetime, Culture Wise guides enable you to quickly find your feet by removing the anxiety factor when dealing with a foreign culture.

Adjusting to a different environment and culture in any foreign country can be a traumatic and stressful experience, and the US is no exception. You need to adapt to new customs and traditions, and discover the American way of doing things; whether it's sharing a few Buds and dogs with your buddies at a ball game; enjoying a neigbourhood BBQ of hog, mutton or ribs, followed by Key lime or pumpkin pie; or a family brunch of bagels, lox, cream cheese and capers – everything in America seems to come with food.

America is a land where many things are done differently: where people drive enormous autos on vast super highways with a dozen lanes, and traffic may join or exit from the left- or the right-hand lane; where people drink iced tea, root beer and bourbon, and eat chitlins, cornbread, hominy grits and black-eyed peas; where you need a few lifetimes to understand ball games such as baseball and gridiron (but can still enjoy them); and where patriotism is a way of life and it's a felony to insult Old Glory (the US flag).

Culture Wise America is essential reading for anyone planning to visit the US, including tourists (particularly travellers planning to stay a number of weeks or months), business people, migrants, retirees, holiday homeowners and transferees. It's designed to help newcomers avoid cultural and social gaffes; make friends and influence people; improve communications (both verbal and non-verbal); and enhance your understanding of America and the American people. It explains what to expect, how to behave in most situations, and how to get along with the locals and feel at home – rather than feeling like a fish out of water. It isn't, however, simply a monologue of dry facts and figures, but a practical and entertaining look at life in America – as it really is – and not necessarily as the tourist brochures would have you believe.

A period spent in America is a wonderful way to enrich your life, broaden your horizons, and hopefully expand your circle of friends. We trust this book will help you avoid the pitfalls of visiting or living in America and smooth your way to a happy and rewarding stay.

Good luck!   *David Hampshire & Anthony Poulton-Smith*

February 2009

American flag & Constitution

1.

A CHANGE OF CULTURE

With almost daily advances in technology, ever-cheaper flights and knowledge about almost anywhere in the world at our fingertips, travelling, living, working and retiring abroad have never been more accessible, and current migration patterns suggest that it has never been more popular. However,, although globalisation means the world has 'shrunk', every country is still a world of its own with a unique culture. Some people find it impossible to adapt to a new life in a different culture – for reasons which are many and varied. According to statistics, partner dissatisfaction is the most common cause; as non-working spouses frequently find themselves without a role in the new country and sometimes with little to do other than think about what they would be doing if they were at home. Family concerns – which may include the children's education and worries about loved ones at home – can also deeply affect those living abroad.

> 'There are no foreign lands. It is the traveller only who is foreign.'
> Robert Louis Stevenson (Scottish writer)

Many factors contribute to how well you adapt to a new culture – for example, your personality, education, language skills, mental health, maturity, socio-economic situation, travel experience, and family and social support systems. How you handle the stress of change and bring balance and meaning to your life is the principal indicator of how well you'll adjust to a different country, culture and business environment.

AMERICA IS DIFFERENT

Many people underestimate the cultural isolation that can be experienced in a foreign country. Even in a country where you speak the language fluently, you'll find that many aspects of the culture are surprisingly foreign (despite the cosy familiarity engendered by cinema, television and books).

Everyone thinks that they know America. Its presence is all-pervasive, in newspapers and magazines, on television and the cinema screen; it even influences much of the clothing we wear, the cars we drive and the food we eat. US politics have more effect on other nations than do those of any other country on earth. However, thinking you know a country and actually living there are two completely different things, and there are many facets of US life which are quite different from those at home. Of course, if 'home' is in China, Africa or parts of the Middle East, then life in the US may feel very alien indeed.

One of the most unsettling aspects of America is its sheer scale. It's a nation which crosses four time zones (six if you count Alaska and Hawaii), where it can take over three days' non-stop driving to travel from the east coast to the west. In spite of its crowded metropolises, much of the country is wilderness and sparsely populated, and the people who live in its rural heartland are very different from the city slickers of New York or Los Angeles.

The United States of America, as its name suggests, is a federation of smaller states. Its people speak the same language – more or less – although those from New England and the Deep South may occasionally struggle to understand each other (not to mention all those who don't speak English at all). Each state also has its own rules and laws. You can settle in one area, then move to another, and almost feel as though you've moved to a completely different country. You may have to learn a new set of driving rules, and maybe even take another driver's test. And, if you're working in, say, teaching or hairdressing, you may need to obtain a new license before you can work in the new state.

The British and Europeans have a close, although not always comfortable, relationship with America. They discovered the New World only to be shown the door when America asserted its independence in 1776, yet since then they have fought alongside each other in wartime, traded widely in peacetime, and the US has opened its doors to immigrants from across the European continent.

Some Americans look to Europe as the fount of all culture; at the same time, there are older US citizens who consider

Europeans to be aloof and snobbish or, worse, left wing bureaucrats, while many Europeans regard Americans as right wing, loud, brash and uncouth.

Americans tend to live by the clock and measure success by achievement, and this attitude is very different from societies where time spent in contemplation is just as valuable as time spent closing a deal. People from Eastern and Middle Eastern cultures may find US life uncomfortably materialistic and fast. Immigrants from societies where family is the central core of life may struggle to understand how an American family, while professing to be close, lives in separate cities, watches television in separate rooms and eats at different times of the day.

Before you try to get to grips with American culture, however, you first need to adapt to a totally new environment and new challenges, which may include a new job, a new home and a new physical environment – which can be overwhelming.

America has many extremes of climate and weather, and you mustn't underestimate the effects that these can have on you. Extreme conditions of heat and cold can lead to a lack of energy, poor sleep and dehydration. In the summer in the southern states, temperatures regularly rise to a physically draining 120°F (50°C), while winters bring freezing conditions and heavy snowfalls to the Midwest and northern states. Dangerous weather phenomena such as tornadoes, hurricanes and hailstones the size of golf balls are an accepted part of life in some parts of the US, where weather patterns are far less predictable than they are, for example, in Europe.

Those who move to a new job or attempt to start a business in America may encounter a (very) steep learning curve – indeed, even finding a job can be a struggle, as you'll be up against a population which lives to work rather than working to live. The chances are that you've left a job in your home country where you held a senior position, were extremely competent and knew all your colleagues. In America, you may be virtually a trainee (especially if your English isn't fluent) and not know any of your colleagues. The sensation that you're starting from scratch can be demoralising.

Even if you move to a part of the US with a large expatriate community – such as Los Angeles or New York – items that you're used to and took for granted in your home country may not be available, e.g. certain kinds of food, opportunities to engage in your favourite hobby or sport, and books and magazines in your language. The lack of 'home comforts' can wear you down. You'll also have to contend with the lack of a local support network; at home you had a circle of friends, acquaintances, colleagues and possibly relatives you could rely on for help

and support. In America, there may be no such network, which can leave you feeling lost.

The degree of isolation you feel usually depends on how long you plan to spend in America and what you'll be doing there. If you're simply on a short holiday, you may not even be aware of many of the cultural differences; although if you are, it will enhance your enjoyment and may save you a few embarrassing or confusing moments. However, if you're planning a business trip, or intend to spend an extended period in the US, perhaps working, studying or even living there permanently, **it's essential to understand the culture, customs and etiquette at the earliest opportunity.**

> **'If you reject the food, ignore the customs, fear the religion and avoid the people, you might better stay at home.'**
>
> James A Michener (American writer)

CULTURE SHOCK

Culture shock is the term used to describe the psychological and physical state felt by people when travelling, living, working or studying abroad, or even moving to a new environment in their home country (where the culture may vary considerably by region and social class). Culture shock can also be regarded as the period of adjustment to a new country or environment, where, in addition to adapting to new social rules, rules of behaviour and values, you may also need to adjust to a different climate, food and dress. It manifests itself in a lack of direction and the feeling of not knowing what to do or how to do things, and not knowing what's appropriate or inappropriate. You literally feel like a 'fish out of water'.

Culture shock is precipitated by the anxiety that results from losing all familiar rules of behaviour and symbols of social intercourse. These rules and symbols are the thousand and one ways in which we orient ourselves to the situations of daily life: when to shake hands and what to say when we meet people; when and how to tip; how to give orders to staff or employees; how to buy goods and services; how to use a cash machine or the telephone; when to accept and refuse invitations; and when to take statements seriously and when not to. These cues, which may be verbal, gestures, or facial or hand expressions, are acquired in the course of our life, and are as much a part of our culture and customs as the language we speak or our beliefs. Our peace of mind and efficiency depends on hundreds of these cues, most of which are unconsciously learned.

The symptoms are essentially psychological – although you can experience real pain from culture shock – and are caused by the sense of alienation you feel when you're bombarded on a daily basis with cultural differences in an environment where there are few, if any, familiar references. However, there are also physical symptoms that may manifest themselves in the form of an increased incidence of minor illnesses (e.g. colds and headaches), or more serious psychosomatic illnesses brought on by depression. You shouldn't underestimate the consequences of culture shock, although the effects can be lessened if you accept the condition rather than deny it.

Stages of Culture Shock

Severe culture shock – often experienced when moving to a new country with a different language – usually follows a number of stages (the names of which may vary) and forms, but is typically as follows:

1. The first stage is known as the 'honeymoon' stage, and usually lasts from a few days to a few weeks after arrival (although it can last longer, particularly if you're insulated from the usual pressures of life). This stage is essentially a positive (even euphoric) one, when a newcomer finds everything is an exciting and interesting novelty. The feeling is similar to being on holiday; therefore, when you're on holiday or a short trip abroad, you generally experience only the positive effects of culture shock (although this depends very much on where you're from and the country you're visiting – see '**Paris Syndrome**' box).

Paris Syndrome

A dozen or so Japanese tourists a year have to be repatriated from the French capital, after falling prey to what's become known as the 'Paris Syndrome'. This is what some polite Japanese tourists suffer when they discover that Parisians can be rude or that the city doesn't meet their expectations. The experience can apparently be so stressful for some people that they suffer a psychiatric breakdown and need to be hospitalised or repatriated under medical supervision.

2. The second (rejection or distress) stage is usually completely opposite to the first; and is essentially negative, and a period of crisis as the initial excitement and holiday feeling wears off, and you start to cope with the real conditions of daily life – except, of course, life is nothing like anything you have previously experienced. This can happen after only a few weeks, and is characterised by a general feeling of disorientation, confusion and loneliness. Physical exhaustion brought on by jet lag, extremes of hot or cold, and the strain of having hundreds of settling-in tasks to accomplish is an important symptom of this stage.

   You may also experience regression, where you spend much of your time speaking your own language, watching television and videos, and reading newspapers from your home country, eating food from home and socialising with expatriates who speak your own language. You may also spend a lot of time complaining about the host country and its culture.

   Your home environment suddenly assumes a tremendous importance and is irrationally glorified. All difficulties and problems are forgotten, and only the good things back home are remembered.

3. The third stage is often known as the 'flight stage' (because of the overwhelming desire to escape), and is usually the one that lasts the longest and is the most difficult to cope with. During this period you may feel depressed and angry, as well as resentful towards the new country and its people. It may include difficulties such as not being understood, and feelings of discontent, impatience, anger, sadness and incompetence. This is inevitable when you're trying to adapt to a new culture that's very different from your home country.

   Depression is exacerbated because at this stage you can see nothing positive or good about the new country and focus exclusively on the negative aspects, refusing to acknowledge any positive points. You may become hostile and develop an aggressive attitude towards the country.

   Other people will sense this and, in many cases, either respond in a confrontational manner or try to avoid you. There may be problems with the language, your house, job or children's school, transportation … even simple tasks like shopping may be fraught with problems, and the fact that the local people are largely indifferent to all these problems only makes matter worse.

They try to help but they just don't understand your concerns, and you conclude that they must be insensitive and unsympathetic to you and your problems. The transition between your old culture and customs and those of your new country is a difficult process and takes time to complete, during which there can be strong feelings of dissatisfaction.

The period of readjustment can last as long as six months, although there are expatriates who adjust earlier and (although rare) those who never get over the 'flight' stage and are forced to return home.

What are the most annoying aspects of living in America? The following comments (in no particular order) are taken from expatriate web logs.

1. Healthcare – and the need for very expensive insurance.
2. The way that rules and regulations change from state to state.
3. Disregard for other nations.
4. Tacky television and the endless ads.
5. Tipping – even when the service is bad.
6. Tasteless beer.
7. Fast 'junk' food with no flavour and vast portions.
8. Total reliance on cars.
9. Poor work-life balance.
10. Overweening patriotism.

---

accept the customs of the country as simply another way of living. **The environment doesn't change – what changes is your attitude towards it.** You become more competent with the language, and you also feel more comfortable with the customs of the host country and can move around without feeling anxiety. However, you still have problems with some of the social cues, and you won't understand everything people say (particularly colloquialisms and idioms).

Nevertheless, you have largely adjusted to the new culture, and start to feel more at home and familiar with the country and your place in it, and begin to realise that it has its good and bad points.

The same web logs reveal that however much expats may complain about America, they also have some valid reasons for loving the place:

1. Friendliness and welcoming attitude.
2. The 'can-do' attitude and belief that 'anything is possible.'
3. Wide variety of entertainment.
4. Lower cost of living.
5. Customer service with a smile.
6. Diversity and equality.
7. Wide open spaces and great national parks.
8. The 24-hour culture.
9. Freedom of choice.
10. People's pride in their country.

---

4. The fourth (recovery or autonomy) stage is where you begin to integrate and adjust to the new culture, and

5. The fifth stage is termed 'reverse culture shock' and occurs when you return to your home

country. Depending on how long you've been away, you may find that many things have changed (you'll also have changed) and that you feel like a foreigner in you own country. If you've been away for a long time and have become comfortable with the habits and customs of a new lifestyle, you may find that you no longer feel at ease in your homeland. Reverse culture shock can be difficult to deal with, and some people find it impossible to re-adapt to their home country after living abroad for a number of years.

The above stages are present at different times, and everyone has their own way of reacting to them, with the result that some stages are longer and more difficult than others, while others are shorter and easier to cope with.

Reducing the Effects

Experts agree that almost everyone suffers from culture shock, and there's no escaping the phenomenon; however, its negative effects can be reduced considerably, and there are certain things you can do before leaving home:

● **Positive attitude.** The key to reducing the negative effects of culture shock is a positive attitude towards America (whether you're visiting or planning to live there) – if you don't look forward to a holiday or relocation, you should question why you're doing it! There's no greater guarantee of unhappiness in a foreign environment than taking your prejudices with you. It's important when trying to adapt to a new culture to be sensitive to the locals' feelings, and to try to put yourself in their shoes wherever possible, which will help you understand why they react as they do. Bear in mind that Americans have a strong, in-bred cultural code, just as you do, and react in certain ways because they're culturally 'trained' to do so. If you find yourself frustrated by an aspect of the local culture or behaviour, the chances are that they will be equally puzzled by yours!

● **Research** – Discover as much as possible about America before you go, so that your arrival and settling-in period doesn't spring as many surprises as it might otherwise. Reading up on the US and its culture before you leave home will help you familiarise yourself with the local customs, and make the country and its people seem less strange on arrival. You'll be aware of many of the differences in America and be better prepared to deal with them. This will help you avoid being upset by real or imaginary cultural slights and also reduce the chance of your offending the locals by cultural misunderstandings. Being prepared for a certain amount of disorientation and confusion (or worse) makes it easier to cope with it. There are literally hundreds of publications about the US as well as dozens of websites for expatriates (see **Appendices B** and **C**). Many sites provide access to expatriates already living in America, who can answer questions and provide useful advice. There are also 'notice boards' and 'forums' on many websites, where you can post messages or questions.

● **Visit America first.** If you're planning to live or work in America for a number of years or even permanently, it's important to visit the country to see whether you think you would enjoy living there and be able to cope with the culture before making the leap. Before you go, try to find someone in your local area who has visited the US – or, even better, lived and worked there – and talk to them about it. Some companies organise briefings for families before departure. Rent a property before buying a home and don't burn your bridges until you're sure that you have made the correct decision.

● **Learn the language.** As well as a positive attitude, overcoming the language barrier will probably be the most decisive factor in combating culture shock and enjoying your time in America. The ability to speak English isn't just a practical and useful tool (the one that will allow you to buy what you need, find your way around, etc.), but the key to understanding a country and its culture. If you can speak the language, even at a low level, your scope for making friends is immediately widened beyond the usual limited expatriate circle. Obviously not everyone is a linguist, and learning a language can take time and requires motivation. However, with sufficient perseverance virtually anyone can learn enough of another language to participate in the local culture.

Certainly the effort will pay off, and expatriates who manage to overcome the language barrier find their experience in America much richer and more rewarding than those who don't. America is unusual

Honolulu, Hawaii

in the allowances it makes towards people who don't speak English. Many government and state organisations make information available in a wide range of languages, and in parts of the US, Spanish is as widely spoken as English. However, on a social and work level, you'll find it difficult to get close to people if you don't speak English. If you make an effort at communicating with the local people in their own language, you'll also find them far more receptive to you and your needs.

While it may seem odd to forewarn English speakers of a language barrier when thinking about living and working in the US, there are many differences between Standard English and American English, in terms of pronunciation, grammar and terminology – see **Appendix D** for a few examples – and it's important to be aware of these differences. Even within the US, there are a surprising number of differences between the northern and southern states (and, to a lesser degree, east and west). You cannot be expected to recognise and learn every regional nuance in grammar and dialect – even the Americans don't – but you should be aware that they exist.

> '**Americans who travel abroad for the first time are often shocked to discover that, despite all the progress that has been made in the last 30 years, many foreign people still speak in foreign languages.**'
>
> Dave Barry (American writer & humorist)

● **Be proactive** – Make an effort to get involved in your new culture,

and go out of your way to make friends. Join in the activities of local people, which could be a religious holiday, local festival or social activity. Americans will make an effort to invite you to events, although this doesn't mean they regard you as friends – true friendship takes time. In some areas of the US, people are more welcoming to outsiders; in others, they may take time to get to know and trust you. Americans like people who 'join in' and there are often local clubs where you can engage in sport or keep fit, draw and paint, learn to cook regional dishes, make handicrafts, etc. Volunteering is an important activity – around a quarter of people give up some of their time to a good cause – and there are many groups where you can volunteer. Not only will this fill some of your spare time, giving you less time to miss home, but you'll also meet people and make new friends.

If you feel you cannot join a local club, perhaps because the language barrier is too great, then you can always participate in activities for expatriates, of which there are many in the most popular destinations. Look upon a period spent abroad as an opportunity to redefine your life objectives and acquire new perspectives. Culture shock can help you develop a better understanding of yourself and stimulate your creativity.

● **Talk to other expatriates** – Although they may deny it, they've all been through exactly what you're experiencing, and faced the same feelings of disorientation.

Even if they cannot provide you with advice, it helps to know that you aren't alone and that it gets better over time. However, don't make the mistake of mixing only with expatriates, as this will alienate you from the local culture and make it much harder to integrate. Don't rely on social contact with your compatriots to carry you through, because it won't.

- **Keep in touch with home** – Staying in touch with your family and friends at home and around the world by telephone, email and mail will help reduce and overcome the effects of culture shock.

- **Be happy** – Don't rely others to make you happy, otherwise you won't find true and lasting happiness. There are things in life which you can change, and if you need them to change you must do it yourself. Every day we are surrounded by things over which we have little or no control, and to wail about them only makes us unhappier. So be your own best friend and nurture your own capacity for happiness.

Culture shock is an unavoidable part of travelling, living and working abroad, but if you're aware of it and take steps to lessen its effects before you go and while you're abroad, the period of adjustment will be shortened and its negative and depressing consequences reduced.

FAMILIES IN AMERICA

Family life may be completely different in the US, and relationships can become strained under the stress of adapting to culture shock. Your family may find itself in a completely new and possibly alien environment, your new home may scarcely resemble your previous one (it may be much more luxurious or significantly smaller), and the climate may be dramatically different from that of your home country. If possible, you should prepare yourself for as many aspects of the new situation as you can, and explain to your children the differences that they're likely to encounter, while at the same time dispelling their fears.

Culture shock can affect non-working spouses and children more than working spouses. The husband (though it could equally be the wife in equality-conscious America) has his work to occupy him, and his activities may not differ much from what he had been accustomed to at home. On the other hand, the wife may have to operate in a totally new environment that differs considerably from what she's used to. She will find herself alone more often, a solitude intensified by the fact that there are no close relatives or friends on hand. However, if you're aware that this may arise beforehand, you can act on it and reduce its effects. Working spouses should pay special attention to the needs and feelings of their non-working partners and children, as the success of a family relocation often depends on the ability of the wife and children to adapt to the new culture.

Good communication between family members is vital, and you should make time to discuss your experiences and feelings, both as a couple and as a family. Questions should always be raised and, if possible answered, particularly when asked by children. However difficult the situation may appear at the beginning, it will help to bear in mind that it's by no means unique; and that most expatriate families experience exactly the same problems, and manage to triumph over them and enjoy their stay abroad.

> Children can find their lives radically altered by a move to America. American children appear to have more freedom and possessions than those in other countries, but they also face more pressure – from their peers, their parents, their teachers and society as a whole. Teenagers from a more family-orientated country may struggle to find acceptance in a large US high school, especially if their language skills are shaky, and they will need plenty of support at home.

A MULTICULTURAL SOCIETY

The good news for newcomers is that America is a multicultural society, where people from many nationalities live, work and play together in harmony. This has not only greatly enriched the American way of life and added to its diverse range of foods, religions, businesses and ideas, but makes it much easier for immigrants to integrate into society. Virtually all ethnic groups in America maintain active clubs and societies where newcomers are warmly welcomed.

Coined in Canada in the '70s, multiculturalism is an ideology of racial, cultural and ethnic diversity, and its policies advocate that immigrants can integrate into society while retaining and valuing the most important elements of their own culture (including speaking their own language and teaching it to their children where applicable). In America, migrants are encouraged to maintain ties with their homeland and its culture – rather than abandon them – while simultaneously being urged to embrace US values, including introducing foreign cultural ideas. Consequently, America has one of the most ethnically diverse societies in the world, and a low level of inter-ethnic conflict and high levels of cooperation. Intermarriage between different ethnic groups is high, and extends to indigenous and non-indigenous people.

A NEW LIFE

Although you may find some of the information in this chapter a bit daunting, don't be discouraged by the foregoing negative aspects of travelling and living in America; these have only been highlighted in order to help you prepare and adjust to a new life. The vast majority of people who travel and live abroad naturally occasionally experience feelings of discomfort and disorientation, **but most never suffer the most debilitating effects of culture shock.**

As with settling in and making friends anywhere, even in your home country, the most important thing is to be considerate, kind, open and genuine – qualities that are valued the world over. Selfishness, rudeness and arrogance will get you nowhere in America or in any other country. Treat the US and its people with respect, and they will do likewise.

The majority of people living in a foreign land would agree that, all things considered, they love living there – and are in no hurry to return home. A period spent abroad is a wonderful way to enrich your life, broaden your horizons, make new friends and maybe even please your bank manager. The authors and publisher trust that this book will help you to avoid some of the pitfalls of life abroad and smooth your way to a happy and rewarding future in your new home.

> **'Twenty years from now you will be more disappointed by the things you didn't do than by the ones you did do. So throw off the bowlines. Sail away from the safe harbour. Catch the trade winds in your sails. Explore. Dream. Discover.'**
>
> Mark Twain (American writer)

Antelope Canyon, Arizona

2.

WHO ARE THE AMERICANS?

Biggest, loudest, fastest, richest, strongest, brashest, fattest – America is the land of the superlative, the nation to which much of the rest of the world is constantly comparing itself. America is a place of extremes, where the climate seesaws from heat wave to snowbound, even in the same city, and the environment ranges from overcrowded cities to unpopulated wilderness. It's the home of innovation and invention, and the birthplace of many great pioneers in the arts, entertainment, industry and sport. However, it also spawned junk food, soap operas and political correctness, and is home to some of the most self-absorbed people on the planet.

> 'America is a vast conspiracy to make you happy.'
> John Updike (American novelist)

Americans are overtly patriotic, and most believe that their country really is the Promised Land. Not everyone agrees. Some people in Europe, Asia and the Middle East regard today's US as a beached whale, and a fading player on the world's stage. However, their disdain is tinged with envy, since even its detractors cannot deny its influence, and America is still the number-one destination for many would-be emigrants from across the globe.

Almost since it was discovered, some 500 years ago, America has been a magnet for travellers seeking a better life. The first settlers began arriving from Europe in the 16th century – with Spain, Britain, France and the Netherlands leading the way. They brought with them slaves from Africa, and were followed by many more waves of immigrants – the Irish in the 19th century, Jews and Eastern Europeans in the wake of the Second World War and, more recently, economic migrants from Latin America and Asia. By the 21st century, every nation on Earth has at least one community somewhere within the 50 states.

As a result of such sustained foreign invasion, the US is one of the most culturally diverse nations in the world. Americans are fiercely proud of their heritage – or their heritages – and of the fact that their 'land of opportunity' still offers incomers a great chance for success, even though strict immigration controls mean it's no longer so easy to join the club.

Not everyone wants to live in America, but many desire to visit. In recent years, the advent of cheaper flights, and the weakening of the

Demographics

Full country name: United States of America

Capital city: Washington, DC

Population: 306m

Population density: 31 people per km² (80 per mi²). New York City has a population density of 10,300 per km² (26,700 per mi²).

Largest cities: There are nine cities with a population exceeding 1mn – New York City (8.1mn), Los Angeles (3.8mn), Chicago (2.8mn), Houston (2.0mn), Philadelphia and Phoenix (1.5mn), San Antonio and San Diego (1.3mn) and Dallas (1.2mn).

Race: Caucasians 74 per cent; African-Americans 12 per cent; Asians, Native Americans and others 14 per cent. Hispanic people (white and black) account for 12 per cent of the population.

Foreign population: 37mn people were born outside the US. Of these, 52 per cent are from Latin America, 27 per cent from Asia and 15 per cent from Europe. The remainder are from Africa, Oceania – and Canada.

Largest expatriate groups: Mexicans, Puerto Ricans, Cubans

State religion: The US is a secular country – the First Amendment to the Constitution guarantees the right to freedom of religion for everyone.

Most popular religion: Just over 75 per cent of Americans are Christian, while other religions such as Judaism, Islam, Buddhism and Hinduism account for less than 4 per cent; some 14 per cent of people claim no religion.

tourist destination in the world, with over 50mn arrivals in 2007. Many foreigners also buy American property, with Florida and California especially popular with investors. What appeals to them is the American Dream, which is a tantalising promise of the freedom to do what you want to do and the prosperity to afford it. Whether your stay in the US is long or short – and whether or not you live the Dream – the experience is sure to be unforgettable.

To help you understand America and the Americans, this chapter provides information about the country's history, the characteristics of its people, and the icons which mostly aptly represent it.

A POTTED HISTORY

Although man has lived on American soil for thousands of years, there's a distinct line between the history of the country's indigenous people and modern recorded history – and that line was drawn late in the 15th century, when the continent was 'discovered' by Columbus. A colossal amount of change has taken place at a breathtaking pace in just over 500 years, the main events of which are listed below.

Indigenous People

ca 20,000 BC – Man begins migrating to the North American continent from Asia on a land bridge across the Bering Strait. This first wave of immigration by Asiatic people to the New World continues without pause until the route is cut off by a rise in sea levels at the end of the last Ice Age, 11,000 years ago.

2500 BC – The demise of the hunter-gatherer as agriculture is developed.

dollar, has made the US an attractive holiday destination, especially for Europeans. It's the third most popular

1200 BC – Emergence of the first ancient cultural groups, such as the Anasazi in south-west America and the Adena in the east.

1000 AD – Arrival of the first Europeans as the Vikings, under Leif Ericson, establish a short-lived settlement on what is today Newfoundland.

From Early Settlers to the Birth of the United States

'Discovery' of the New World (1492) – Columbus sails west in search of a new route to the Far East. Instead, he lands at Hispaniola (now Haiti) and, shortly after, lands on American soil. The following year, Pope Alexander VI 'gifts' the Americas to Spain, on the condition that the natives are converted to Christianity.

1500 – The first permanent European settlements are founded in modern-day Florida by the Spanish.

1607 – English settlers found the colony of Jamestown on an island off Virginia. It later relocates to Williamsburg.

1614 – Dutch settlers buy an island from local Indians for just 60 guilders and name it New Amsterdam. The British will later capture this prize and rename it New York.

1620 – Pilgrim Fathers aboard the ship *Mayflower* land at Cape Cod in Massachusetts and set up the Plymouth Colony, named after their port of departure in England. Other Puritan exiles follow, escaping religious persecution, to settle around Boston.

1692 – Witch hunts take place in Salem, New England – 19 'witches' are hanged.

1773 – The Boston Tea party. Protestors dump over 300 chests of tea

into the sea in the first act of defiance by the new settlers against Britain. This action sparks the American Revolution.

Slavery

From the early 17th century through to its abolition in 1865, slavery was legal and an accepted part of life. The vast majority of slaves were Africans, shipped to the west to be put to work farming cotton, sugar and tobacco, although some Native Americans were also held as slaves. A census in 1860 revealed nearly 4mn slaves in the 15 states where the practice was still legal, accounting for a third of the total population. By the early 1800s, many Americans were uncomfortable with the idea of slavery and the best-selling book in the 19th century (after the Bible) was *Uncle Tom's Cabin*, by Harriet Beecher Stowe, which revealed the cruelty of slavery and helped fuel the abolitionists' cause.

The American Revolution (1775-1783) – The original 13 settlements gain their independence from the British Empire. What began as a protest against taxes escalates into armed conflict. The revolutionaries, or 'Patriots', are led by such notables as George Washington and Thomas Jefferson.

4th July 1776 – The Declaration of Independence is signed by the 13 colonies which become the first 'United States'.

1788 – The new US Constitution is ratified.

1789 – George Washington becomes the first President of the United States.

1791 – The Bill of Rights guarantees the freedom of the individual.

1803 – The Louisiana Purchase of 828,000mi² (2,140,000km²) of territory from France, for a sum of $15m, effectively triples the size of the nation at a stroke.

1830-1900 – The settlers move westward, claiming land and control over the US, as the number of states rises to 45. This increases conflict with Native American tribes over land and resources, and spells disaster for the American buffalo (bison) which are hunted almost to extinction – up to 40mn are slaughtered for skins and meat and to prevent them from delaying trains on the ever expanding railroad network.

1846-1848 – Victory in the Mexican War sees the US acquire more land from its southern neighbour, including California.

1860 – Slavery abolitionist Abraham Lincoln is elected President.

The American Civil War (1861-1865) – America is divided as the Confederate States in the south under Jefferson Davis take on Lincoln's Unionists in the north. Victory for the north effectively abolishes slavery throughout the country, 60 years after its eradication in the northern states. Lincoln is assassinated in 1865.

> Four American presidents have been assassinated – Lincoln, James A Garfield, William McKinley and John F Kennedy – and a further 12 have been the targets of unsuccessful assassinations. The job should clearly come with a federal health warning.

1890 – The last battle between the US and Native Americans takes place at Wounded Knee Creek, when a stand off between the Lakota Sioux and the 7th Cavalry Regiment ends in a bloodbath. More than 300 Sioux are killed. The incident, which is later recorded as a massacre, ends over 250 years of fighting – the Indian Wars – in which the settlers slowly but surely took the land from the Native Americans.

1892 – The federal immigration station opens on Ellis Island in New York and becomes the traditional door to America. By the time it closes in 1954, some 12mn individuals have passed through its doors.

1898 – Victory for the US in the Spanish-American War ends Spain's empire in the Caribbean and Pacific. The Treaty of Paris, marking the end of hostilities, hands control of Puerto Rico, the Philippines and Guam to America.

20th Century

1917 – Having stayed neutral since the outbreak of the First World War in 1914, the US joins the Allied Powers. This is a pivotal point in their victory and the first hint of the power that the US will wield in the new century.

1920 – Alcohol is outlawed under the Prohibition Law, and the gangster culture grows out of the trade in illegal booze. In the same year, women get the vote.

1924 – Indigenous people finally gain the right to become American citizens.

1929 – The Wall Street Crash. The US stock market plummets and this, combined with a rise in debt and a series of crop failures, leads to the Great Depression, an economic slump affecting not just America but the world. President Franklin D. Roosevelt tries to put the US back on track in 1933, with his New Deal recovery programme, creating public works and re-legalising alcohol.

1941 – A shock attack by the Japanese on Pearl Harbour in Hawaii pulls America into the Second World War. Ironically, the increased production for the war effort creates jobs and is a major factor in ending the economic slump.

1945 – Japan surrenders after the US drops atomic bombs on Hiroshima and Nagasaki.

1947 – America turns against communism, and the Cold War begins.

1950 – Senator Joseph McCarthy's crusade to root out communists in the government and public life spawns the word McCarthyism – the campaign lasts until 1954 and targets many famous people, including Charlie Chaplin and Orson Welles (most of whom weren't communists). Meanwhile, America is back at war, this time aiding the South Koreans against communist China and North Korea.

The Dust Bowl

Drought and dust storms devastated the Great Plains region, stretching from Kansas to Texas, from 1930 to 1936, as a result of bad farming techniques. This drove many farmers and sharecroppers off the land, exacerbating the effects of the Great Depression. Their dreadful plight was immortalised in John Steinbeck's novel *The Grapes of Wrath*.

1955 – A tired black woman called Rosa Parks refuses to give up her seat to a white passenger on an Alabama bus. Her actions are seen as the first act of non-violent civil disobedience which will characterise the Civil Rights movement in the coming decade.

1960 – Democrat John F. Kennedy is elected the 35th President of the United States.

1961-1962 – America teeters on the brink of war with the Soviets after the Bay of Pigs invasion, a US-backed plan by Cuban exiles to invade the island, backfires. A communist missile base

John F Kennedy

so close to US soil sends shivers down America's spine, until Kennedy forces the Soviets to back down.

1963 – Kennedy is assassinated in Dallas. His killer, Lee Harvey Oswald, is arrested but then shot dead by Jack Ruby.

The Vietnam War (1964-1973) – One of America's darkest hours. The US steps into the Vietnam conflict, backing the republican south against the communist north. Support at home soon dwindles as the bodies of young conscripts return home. The war claims 58,000 American lives, a small fraction of the 2m-plus Vietnamese (soldiers and civilians) who perish in the conflict.

1964 – The Civil Rights Act becomes law, promising to end racial discrimination.

1968 – Civil Rights leader Martin Luther King is assassinated in Memphis, Tennessee, sparking race riots in more than 60 cities across America. Later that year, presidential candidate and brother of the late John, Robert F. Kennedy, is assassinated by Palestinian Sirhan Sirhan.

1969 – America regains its pride vis-à-vis its Soviet rivals in the Space Race on 20th July, when astronauts Neil Armstrong and Buzz Aldrin become the first men on the Moon. More than 700mn viewers watch the event on television.

> **'That's one small step for man, one giant leap for mankind.'**
>
> Neil Armstrong (astronaut, as he became the first man to set foot on the Moon)

1974 – A break-in at the Watergate hotel in Washington, DC reveals the illegal activities of President Nixon's staff and, given the near certainty of his impeachment (being brought up on charges), Nixon resigns from office. Such is the impact of Watergate that the suffix '–gate' has been tagged to many subsequent political scandals.

1979 – The hostage crisis at the American embassy in Iran marks the first downturn in relations between the US and the Islamic world. The hostages are finally released after 444 days, ironically on the day of President Ronald Reagan's inauguration in early 1981.

The Reagan Years (1981-1989) – The Republican ex-movie star serves two terms as one of America's most popular and successful presidents, boosting the economy and presiding over the end of the Cold War. His ability to deflect criticism earns him the nickname 'The Teflon President'.

1986 – The space shuttle Challenger explodes, killing all on board and halting the space programme for two years.

1988 – George H. W. Bush, Reagan's vice-president, is elected President.

1991 – The Gulf War. A coalition force led by the US and mandated by the United Nations, liberates Kuwait after the small oil-rich state is invaded by Iraq.

1992 – Democrat Bill Clinton is elected president.

1993 – A truck bomb parked below the North Tower of New York's World Trade Centre explodes, killing six and injuring over 1,000, in a chilling foretaste of the September 11th attacks eight years later.

The Waco 'siege' in 1993, and the Oklahoma City bombing in 1995, proved that terrorists and anti-government insurgents also exist on American soil and don't always have Arab surnames. Waco was the home of the Branch Davidian cult, whose leader David Koresh held out against the Federal Bureau of Investigation (FBI) for 51 days. The siege ended in a fire, in which 76 people died, including Koresh, following a controversial FBI assault on the compound. Two years later, an explosion at a government building in Oklahoma City killed 168 people – the worst ever act of terrorism on American soil – until 9/11. It was the work of ex-US soldier Timothy McVeigh, who claimed his anti-government feelings were fired by events at Waco and his experiences during the Gulf War. He was executed in 2001.

1998 – Bill Clinton is the second serving American president to be impeached by the House of Representatives following evidence that he had lied before a grand jury when he denied having sexual relations with White House intern Monica Lewinsky. Clinton is acquitted the following year,

and ends his term of office as one of America's more popular presidents.

21st Century

2000 – George W Bush (Bush Junior) narrowly beats Al Gore in a disputed vote (who can ever forget the drama of the 'hanging chads') to snatch the presidency back for the Republicans.

9/11 – On 11th September 2001, terrorists hijack four passenger planes and succeed in flying them into both towers of the World Trade Centre and the Pentagon; the fourth plane crashes in Pennsylvania. The death toll reaches 2,998 (not including the terrorists) with over 6,000 injured. Many are from the emergency services. The attacks are identified as the work of al-Qaeda, led by Osama Bin Laden. The US launches its war on terrorism to bring those who planned the attacks to justice, beginning with an offensive to liberate Afghanistan from the ruling Taliban.

2002 – Bush makes his 'axis of evil' speech, naming Iraq, Iran and North Korea among America's most dangerous enemies.

Iraq War (April-May 2003) – On suspicion that Iraq is producing weapons of mass destruction, Bush turns his attention to Saddam Hussein and orders an invasion of the country. The initial skirmishes are brief. American forces advance into Baghdad in early April, and on 1st May, Bush declares that the main part of the war is over. However, the 'peace' will prove more elusive.

2004 – The US suffers fall-out from the Iraq war, amid allegations of mistreatment of prisoners at Guantánamo Bay, and Senate reports claiming that the US and its allies went into the war on 'flawed' information.

2005 – In August, hundreds of people are killed or left homeless when Hurricane Katrina hits the Gulf Coast states. One of the worst-affected cities is New Orleans.

2006 – Plans to criminalise illegal immigrants lead to mass protests. Meanwhile, the only man to be charged in connection with the 9/11 attacks, Zacarias Moussaoui, is sentenced to life in prison. In November, the Democrats win control of the Senate and the House of Representatives in mid-term elections.

2007 – President Bush announces that more troops will be sent to increase security in Baghdad. Despite public protest, Congress later approves more funding for the ongoing conflict in Iraq.

August 2007 – Start of the 'credit crunch' as the sub-prime mortgage crisis leads to a downturn in the housing market, and raises the threat of US – and worldwide – recession.

2008 – Election year kicks off. John McCain wins the Republican ticket, while Hillary Clinton and Barack Obama battle to represent the Democrats, boosting the prospect of the first female or black American president.

March 2008 – The 4,000th American soldier is killed in Iraq. Estimates of the death toll among Iraqi civilians are estimated at over 100,000.

June 2008 – Barack Obama is declared the Democrats' presidential candidate.

September 2008 – The credit crunch bites hard and the US faces its biggest financial crisis since the Great Depression of the '30s, as major investment bank Lehman Brothers collapses and other large US financial institutions are taken over by rivals. The government bails out the bankers with a $700bn rescue plan, but the crisis is far from over.

November 2008 – Barack Obama is elected the 44th President, and will be the first African-American to hold the post.

THE PEOPLE

In a country with such a diverse ethnic mix, there's no such thing as a typical American. The US may be a young country, but its people have a sense of national pride the equal of anywhere in the world, and their cultural ancestry is just as important to them as being American. When the individual has a lineage from a number of differing cultures and nationalities, they proudly acknowledge every one of them, and readily welcome those of a spouse or other new member of the family.

> Americans are rarely just Americans. Many refer to themselves as Irish-Americans, Italian-Americans, or give a similar acknowledgement of their roots. Blacks are almost universally known as African-Americans.

Another important, although less obvious, factor is location. The lifestyles of families, or individuals, who've emigrated together from the same country, or even the same city, can be very different, depending on where they settle. Influential factors, such as climate, pace of life, population density, employment options, other communities, and many other cultural nuances, have an influence. These regional differences are noticeable within any country, yet the sheer size and cultural mix of the US accentuates them.

Generally, the larger cities are more open to, and accepting of, foreign cultures – New York's dynamism comes in part from being a varied and vibrant cultural melting pot. The smaller the community, the less likely you are to find cultural differences and the more likely you are to encounter an insular and less tolerant society – this is particularly true of parts of the Midwest and the southern states. Where tourism is a major part of the economy, there's a greater open-mindedness towards foreigners, as is the case in California, Florida and Hawaii, which have thrived as a result of tourism.

Whatever their ancestry, there are also cultural traits which are common to all Americans who exhibit them to differing degrees. These include national and individual pride, optimism, self-reliance and a 'can do' attitude, generosity, strong family values and an almost overwhelming desire for self-improvement.

Most Americans are informal and easy going, and can appear disconcertingly casual to Europeans and Asians, who have a more formal code of conduct. Their self-belief is sometimes misread as arrogance, and their eager acceptance of change – newer, bigger, better – misconstrued as dissatisfaction or greed. Americans can appear self-centred and self-indulgent, traits which are underlined by their attitudes to consumerism and food.

America is fat! Cheap food and reliance on the car has created a nation of overweight people, with over one-third of American adults officially categorised as obese.

Meanwhile, recent US governments' tendency to leap into international affairs – America is often labelled as the 'world's policeman' – has lead other nations to view the country as a collective control freak, a personality trait which is also demonstrated by many individuals.

Bold and brash, 'Yanks' have a great capacity for upsetting people, but they also have more than enough charm to smooth ruffled feathers, and their openness and easy acceptance makes their country a welcoming place to live.

Patriotism & Pride

Patriotism resembles a religion in the US, where both are instilled from an early age. God is an American, at least in most Americans' hearts. Schoolchildren pledge their allegiance to the Stars and Stripes every day, and almost every American can sing along to the national anthem (*The Star-Spangled Banner*) which kicks off every sporting event.

Pride in their homeland is matched only by Americans' pride in their family and status. Almost nowhere will you find people more willing to talk about, show or share what they have with others. Any purchase, family event or achievement is an excuse to entertain friends and neighbours, encouraging them to delight in their accomplishments. Work colleagues, distant relatives and neighbours, whether you know them well or not, will invite you to social gatherings, and you must be prepared to return the invitation should fortune smile on you.

Family Values

The fundamental unit in American life is the family, however dysfunctional it may be. There are many television sitcoms, such as *Married with Children*, which revolve around the ideal of Mom, Pop and the children, and you hear the opinion that 'nothing is more important than family' from every class, culture and community. This family 'model' dates back to the '50s, and is now somewhat outmoded – only a quarter of American households consist of married couples with kids, as one-parent, unmarried, gay and lesbian families become more common with every passing year – but this doesn't dent its popularity.

To Americans, the 'family' isn't the extensive unit that it is in Latin American or Middle Eastern countries. Grandchildren are considered part of the family fold, but grandparents, uncle and aunts, in-laws and cousins are one step distant, and often described simply as 'relations'.

Me, Myself & I

The pioneer spirit, which sent wagon trains full of adventurers in search of a new life in the West, has created a nation of free-spirited individuals, whose self-reliance is matched only by their self-absorption. Americans don't like to be told what to do, and they admire 'lone cowboys' who blaze a trail or stand up for their beliefs. Not for nothing is

Frank Sinatra's *My Way* one of the most popular karaoke requests.

Self-reliance can make for uncomfortable life transitions. Children are pushed out of the nest when their full-time education is over, and the elderly live alone rather than become a burden on their offspring. This can also create an excessive amount of navel-gazing, which is why American bookshelves are crammed with tomes on self-help and self-improvement.

The Moral Majority

For such a free-thinking, open society, Americans can be surprisingly tightly buttoned up. The legacy of the Puritans lives on in the relentless work ethic (which drives middle managers into the coronary care ward) and in the schizophrenic attitude towards sex. Americans are always seeking more and better sex, but not in front of the children. (Violence on television shows is acceptable, but sexual activity is not.)

At its extreme, some Americans (particularly Republicans) lean towards fundamentalism, with homosexuality, abortion and anything vaguely 'anti'-family treated as a danger to the moral health of the US. On an everyday basis, people are gagged by the spectre of political correctness, which takes egalitarianism to new lengths by seeking to stifle any vaguely 'personal' comments or off-colour jokes.

> **'My fellow Americans, ask not what your country can do for you, ask what you can do for your country.'**
>
> John F Kennedy (35th US President)

Charity & Good Works

Americans are generous. A large number of people donate money to charities and good causes or, even more tellingly, give their time to help others. Good works have their roots in the days of the early settlers when people depended on each other; today it may have more to do with guilt at living in one of the world's most prosperous economies. Whatever the reason, around a quarter of Americans are regular volunteers, while in 2006, people handed over an amazing $300bn in charitable donations.

Fears & Insecurity

Life in America isn't always sunny-side up. The pressure to succeed, to win and be the best, means that people are often dissatisfied with their lives, or fearful that it could all come crashing down. Americans fear many things, from losing their status to losing their hair. They're especially concerned about their health – a reasonable worry in a country where surgery can cost as much as a house – and will clutch at any health fads, from wheatgrass juice to pole-dancing. Americans are also concerned (paranoid) about security, which isn't surprising with an entrenched gun culture and the American's 'right to bear arms' and defend his property enshrined in the constitution (those who can afford it live in compounds with 24/7 security).

America's insecurities were proved all too real by the events of 9/11. Until that day, many felt safely insulated from the crazy outside world – people in the US are not well travelled and, according to *USA Today*, only some 20 per cent even have a passport. However, most are now only too aware that being inhabitants of the biggest country in the world is no insurance against the effects of the global terrorism.

Eternal Optimists & Great Achievers

When the going gets tough, Americans get going. They're eternal optimists who always look on the bright side, and refuse to bow to adversity, putting on Oscar-worthy performances in impossible situations. They've had plenty of experience – the early settlers coped with great hardships, and even today, natural disasters such as hurricanes and tornados regularly test people's endurance. Their ability to make the best of things also affects their attitudes to people. Americans are quick to forgive and forget the bad behaviour of their leaders. Or maybe they just have short memories!

Americans scorn fate and idolise achievement. They believe that nothing is impossible and great gains can be made by effort and endeavour. Top businessmen and celebrities are admired for their money and their success, while failure is a dirty word. To fail at something is the closest an American will come to feeling shame or losing face, and it's something he will endeavour to keep hidden – like his expanding waistline.

The sheer size of the US means that the different regions are almost like separate countries, so while Americans display some universal attitudes, there are also some strong regional characteristics:

◆ New Yorkers appear abrupt or even rude and are never lost for words, but they're sharp and witty, and often kind towards strangers;

◆ Southerners appear warm and welcoming, but the politeness can be surface gloss, and it takes a while before y'all get to know them;

◆ The Midwest is cowboy country, and its inhabitants don't have time for frills – blunt and honest, they tell it as it is and prefer you to do the same;

◆ New Englanders can be dour and straight-laced (it's the Puritan background) but are loyal and gracious once they unbend;

◆ Not all Californians desire to be in the movies or practise alternative lifestyles. The last stop on the settlers' trek is still a place to which Americans escape – many are there through choice rather than birth, which may be why they appear so open to new people and ideas.

Have a Nice Day!

This ultra-American greeting has become a cliché but is usually genuinely meant. Most people really do want you to have a nice day. Americans have a natural affinity for helping people – the service industry is a career choice rather than a stopgap. It utilises their most positive characteristics, which are friendliness, openness, oodles of charm and a genuine desire to assist – and these are the qualities which most visitors take home with them.

SENSE OF HUMOUR

American humour isn't complex – much of it relies on situation comedy (sitcom), slapstick, ridicule or innuendo (often of a sexual nature). Irony and sarcasm are rarely encountered and may even be frowned upon, since many Americans simply don't understand it. The world is familiar with the things which make Americans laugh – the country has broadcast its humour around the world since the invention of television. Viewers recognise *Cheers*, *Frasier* and *Friends* from Texas to Turkey, while classic TV series, such as *The Golden Girls* and *The Cosby Show*, have spawned remakes in different languages and cultures.

As long as you understand the language, you should get the joke. However, American jokes often make references to well-known individuals and events. For example, former president Richard Nixon is synonymous with all that is untrustworthy and undesirable in a politician, and is a favourite butt of American jokes. But

to a foreigner who missed out on the Watergate scandal, or is unaware of Nixon's part in it, these gags may be utterly meaningless. Similarly, anyone unaware of Bill Clinton's alleged affair with a White House intern would be nonplussed by the many quips about the ex-president's sexuality.

In a survey of American women, when asked, 'Would you sleep with former President Bill Clinton?', 86 per cent replied, 'Not again'.

Rude and lewd humour is popular – almost irrespective of people's social standing, background, age, creed, gender, race, or religion. It rarely causes embarrassment, as hardly anyone you meet will be hearing or using the terminology for the first time. Visitors should be aware of the 'ass' factor. Around 50 per cent of all retorts include this word, which refers not to a donkey but to a particular part of the human anatomy. One of the most popular slapstick stunt shows is called *Jackass*.

In such a multi-cultural and multi-racial society, many people now steer clear of poking fun at ethnic groups, women or anyone socially or physically disadvantaged, for fear of being considered racist, sexist or in any other way politically incorrect. Some people still tell Polish jokes (the Poles are the butt of American humour in the way that the Irish are for British comedians) and many will risk telling tales about dumb blondes and dumber rednecks – but such humour may not be acceptable in all company. Jokes about blacks and Jews are only OK if it's a black or Jewish comedian telling them.

Jokes about folk from adjoining states – and Canadians – are acceptable.

It's also fine to poke fun at lawyers and politicians who are considered fair game.

Telling jokes isn't an easy skill to master in the country of your birth, and attempting it on foreign soil is a risky business. Even if you speak the language like a local, the differences in humour are such that it's best to content yourself with listening. Never attempt translation of a joke from your home country or native tongue – these rarely work!

CHILDREN

Nothing is more important than the American family, and the children are the future of the family. As a result, they receive a great deal of encouragement and support from their parents, many of whose lives appear to revolve around their offspring. Parents take on extra jobs to put their kids through college and sacrifice evenings and weekends to accompany them to extra-curricular activities, from dance classes to Little League (children's baseball). Children become consumers before they're out of their diapers, and all teenagers expect their own television, computer, mobile phone – and car.

Many parents are over-protective – often referred to as 'helicopter parents'. America is the epitome of the 'nanny' state, and nowhere is that more apparent than in the care and concern which parents show towards their children's health and safety. American children often have their own doctor, a paediatrician, in addition to the family doctor. They have prime responsibility for the health of a child until he or she is at least two and, depending upon the preferences of the family, up to the age of 16. In addition, most kids also have an orthodontist. Nothing is more essential to success in the US than a set of shiny white, perfectly straight teeth.

Do American children deserve all this indulgence? Most parents expect – and receive – respect from their offspring, who must exhibit a sense of responsibility from an early age towards their families, their peers and their grades. They are as goal-orientated as their parents, and many work part-time from an early age. They also have to deal with the social demands of school friends – popularity within their peer group is paramount. With all this pressure, some go off the rails. Rates of drug abuse and pregnancy are high among American teenagers, and the kind of respect accorded to elders in   Asian or

Mediterranean cultures is much less rarely seen.

But in the main, you'll find American children are polite and respectful, if a little more confident and extrovert than children elsewhere. Many resemble miniature versions of their older relatives – or maybe it's the other way around! A lot of Americans are, in their superficiality and eagerness to please, very like big kids, and some have never succeeded in outgrowing their teenage years.

> '**The thing that impresses me most about America is the way the parents obey their children.**'
>
> King Edward VIII (British monarch)

THE CLASS SYSTEM

America has no class system in the traditional sense. Americans take great pains to tell you that theirs is the self-proclaimed land of opportunity, where everyone has an equal chance to succeed. There's no nobility or feudal system, so no one inherits their social standing (unless they're the offspring of the rich and famous). However, in spite of its egalitarian attitudes, the US has invented its own kind of class system, which is based on an individual's assets – their possessions, their money and their educational attainments.

Within this meritocracy, there are five different levels or 'classes', which can be summed up as follows:

- **Upper Class** – These are the power brokers, owners of major businesses, benefactors, leading politicians and the bosses of great institutions, who influence the nation's decisions.

- **Upper Middle Class** – White-collar professionals with degrees and comfortable incomes, who enjoy job satisfaction, security and a good deal of influence in their place of work.

- **Middle Class** – This group encompasses semi-professionals, craftsmen, and others with a college education. Families may include two workers, and their combined income will often rival the lower reaches of the Upper Middle Class, but this is offset by the insecurity of their jobs. When there's only one wage-earner in the home they may well find it difficult to make ends meet, and slip towards an intermediate Lower Middle Class.

- **Working Class** – This group constitutes the majority of the population, including semi-skilled blue collar workers alongside lower-paid white collar workers. Most of the 45 per cent of Americans without any college education are deemed to be working class.

- **Lower Class** – The majority of this group are on or below the poverty line. While many are employed, their jobs lack stability and their luck fluctuates with the economy. They may live in trailer parks or government-subsidised housing projects. Many are from more recent migrant cultures – and all are more vulnerable to crime and other social problems. This class also includes people who've been alienated from the rest of society for a number of reasons, such as mental health problems, homelessness, alcoholism or drug addiction.

ATTITUDES TO FOREIGNERS

The sheer size of the US, and its multi-cultural make up, means that there's room for everyone, and the waves of immigration which create friction in many European countries make barely a ripple on American soil. Most people's ancestry is no more than a handful of generations old, so they're invariably open to newcomers and to the influx of new ideas and cultures, and happy to adopt the more attractive aspects of those cultures, from their foods to their fashion. It's only within areas where non-nationals tend to gather that there's resistance to foreign cultures or even to the stereotypical American way of life.

Race Relations

Like many western nations, the US has been guilty of racism, which has particularly affected its Native American and African-American populations. Blacks were victims from the early days of the slave trade until well into the latter half of the 20th century, when segregation and the emergence of white supremacists, such as the Ku Klux Klan, sparked the Civil Rights movement. Native Americans have been second-class citizens since the first settlers arrived, losing their land rights and being relegated to reservations – they're still one of the most isolated and socially-disadvantaged groups in the US.

> **'America is the only country that went from barbarism to decadence without civilisation in between.'**
>
> Oscar Wilde (Irish writer & wit)

Even in an enlightened America, blacks, Hispanics and indigenous people are often at the back of the queue when it comes to jobs and education, and in the front line for dangers such as crime and drugs. However, few other countries offer such a chance for self-advancement, as the success of individuals such as actress and singer Jennifer Lopez and US president Barack Obama attests.

It would be entirely wrong to say racism no longer exists – there are racists and bigots in America, as there are all over the world. However, at least publicly, racism is now one of the most heinous cultural misdemeanours anyone can make. Prejudices of any kind are akin to a taboo in the US – this is the nation which gave birth to political correctness in all its many and sometimes confusing forms – and most people go out of their way to avoid racist comments or actions. However, organisations such as the Minutemen attest to strong anti-immigration sentiment, and the racist Ku Klux Klan (KKK) is still going strong in some southern states.

Xenophobia – fear and loathing of foreigners – is rare in America, where everyone is, to an extent, foreign. Nevertheless, most Americans have little interest in cultures outside their own (except for food).

State Patriotism & Civic Pride

Most US states are comparable in area to many European nations, and each has its own sense of identity, along with an individuality which resembles patriotism. Each state has its own flag, motto, nickname and other individual symbols, along with its own government, taxes and laws – they're almost small countries in their own right, and their inhabitants take great pride in their state, as well as in their city, town or community.

Americans who move from one state to another usually do so to improve their lives, and they almost instantly take on a sense of pride in their newly adopted state. Moving to America, a non-national will take on the guise of a resident of the state as quickly as he will the nation – so by the time the newcomer refers to himself as an American, he will already consider himself to be a Texan, Californian or

the like. Note that by choosing to live in a particular state, you'll be defined by the characteristics and reputation of that state, e.g. California's obsession with appearance and fads.

This sense of belonging to a region or a community also extends to the spoken word. While English is the principal language, settlers from Cuba, Mexico, Puerto Rico and other well-represented Spanish-speaking countries continue to speak their mother tongue within their community, even when the individual is a second or third-generation American national.

The American states each have a long list of symbols which are special to the area, such as state flower, state bird and even state vegetable (in Tennessee it's a tomato), some of which are quite bizarre; for example, Texas nominates the Dutch Oven as its 'state cooking implement', while Utah's 'state snack food' is Jell-o.

ICONS

Every country has its icons – people, places, structures, symbols, flora and fauna, food and drink – which are revered or unique to that country and have special significance to its inhabitants. The following is a list of some of America's icons that you can expect to see or hear reference to. (The authors apologise for the many worthy people missing from this list due to lack of space; it's a tribute to the US that is has so many people worthy of the title 'icon'.)

Icons: People

Filmmakers & Movie Stars

Fred Astaire (1899-1987) – Tagged the greatest dancer of the 20th century, Astaire is best remembered for his partnership with Ginger Rogers, who featured in ten of his 31 musical films.

Humphrey Bogart (1899-1957) – An unlikely leading man, 'Bogey' nonetheless starred in some classic romantic films, including *Casablanca* and *The African Queen*, and his marriage to Lauren Bacall was a genuine Hollywood love match. Bogart transcended the movies to become a true icon, and his name turns up as a reference throughout US popular culture – from song lyrics to a type of hat. In 1999, the American Film Institute named him the Greatest Male Star of All Time.

Marlon Brando (1924-2004) – Acclaimed actor with attitude, who began his career as a brooding sex symbol in *A Streetcar Named Desire* and later menaced his audience as *The Godfather*. Brando was also an activist for Civil and Native American rights.

James Dean (1931-1955) – Dean had achieved just three starring roles when he died in a car crash in California. His movies, which included *Rebel without a Cause*, had already turned him into an icon for America's youth – his death made him immortal.

The car James Dean died in, a Porsche 550 Spyder, was known as 'Little Bastard', and some people believe the car was cursed. Several drivers were later killed or injured in vehicles which incorporated parts from the infamous car and thieves were also hurt while trying to steal trophies from the car. In 1960 it disappeared during transportation and has never been seen since.

Clint Eastwood (b.1930) – Tough-guy movie star, whose best-known roles include the 'Man with No Name' in Sergio Leone's spaghetti westerns, and Harry Callahan in the *Dirty Harry* action flicks. He served as the mayor of Carmel in California and is considered Hollywood 'royalty'.

Rita Hayworth (1918-1987) – 'Love goddess' Hayworth was the number one screen sex symbol in the '40s, with a private life as exotic as her on-screen performances. She married five times, her husbands including maverick director Orson Welles and Prince Ali Khan.

Bob Hope (1903-2003) – Legendary comic actor, Hope is best remembered for his *Road to…* movies, in which he starred alongside Bing Crosby, and for entertaining US troops on their overseas campaigns. These ultra-American activities belie the fact that he was born in south London (England).

Marilyn Monroe (1926-1962) – History's most famous blonde, Monroe is better remembered for her three failed marriages and the conspiracy theories surrounding her untimely death, than her undeniable acting talent, which she demonstrated in classic films, such as *The Misfits* and *Some Like It Hot*.

George Lucas (b. 1944) – Film-maker who made light sabres desirable and archaeologists sexy with his *Star Wars* and *Indiana Jones* movies.

Paul Newman (1925-2008) – Hollywood's blue-eyed boy had a string of memorable roles, including *Cool Hand Luke*, *The Hustler*, and Butch Cassidy to Robert Redford's Sundance Kid. Married to actress Joanne Woodward for over 50 years, he also ran his own food company, Newman's Own, which donates all its profits to charity.

Stephen Spielberg (b. 1946) – Feted as the most powerful figure in the American film industry, Spielberg's name is synonymous with 'Hollywood blockbuster', from his sci-fi classics such as *ET* to historical epics like *Schindler's List*.

James Stewart (1908-1997) – Versatile and self-effacing, 'Jimmy' Stewart's career spanned seven decades and five Oscar nominations (he won Best Actor for *The Philadelphia Story*). He was also a war hero, flying missions over Nazi Germany. Most fans remember him best in the Christmas classic *It's a Wonderful Life*.

Spencer Tracy (1900-1967) – Despite his premature death, Tracy still appeared in 74 films. He received a record-breaking nine Best Actor Oscar nominations, and starred with Katharine Hepburn in an enduring screen partnership, which also continued off screen for over 20 years.

John Wayne (1907-1979) – The ultimate American 'tough guy', Wayne battled Wild West outlaws and Japanese troops as the first all-action hero. Controversial for his ultra-conservative, anti-communist views, he nonetheless captured the hearts of US movie-goers, who remember him for his gruff voice and distinctive bow-legged walk.

> 'Get off your horse and drink your milk' is a line attributed to one of John Wayne's characters, though the actor never actually said it. Another famous misquote is 'A man's gotta do, what a man's gotta do'. The correct line, spoken by Wayne in *Hondo*, was 'A man ought'a do what he thinks is best.'

Musicians & Singers

Louis Armstrong (1901-1971) – Nicknamed 'Satchmo' (satchel mouth), Armstrong was an innovator of early jazz. An excellent trumpeter, he later developed the unique singing style known as 'scat', and his gravelly voice is instantly recognisable, many years after his death.

James Brown (1933-2006) – Known as the 'Godfather of Soul', Brown was also one of the founding fathers of funk – his frenetic rhythms influenced many of today's dance and hip hop acts.

Nat 'King' Cole (1919-1965) – Jazz pianist turned popular crooner, Cole was the first black entertainer to cross into the white mainstream – he hosted his own TV show on NBC in the mid-'50s.

Bing Crosby (1903-1977) – The man who inspired Sinatra, Bing is the voice behind *White Christmas,* and one of the most admired singers of all time (also an accomplished actor). At his peak in the '40s, almost half of all radio broadcasts featured his

WORLD PREMIERE NOW SHOWING

songs, and one poll declared him more popular than the Pope.

Bob Dylan (b. 1941) – Singer-songwriter, poet and the voice of '60s protest, Dylan's best-known songs, such as *Blowin' in the Wind*, incorporated political and social commentary. He remains a rock figurehead. In 2004, Rolling Stone magazine ranked him second only to the Beatles in its list Great Artists of all Time.

Duke Ellington (1899-1974) – One of the originators of jazz, pianist and bandleader Ellington lead the most influential jazz orchestra of the 20th century for over 50 years.

Ella Fitzgerald (1917-1996) – Known as 'The First Lady of Song', Fitzgerald was an American jazz vocalist with a vocal range spanning three octaves. She's widely considered one of the supreme interpreters of the Great American Songbook, and during a recording career that lasted 57 years, she won 13 Grammy Awards.

Eminem (b. 1972) – Also known as Marshall Mathers or Slim Shady, his clever observations and 'so what!' attitude have made him one of the highest-selling rap artists of all time – despite being white.

Aretha Franklin (b. 1942) – The 'Queen of Soul', Franklin is also renowned for her jazz, rock and gospel output, and is the only female recording artist to notch up 20 number one rhythm and blues (R&B) singles. Her greatest hit was her 1967 cover of Otis Redding's *Respect*.

George Gershwin (1898-1937) – Versatile and prolific, Gershwin was America's greatest composer, writing opera, classical compositions and popular Broadway hits. His brother Ira contributed many of the lyrics, and his

work was recorded by some of the world's greatest singers, from Bing Crosby to Barbra Streisand. Gershwin died from a brain tumour shortly before his 39th birthday.

Jay-Z (b. 1969) – The most successful man in hip hop, Jay is an artist and entrepreneur with over 30mn record sales to his name. He's so prolific, he's said to have written one album in a couple days – and can compose without pen or paper.

Judy Garland (1922-1969) – Singer-actress Garland achieved stardom as a teenager as Dorothy in *The Wizard of Oz*, and became one of America's best-loved musical stars, despite her chaotic love life and addiction to painkilling drugs.

Woody Guthrie (1912-1967) – A survivor of the Dust Bowl and the Great Depression, folk musician Guthrie chronicled American history through his music. His most famous song, written in 1940, is *This Land is Your Land*, which is still sung by American students.

Jimi Hendrix (1942-1970) – The man who made his guitar 'sing', Hendrix's amplified, feedback-heavy style became a blueprint for rock guitarists. *Rolling Stone* magazine voted him number one in their list of great guitarists.

Michael Jackson (b. 1958) – Although his name is now a byword for eccentricity, Jackson's musical influence is undisputable. Since his debut with the Jackson Five, he has dominated the charts – 1982's *Thriller* remains the best-selling album of all time. His complex dance routines were a big influence on hip hop, and his imaginative videos helped put MTV on the map.

Madonna (b. 1958) – The top-earning female singer in the world, Madonna has sold in excess of 200mn records and is worth over $500m. Nicknamed the 'Material Girl' by the media, she has courted controversy with her overtly sexual performances and well-aimed pot-shots at the Catholic Church, and her talent just gets better with age.

Elvis Presley (1935-1977) – Along with Marilyn Monroe, Presley is the definitive American icon – larger than life, sexy as hell and dead before his time. He brought the music of black Americans to a white audience with songs like *Hound Dog*, but could bend his voice to any style, and his looks made him a sure-fire hit as a movie star. Even his controversial and untimely death couldn't dent his reputation as 'The King of Rock & Roll'.

Elvis Presley has consistently sold more records in each year since his death than he ever did when still alive. Imitation of 'The King' has become a mini industry, and his Memphis home, Graceland, a place of pilgrimage. It's unlikely that Elvis will ever really die.

Frank Sinatra (1915-1998) – Known as 'Ol' Blue Eyes', Sinatra was the king of swing – an easy-listening superstar with hits like *Strangers in the Night*. As an actor, he won a Best Supporting Actor Oscar for *From Here to Eternity* in 1953. In the early '60s, as leader of the Rat Pack, the Hollywood 'in crowd', and (loosely) linked with organised crime, he was, for a while, quite possibly the coolest man in America.

Phil Spector (b. 1939) – Song-writer, producer and inventor of the 'wall of sound', Spector was a hit factory in the '60s, especially with his girl groups such as the Crystals and the Ronettes. He also co-wrote the most-played (in the US) song of the 20th Century, the Righteous Brothers' *You've Lost That Lovin' Feelin'*. He was arrested in 2003 on suspicion of murder, but the jury at his first trial couldn't reach a verdict (the re-trial had still to be concluded when this book went to press).

Bruce Springsteen (b. 1949) – Singer, songwriter and multiple Grammy award winner, 'The Boss' sets to music the hopes and fears of America's working-class. Appropriately, one of his biggest hits was *Born in the USA*.

Sportsmen, Sportswomen & Sporting Events

Muhammad Ali (b. 1942) – Few challenge Ali's claim to be 'the greatest' boxer of his generation, if not the greatest ever. Never before had a boxer of his weight fought with such speed and grace, nor been so outspoken. A gold medal winner at the 1960 Rome Olympics, four years later Ali beat Sonny Liston to become the undisputed world heavyweight champion. He lost and regained the biggest prize in boxing

Joe DiMaggio's brief marriage to Marilyn Monroe in 1954 captivated the nation. It lasted less than a year, but he continued to deliver red roses to her crypt for 20 years after her death.

Michael Jordan (b. 1963) – Considered the greatest basketball player ever, Jordan's average score was over 30 points per game during his professional career. He played for the Chicago Bulls and Washington Wizards and has come out of retirement on two occasions. Jordan is also one of the most heavily marketed sports stars in American history.

Billie Jean King (born 1943) – Tennis player who won a total of 39 Grand Slam titles: 12 singles, 16 doubles titles and 11 mixed doubles. King is an outspoken advocate against sexism in sports and society, and is the founder of the Women's Tennis Association, the Women's Sports Foundation and World Team Tennis.

three times, and his victory against reigning champion George Foreman in Zaire in 1974 (known as 'The Rumble in the Jungle') was one of the greatest sporting events of all time. Born Cassius Clay, Ali converted to Islam in 1975. He retired in 1981.

Baseball – Known as 'the beautiful game', baseball is America's national sport, and was first played in its modern form in 1839 at Cooperstown, New York. If one sport defines America, it's baseball, which is uniquely American. It has spawned a language all of its own, and many of its terms have found their way into the American lexicon, such as curve ball, rain check and strike out. Only when you've mastered 'baseball' talk can you consider yourself a real American.

Joe DiMaggio (1914-1999) – Star baseball player for the New York Yankees, DiMaggio's 56-game hitting streak during 1941 is still recognised as the greatest-ever achievement in baseball, and he's been nominated the leading baseball player of all time.

Joe Louis (1914-1981) – King of the ring through the '30s and '40s, Louis fought 71 matches, and lost just three. Nicknamed the 'Brown Bomber', he was heavyweight champion for nearly 12 years, from 1937 to 1949, and a hero to both blacks and whites.

Rocky Marciano (1923-1969) – Born Rocco Francis Marchegiano, Marciano was the heavyweight champion of the world from 1952 to 1956. With 43 knockouts to his credit (87.8 per cent knockout rate), he remains the only heavyweight champion in boxing history to retire having won every fight of his professional career.

John McEnroe (b. 1959) – Tennis brat McEnroe won three Wimbledon and four US Open titles in the '80s. America's most entertaining tennis star, Mac is best known for his matches against his main rival Bjorn Borg, and for his on-court outbursts, during which he frequently told the umpire, "You cannot be serious!"

Joe Montana (b. 1956) – The greatest quarterback in the history of the National Football League (NFL), 'Joe Cool' led the San Francisco 49ers to four Super Bowl victories, becoming the only player ever to collect three Super Bowl 'Most Valuable Player' awards. His 49ers career ended in 1992, although he played two seasons for the Kansas City Chiefs before retiring.

Jesse Owens (1913-1980) – Owens' participation in the 1936 Berlin Olympics was as much a shock for Hitler as a triumph for black America. Nazi Germany saw the Games as the ideal vehicle for showcasing the rebirth of their nation's power, but no one planned for Owens, the grandson of a slave, who shook the sports world by winning four gold medals: 100 metres, 200 metres, long jump and 4x100 relay.

Babe Ruth (1895-1948) – Born George Herman Ruth, Jr and also know as 'The Bambino' and 'The Sultan of Swat', Babe was an American Major League baseball player from 1914-1935, and one of America's greatest sports heroes and the most celebrated player in American baseball history. He was the first player to hit 60 home runs in a season (1927), a record which stood for 34 years; and his lifetime total of 714 home runs, on his retirement in 1935, was a record for 39 years.

Petros 'Pete' Sampras (born 1971) – 'Pistol' Pete is widely considered the greatest tennis player in the sport's history. During his 15-year career, he won a record 14 Grand Slam men's singles titles in 52 appearances (2

Australian Opens, 7 Wimbledons, 5 US Opens). He was also the year-end world number one for six consecutive years (1993-1998), a record for the open era; and tied for third all-time.

Super Bowl

The season-ending championship game of the National Football League (NFL), played in February on 'Super Bowl Sunday', between the champions of the National and American Conferences. It's the most watched TV broadcast of the year, and to Americans is the 'most important sporting event in the universe'.

Tiger Woods (b. 1975) – The world's number one golfer, Woods is so successful at his sport that he has quite simply won more money and trophies than any other sportsman – it's been predicted he'll be the first billionaire athlete by 2010. His talent on the green has revitalised America's interest in golf.

Other Famous Americans

Susan B. Anthony (1820-1906) – Campaigner who fought for American women's right to vote. Her exhausting schedule included up to 100 speeches a year for some 45 years – and finally bore fruit when, in 1920, 14 years after her death, the US ratified the 19th Amendment allowing women the vote.

P. T. Barnum (1810-1891)

Showman, entrepreneur and creator of the 'Greatest Show on Earth'. Best-known for the Barnum & Bailey Circus, Barnum was acutely tuned into America's growing desire for entertainment, introducing dog shows and beauty pageants alongside his dwarfs, magicians and exotic animals.

Charles 'Charlie' Brown (created 1950) – Charlie is the main character in the comic strip Peanuts, created by Charles M. Schulz (1922-2000). The strip is one of the most popular and influential in the history of the medium, with 17,897 strips published in all; at its peak, it ran in over 2,600 newspapers, with a readership of 355mn in 75 countries, and was translated into 21 languages.

Warren Buffett (b. 1930) – Not just the richest man in America but, according to Forbes Magazine in 2008, the richest man in the world. Buffett made his fortune from the stock market, and spends much of his energy giving his money away – he pays himself a frugal annual salary of $100,000 and has lived in the same house in Nebraska for the last 50 years.

Sitting Bull (1831-1890) – A holy man with the Lakota Sioux, Chief Sitting Bull devoted most of his life to defending his people's rights to their ancestral lands, using any method he could. His victory over Custer at the Battle of Little Big Horn in 1876 was a great military success in the Indian Wars, but Sitting Bull's main notoriety came from his appearances in 'Buffalo' Bill Cody's Wild West show. He was killed in a struggle with police on his South Dakota reservation.

Andrew Carnegie (1835-1919) – Steel magnate Carnegie emigrated from Scotland to Pittsburgh and made his fortune in industry to become one of the richest men in history. He's famous for his philanthropy – using his riches to found educational establishments throughout the world. One of his best-known monuments is the Carnegie Hall in New York (see photo).

Colonel David Stern Crockett (1786-1836) – A celebrated 19th-century American folk hero, frontiersman, soldier and politician, Davy Crockett (as he is known in popular culture) is also referred to by the title 'King of the Wild Frontier'. He served in the Texas Revolution against Mexico, and died at the Battle of the Alamo (see below).

Walter Elias Disney (1901-1966) – A multiple Academy Award winner, Walt Disney was a film producer, director, screenwriter, animator, entrepreneur and philanthropist. He's most famous in the field of entertainment as the co-founder (with his brother Roy O. Disney) of Walt Disney Productions, one of the best-known movie producers in the world.

Thomas Alva Edison (1847-1930) – An inventor and businessman who developed many devices, including the phonograph and the electric light bulb.

Albert Einstein (1879-1955) – German-born physicist who immigrated to America in 1933. An unremarkable scholar, Einstein went on to become the most famous scientist of the 20th century – his theory of relativity is known (though not necessarily understood) by everyone. His theories were pivotal in the development of the atomic bomb, something he always regretted.

Amelia Mary Earhart (1897-1937) – A noted aviation pioneer and author, Earhart was the first woman to receive the Distinguished Flying Cross, awarded as the first aviatrix to fly solo across the Atlantic Ocean. She set many other records and wrote best-selling books about her flying experiences. Earhart disappeared over the Pacific Ocean in 1937 during an attempt to make a circumnavigation of the globe.

Wyatt Berry Stapp Earp (1848-1929) – A farmer, gambler, miner, teamster and officer of the law in various Western frontier towns, Wyatt Earp is best known for his participation in the Gunfight at OK Corral, along with Doc Holliday, and two of his brothers, Virgil and Morgan. He has become an iconic figure in American folk history

and has been the subject of various movies, TV shows, biographies and works of fiction.

Henry Ford (1863-1947) – Founder of the Ford Motor Company and inventor of the modern assembly line used in mass production, Ford's production of the Model T automobile revolutionised transportation and American industry. He was a prolific inventor and was awarded 161 US patents.

Benjamin Franklin (1706-1790) – A man born of humble beginnings who rose to prominence through several diverse fields, Franklin embodies the American Dream. He was a writer; a scientist who laid down the basis for understanding electricity; the inventor of many things, from bifocal glasses to the lightning rod; a linguist fluent in five different languages; a skilled ambassador and politician; and one of the Founding Fathers of the United States.

Bill Gates (b. 1955) – Chairman of the Microsoft Software Corporation, which he launched with Paul Allen in 1975. Gates remains the largest individual shareholder, with 9 per cent of the stock, and is incredibly wealthy – he topped the Forbes 400 list of richest Americans from 1993 to 2007. With his wife, he started the Bill and Melinda Gates Foundation in 2000, and has since given over $29bn to charities.

Ernest Hemingway (1899-1961) – Novelist, journalist and adventurer, Hemingway was one of the greatest writers of his generation, winning both the Pulitzer Prize and the Nobel Prize for Literature. Hemingway travelled the globe, reporting on world wars and major conflicts, and enjoyed manly pursuits, such as big-game hunting and bull-running in Spain. His sparse and economic writing style, and his novels, which included *The Old Man and the Sea* and *A Farewell to Arms*, had a significant influence on other writers, from Hunter S. Thompson to Bret Easton Ellis.

'For Sale: Baby Shoes, Never Worn.' This was Hemingway's shortest tale, the result of a $10 bet with friends that he could write a complete story in just six words. His friends paid up.

Harry Houdini (1874-1926) – Born in Hungary as Erik Weisz, Houdini was a magician, stunt performer and escapologist, widely regarded as the greatest ever. He performed in Europe and throughout America, where he would free himself from jails, handcuffs, chains, ropes, and straitjackets, often while hanging from a rope in plain sight of audiences.

Howard Robard Hughes (1905-1976) – An aviator, industrialist, film producer/director, philanthropist, and one of the wealthiest people in the world, Hughes gained fame in the late '20s as a maverick film producer, making big budget and often controversial films like *Hell's Angels*, *Scarface* and *The Outlaw*. As an aviator, Hughes set multiple world speed records, and acquired and expanded Trans-World Airlines. However, he's most widely remembered today for his eccentric behaviour and reclusive lifestyle in later life.

Thomas Jefferson (1743-1826) – The third president (1802-1809, Democrat) of the United States, Jefferson was the principal author of the Declaration of Independence and one of the Founding Fathers of the US. Jefferson excelled in everything he attempted, achieving distinction in the fields of horticulture, architecture, archaeology and palaeontology, as well as being an author and inventor, and founder of the University of Virginia. He almost doubled the size of the United States after the Louisiana Purchase, which annexed land now encompassing part of 15 states. He's universally acclaimed as one of the greatest-ever Americans.

John F. Kennedy (1917-1963) – President for less than three years, until his assassination, Kennedy was one of the most charismatic and dynamic leaders of the free world. During his remarkable and all too short political career, he worked tirelessly for peace – he founded the Peace Corps and laid the foundation for the end of the Cold War. Among his inspirational speeches was the promise to put a man on the moon before the end of the '60s, something he achieved but never lived to see.

Martin Luther King, Jr (1929-1968) – Champion of the Civil Rights movement, King was a Baptist minister who rose to prominence through his support of non-violent protest and his rousing speeches – all Americans know his 'I Have a Dream' oratory which he delivered in Washington in 1963. King received the Nobel Peace Prize the following year, its youngest-ever recipient. He was gunned down by an assassin in 1968, and is commemorated by a federal holiday on the third Monday of each January.

Mickey Mouse

The cartoon character, who made his debut in 1928, is as representative of Disney and its founder, Walt, as a crown is of a king. It's said that Mickey Mouse is the most recognisable symbol in the US, second only to the American flag.

The term 'Mickey Mouse' is not a compliment. Americans use it to suggest that something is unimportant, poor quality or trivial, as in 'Mickey Mouse money', which is how some Americans abroad refer to foreign currency.

Abraham Lincoln (1809-1865) – Considered by many to be America's greatest leader, Lincoln was the country's 16th president (1861-1865), and the first Republican president. His status derives from his leadership of the Union states to victory over the Confederate south in the Civil War; his tireless campaign to abolish slavery, and his oft-quoted words which make up the Gettysburg Address. Like many great leaders, he was assassinated.

Charles Augustus Lindbergh (1902-1974) – An aviator, author, inventor and explorer, Lindbergh is famous as the pilot of the first solo, non-stop Transatlantic flight in 1927, from New York to Paris, in the single-engine monoplane, *Spirit of St. Louis*.

Jackson Pollock (1912-1956) – Loved and loathed in equal parts, Pollock was a major force in the abstract expressionist movement, and the most influential American artist of all time. One of his paintings was sold at auction in 2006 for $140mn– the world's most expensive painting.

John Davison Rockefeller (1839-1937) – An industrialist and philanthropist, Rockefeller revolutionised the petroleum industry and defined the structure of modern philanthropy. In 1870, he founded the Standard Oil Company and ran it until he officially retired in 1897. As gasoline grew in importance, his wealth soared and he became the world's richest man, and is often regarded as the richest person in history.

Richard Rodgers (1902-1979) & **Oscar Hammerstein** (1895-1960) – A song-writing duo, usually referred to as Rodgers and Hammerstein, famous for creating a string of immensely popular award-winning Broadway musicals in the '40s and '50s, including *Oklahoma*,

Carousel, *South Pacific*, *The King and I* and *The Sound of Music*.

Franklin Delano (1882-1945) & **Eleanor Roosevelt** (1884-1962) – Often referred to by his initials FDR, Franklin Roosevelt was the 32nd President (Democrat) of the United States, the only president elected to four terms in office (1933-1945) and the only one to serve more than two terms (due to WWII). During the Great Depression in the '30s, he created the New Deal to provide relief for the unemployed, recovery of the economy and reform of the banking system. **Anna Eleanor Roosevelt** was an advocate for civil rights; and after her husband's death in 1945, was an internationally prominent author and speaker for the New Deal coalition.

The Simpsons – An American animated sitcom created by Matt Groening for the Fox Broadcasting Company, first broadcast in 1989. It's a satirical parody of the middle class American lifestyle, epitomised by its titular family, which consists of Homer, Marge, Bart, Lisa and Maggie. The show has won dozens of awards and is the longest-running sitcom and animated programme, and was named by *Time* magazine as the 20th century's best television series.

John Steinbeck (1902-1968) – Internationally acclaimed author of *The Grapes of Wrath* (1939) and *Of Mice and Men* (1937), Steinbeck wrote twenty-five books, including sixteen novels, six non-fiction books and several collections of short stories. He was awarded the Nobel Prize for Literature In 1962.

Superman – From his debut in *Action Comics* in 1938, the boy from the planet Krypton has captivated Americans. Superman/Clark Kent has appeared in movies, television series and video games, and his enduring popularity is due not just to his fantastic powers, but to his never-ending patriotic battle for 'truth, justice and the American way'.

Mark Twain (1835-1910) – The pen name of Samuel Langhorne Clemens, author, lecturer and humorist, and possibly the most quoted American ever. Twain wrote many novels, but two were especially influential: *The Adventures of Huckleberry Finn*, hailed as the Great American Novel, and *The Adventures of Tom Sawyer*.

Andrew Warhol (1928-1987) – Artist and central figure in the movement known as pop art, Warhol achieved worldwide fame for his work as a painter, avant-garde filmmaker, record producer, author and public figure. He was infamous for his membership in wildly diverse social circles which included bohemian street people, distinguished intellectuals, Hollywood celebrities and wealthy aristocrats.

George Washington (1732-1799) – Washington led his new American army to victory over the British during the American Revolution, and then retired to his plantation in Virginia. However, he was tempted back into politics and in 1789 was elected unanimously as the first President of the United States (1789-1797). A humble and dignified man, Washington concentrated on keeping the new America out of conflict and on building the economy, and is still hailed as one of its most successful leaders. He's celebrated as the Father of the Nation, after expanding the Union and overseeing the creation of a taxation system, a national bank and the first Supreme Court judges.

There are numerous memorials to George Washington throughout the US. His face appears on the dollar bill and the quarter (25 cent) coin, and both the capital city Washington, DC and Washington state are named after him. The latter is the only US state named after an American.

Tennessee Williams (1911-1983) – A prominent playwright who received many of the country's top theatrical awards, Tennessee won the Pulitzer Prize for Drama for *A Streetcar Named Desire* (1948) and *Cat on a Hot Tin Roof* (1955); other award-winning plays included *The Glass Menagerie*, *The Night of the Iguana* and *The Rose Tattoo*.

Oprah Gail Winfrey (born 1954) – Often referred to simply as Oprah, Winfrey is an American television host, media mogul and philanthropist. Her talk show, *The Oprah Winfrey Show*, has earned her multiple Emmy Awards, and is the highest-rated talk show in the history of television. Oprah has been ranked the richest African American of the 20th century, and is among the most influential women in the world.

Frank Lloyd Wright (1867-1959) – The world's first modern architect, Lloyd Wright developed a series of highly individual styles, from construction to interior design. His most famous buildings include the Guggenheim Museum in New York and Oklahoma's Price Tower, his only 'skyscraper', while his 'Prairie Houses' introduced Americans to the concept of open-plan living.

Icons – Places & Structures

The Alamo – This former mission in San Antonio, Texas, was the scene of a battle in 1836, when a handful of Texans held out for 13 days against an onslaught by Mexican troops during the Texas Revolution. The Alamo fell, but its brave defenders came to symbolise sacrifice in the pursuit of liberty. The building now receives 2.5mn visitors a year.

Disneyland – The mother of all theme parks, Disneyland was conceived by Walt Disney as a small entertainment centre, and opened in 1955 on a vacant lot in Burbank Studios, California. Famous for its fantastic themed 'lands' and daily parade of Disney characters, it's since grown into a resort, and been joined by Walt Disney World in Florida, plus Disney parks in France and the Far East.

Empire State Building – Still the best-known skyscraper and a landmark on the New York skyline, the Empire State Building was begun in 1930 and completed just 410 days later. At 1,472ft (449m) high, and 102 stories, the art deco tower was the world's tallest building for 41 years until being overtaken by the World Trade Centre. It has survived a plane crashing into it and being climbed by King Kong, and is officially one of the Seven Wonders of the Modern World.

> **More than 30 people have committed suicide by jumping from the Empire State Building. In 1979, would-be suicide Elvita Adams leapt from the 86th floor, but was blown back onto the 85th floor. She survived with just a broken leg.**

Gateway Arch – Built in St. Louis, Missouri, and known as the 'Gateway to the West', this graceful arch is the tallest monument in the US, rising to 630ft (192m) tall. It was completed in 1965 as part of the Jefferson National Expansion Memorial, which commemorates the American settlers' westward migration. Each year, a million visitors ride the trams to the top of the arch.

Golden Gate Bridge – When it opened in 1937, this section of US Highway 101 was the longest suspension bridge in the world. It carries six lanes of traffic for 8,981ft (2,737m) across the Golden Gate – where San Francisco Bay meets the Pacific Ocean. Its distinctive colour, officially known as International Orange, was designed to blend with the scenery while keeping the structure visible in the bay's famous fog.

Grand Canyon – The world's greatest gorge was carved out over millions of years by the Colorado River through the state of Arizona. The first recorded sighting was by Garcia Lopez de Cardenas in 1540, although it took until 1869 for a man (Major John Wesley Powell) to travel through the canyon by river. It measures some 277mi (446km) in length, ranges up to 18mi (29km) in width and is over one mile (1.6km) in depth at its deepest point. The sedimentary layers of rock cut by the river give geologists the opportunity to investigate almost 2bn years of the planet's history.

Hollywood – This district of Los Angeles is famous for being the home of the movies, although most are now shot elsewhere. Its most visible landmark is the famous Hollywood sign, comprising nine 50ft (15m) high white letters. This sign originally read 'Hollywoodland' and advertised a housing development.

Hoover Dam – Opened in 1935 and named for the then president Herbert Hoover, this 726ft (221m) high dam is the second-highest in the United States. It cuts across the Colorado River, where Arizona meets Nevada, and links two time zones.

Lincoln Memorial – Resembling a Greek temple, this shrine to President Abraham Lincoln is on the National Mall in Washington, DC – and is one of the capital's must-see monuments. It was dedicated in 1922 and has been used as a rallying point many times.

Madison Square Garden – The premier venue in New York, if not the entire US, for sports events, concerts and shows, MSG is home to the city's basketball and hockey teams. It seats up to 20,000 spectators, and stages around 320 events every year.

Mall of America – The largest fully-enclosed retail and entertainment complex in the US, Minnesota's Mall of America opened in 1992. It houses over 500 retail stores, and has enough space to park thirty-two 747 airplanes. Additional attractions include an indoor amusement park (complete with a Ferris wheel) and a wedding chapel.

> If a shopper spent 10 minutes browsing every store in the Mall of America, it would take them 86 hours to complete their visit.

Niagara Falls – A massive waterfall on the Niagara River, straddling the border between the US and Canada. While not exceptionally high, Niagara Falls are very wide, and have a flow of over 168,000m³ of water falling over the crest line every minute in high flow.

Times Square – A major intersection in Manhattan at the junction of Broadway and 7th Avenue, famous for its neon billboards. It's the venue for the New Year's Eve ball drop, which has welcomed in the New Year since 1917.

Washington Monument – Built to commemorate George Washington, this graceful structure, 555ft (169m) high,

is the world's tallest obelisk. Located in the capital, near to the White House, it was opened in 1888.

The White House – The official residence of the President of the United States since John Adams in 1800, the White House has been changed and updated by successive leaders – most notably by Harry S Truman and First Lady Jackie Kennedy. It's located at 1600 Pennsylvania Avenue, the most famous address in the US.

The White House, Washington DC

World Trade Centre – The Twin Towers are America's best-known landmark – even more famous for their absence from the New York skyline after the terrorist attack of 9/11 destroyed the World Trade Centre complex. At 1,368ft (417m), the Towers held the record of the world's tallest building for just one year after their completion in 1973.

Yellowstone National Park – Yellowstone was set aside as the world's first National Park in 1872 and covers 3,472mi² (8,987km²). Most of the park is located in Wyoming, but it also extends into Montana and Idaho. It's known for its abundance of wildlife and geothermal features, most notably the geyser called Old Faithful. Yellowstone Lake is sited over the largest (active) super volcano on the continent.

Icons: Symbols

Barbie Doll – The best-selling fashion doll was launched in 1959 by Mattel and remains a major source of revenue for the company. It's estimated that over a billion have been sold worldwide in over 150 countries, with Mattel claiming that three Barbie dolls are sold every second.

The Declaration of Independence – A statement adopted by the Continental Congress on July 4th 1776, announcing that the thirteen American colonies then at war with Great Britain were no longer a part of the British Empire. Written primarily by Thomas Jefferson (see above), the Declaration is a formal explanation of why Congress had voted on July 4th to declare independence from Great Britain, more than a year after the outbreak of the American Revolutionary War. The birthday of the declaration – Independence Day – is celebrated on July 4th.

Ford Model T – Colloquially known as the Tin Lizzie and the Flivver, the Model T was an automobile produced by the Ford Motor Company from 1908 to 1927. It's widely regarded as the World's first affordable automobile and the car that 'put America on wheels', largely due to Ford's innovative assembly line and production methods.

Great Seal of the United States – Used to authenticate certain documents issued by the United States federal government, the phrase 'great seal' is used both for the physical seal itself (which is kept by the United States Secretary of State), and more generally for the design impressed upon it, which has the national coat of arms on the obverse. It's officially used on documents such as US passports, military insignia, embassy signs and various flags.

The Liberty Bell – Located in Philadelphia (Pennsylvania), the Liberty Bell is one of the most prominent symbols of the American Revolutionary War. It's a familiar symbol of independence within the United States, and has been described as an icon of liberty and justice. According to tradition, its most famous ringing occurred on July 8th 1776 to summon citizens of Philadelphia for the reading of the Declaration of Independence (although this is disputed).

Mount Rushmore – Cut into the rock near the top of a mountain in South Dakota are the faces of four US presidents. The memorial represents the first 150 years of the nation's history, with 60ft (18m) high sculptures of George Washington, Thomas Jefferson, Theodore Roosevelt and Abraham Lincoln. It was carved between 1927 and 1941 by Belgian sculptor Gutzon Borglum, with the help of 400 workers, and is visited by over 2mn people annually.

Stars & Stripes – Consisting of 13 horizontal stripes and 50 white five-pointed stars, representing the original 13 colonies and the current number of states respectively, the flag is the symbol of Americanism and patriotism. Traditionally designed by Betsy Ross, it's flown all-year round on government buildings (including every classroom) and some private homes also display it (although most only do so on specific national days). There are many rituals and traditions connected with the flag, including a specific way of folding it.

Statue of Liberty – As instantly recognisable as the Eiffel Tower, with which it shares its designer, the Statue of Liberty was presented to the US by the French in 1886, to mark the nation's centennial. Made from copper sheeting over a steel framework (only the torch is coated in gold leaf), the statue stands on Liberty Island in New York, and was the first glimpse of America for new immigrants.

Uncle Sam

A national personification of the United States, the first usage of Uncle Sam dates from the War of 1812, and the first illustration from 1852. He's often depicted as a serious elderly white man with white hair and a goatee beard, and dressed in clothing that recalls the design elements of the Stars & Stripes, typically a top hat with red and white stripes and white stars on a blue band, and red and white striped trousers.

Icons: Flora & Fauna

Bald Eagle – Also known as the American Eagle, this is the national bird of the US and one of its most enduring symbols. A sacred bird to the Native Americans, who believed it to be a messenger of the gods, its image appears on much American insignia, including the Great Seal of the United States.

Buffalo – Vast herds of American buffalo (bison) once roamed across America, and were essential to the indigenous people who ate their meat, used their hides for clothing and tents, their bones for tools, and even dried their dung to use as fuel. Their numbers were devastated by hunting, and have never recovered.

Grizzly Bear – These powerful and impressive creatures are native to the North American continent and are still found in Alaska and around Yellowstone. Current numbers are estimated at around 60,000. Massive creatures, which can stand 8ft (2.44m) tall, they sometimes come into conflict with man, especially over food – grizzlies are omnivorous and will eat just about anything.

Experts say that if you're confronted by a grizzly you should either climb a tree or submit and remain still – the bear will often lose interest. Running away encourages the bear to give chase and they can move much faster than humans.

Groundhog – February 2nd is known as Groundhog Day when this rodent emerges from hibernation – it's said that if the weather is clear enough for him to see his shadow, there will be six more weeks of winter. There are several weather-hogs, the most famous of which is Punxsutawney Phil, who appears in the Bill Murray movie, *Groundhog Day*.

Prairie Dog (Cynomys) – A small, burrowing rodent native to the grasslands of North America, the prairie dog is a type of squirrel of which there are five different species.

Rattlesnake – Belonging to the class of venomous snakes known commonly as pit vipers, rattlesnakes are characterised by the presence of a 'rattle' at the tip of the tail, used to warn off predators and threats.

The Rose – The rose has been the national flower of the US since 1986, when Ronald Reagan signed its significance into law in the White House rose garden.

Saguaro – The archetypal three-pronged desert cactus, saguaro, only grows in the Sonoran Desert of Arizona, California and northern Mexico. Saguaros can live for over a century, and take up to 75 years to grow one 'arm'. They're protected by law – if a cactus is in the way of any planned construction, a special permit is required before work can begin.

Sequoia – Also known as California Redwoods, these are the tallest trees in the world – the record for the world's tallest living thing is held by Hyperion, a 379.1ft (115.55m) sequoia in California's Redwood National park. They also have a massive diameter, up to 23ft (7m) across, large enough for people to cut tunnels through their base. Sequoia can live to over 2,000 years old.

Icons: Food & Drink

Apple Pie – Settlers brought the apple to America, so the term 'as American as apple pie' is a little inaccurate. Pumpkin pie, served as a dessert at Thanksgiving, is probably more appropriate, as is the Key Lime pie, made from Key lime juice and uniquely American.

Big Mac – The Big Mac is a hamburger sold by McDonalds hamburger restaurants, consisting of two 1.6oz (45.4g) beef patties, iceberg lettuce, American cheese, pickles, onion and special McDonalds 'Mac' sauce (a variant of thousand island dressing), served on a three-part sesame seed bun. It has become a symbol of fast food and junk food, with millions sold at the ubiquitous McDonalds' restaurants every day around the world.

Cajun Food – From the French-speaking Acadiana region of Louisiana, the cuisine could well be defined as three-pot cookery: one for the main dish, one for the grain (such as rice or corn), and one for whatever vegetable is currently plentiful. The ingredients are locally available; historically Cajun food developed through the expulsion of the Acadian refugees by the British, forcing them to live off the land.

Chocolate brownies – A chocolate brownie is a flat, baked square or bar, sliced from a type of dense, rich chocolate cake. They come in a variety of forms, and are either 'fudgy' or 'cakey', depending on their density, and may include nuts, icing, cream cheese, chocolate chips or other ingredients. Brownies are typically accompanied by either milk or coffee. They were first recorded around 1906, although they are thought to have been made earlier than this.

Coca-Cola (Coke) – A carbonated soft drink sold in stores, restaurants and vending machines in over 200 countries, it's produced by the Coca-Cola Company in Atlanta(Georgia), and is often referred to simply as Coke, or (in European and American countries) as Cola or Pop. Originally intended as a patent medicine when it was invented in the late 19th century by John Pemberton, Coca-Cola was bought out by businessman Asa Griggs Candler, whose marketing led Coke to its dominance of the world soft drink market throughout the 20th century.

Cotton candy – This spun-sugar snack was introduced to the world in 1904 at the St Louis World's Fair by William Morrison and John C. Wharton. They called it 'Fairy Floss' and sold it for the then expensive price of 25 cents a box. Despite this, they sold over 68,000 boxes.

Donut – The American donut (or doughnut) is a sweetened piece of deep-fried batter, either ring shaped or a flattened sphere filled with cream or jam. They've been eaten since the 19th century, and may have been introduced by Dutch settlers. The fast food chain Dunkin' Donuts sells 52 varieties in nearly 8,000 outlets around the world.

Grits – An American Indian corn-based food common in the southern United States, grits consists of coarsely ground corn and is traditionally served for breakfast. Hominy grits is grits made from nixtamalised corn or hominy (dried maize or corn kernels that have been treated with an alkali).

Hot dog – A soft cured sausage of beef and/or pork, served in a soft bread roll and liberally doused in mustard and relish. Hot-dog stands are found all over America, where a 'dog' is the traditional *hors d'oeuvre* to a baseball game.

Iced tea – A form of cold tea often served in a glass over ice, iced tea may or may not be sweetened. It can be mixed with flavoured syrup, with common flavours including cherry, lemon, lime, peach and raspberry. Apart from tea, other herbs are also sometimes served cold, and referred to as herbal iced tea.

Martini – A cocktail made from gin and vermouth, garnished with an olive. The origin of the martini is uncertain, but it's believed to have been invented in Martinez, California in the latter half of the 19th century.

Peanut butter – A food paste made primarily from ground roasted peanuts, with or without added oil. It's primarily used as a sandwich spread, and is often eaten at breakfast.

Popcorn – A type of corn which explodes (it's also called popping corn) from the kernel and puffs up when heated. The process of making popcorn was first discovered by Native Americans, thousands of years ago. During the Great Depression, popcorn was comparatively cheap at 5-10 cents a bag and became popular – today it's traditionally eaten at the movies.

Root Beer – Also known as sarsaparilla, this soft drink was originally a herbal preparation used to treat coughs and mouth sores. Commercially prepared root beer was developed by Charles Elmer Hires in 1866, and was popular during the Prohibition period, when alcohol was banned.

Spam – First produced in 1937 by the Hormel Company in Austin, Minnesota, this canned meat is made from chopped shoulder of pork with ham – hence the name. Sales soared during the Second World War, and by 1959, one billion cans had been sold worldwide. The US is still the largest consumer of Spam, and it's especially popular in Hawaii, where it features on the menus of McDonalds and Burger King.

Turkey – It's estimated that of 270mnturkeys raised annually in the US, about one-sixth are eaten at Thanksgiving. Benjamin Franklin wanted the turkey, not the bald eagle, to be chosen as America's national bird.

> **Turkeys are said to be stupid birds. It's claimed that those kept outside have been known to drown during heavy rain, when their lungs fill up with water while they are staring up with open beaks.**

Whiskey – A very different spirit from Scotch, American whiskeys include bourbon and rye, which are distilled from corn or rye and aged in oak barrels. Bourbon gets its name from the county in which it was first produced, which itself was named after the French royal family.

General George Washington

3.
GETTING STARTED

One of the most difficult stages of adjustment to a new country is those first few days when you have a million and one things to do. This is stressful enough without the addition of the cultural differences that you'll encounter in America. This chapter will help you overcome some of the challenges of arriving and settling in the US, including those posed by obtaining a residence permit, finding accommodation, renting or buying a car, opening a bank account, registering for taxes, obtaining healthcare, council services and utilities, finding schools for your children, getting online and staying informed.

> 'In the United States, there is more space where nobody is than where anybody is. This is what makes America what it is.'
>
> Gertrude Stein (American writer)

IMMIGRATION

It's estimated that every year, about a million newcomers arrive on US soil, although the door isn't as wide open to immigrants as it used to be. The American public's attitude has changed greatly since the terrorist attacks on 11th September 2001 (9/11), and foreigners, especially those of a Middle-Eastern appearance, are being viewed with suspicion for possibly the first time in the country's history.

Since 9/11, tighter controls have been imposed on foreign visitors, as Americans worry about the effect of immigrants on national security, the labour market and the availability of illegal drugs. One of their greatest concerns is over the number of illegal immigrants, in particular those from Mexico – a survey in 2006 estimated numbers at some 11.5mn, with just under half living in California,

Florida and Texas. More than half of all 'illegal aliens' are Mexican.

All US nationals now require a passport to re-enter America by air or land, which includes those returning from neighbours Canada and Mexico.

Visas

There are two types of visa: immigrant visas, which allow you to live and work permanently in the US, and non-immigrant visas, which allow you to visit the US for between six months and five years and, in some cases, work. Each has countless sub-categories, so you may need expert help in navigating the system.

Non-immigrant (Visitor) Visas

The Visa Waiver Program allows citizens of certain countries to visit America for business or tourism purposes for up to 90 days without obtaining a visa – as of 2006, eligible countries included Australia, Japan and most (but not all) of the European Union (EU) countries. All other nationals must apply at a US Consulate in their home country.

Immigrant Visas or Resident's Permits

It's notoriously difficult to obtain a visa which allows you to live and work in the US. This is known as lawful permanent residency (LPR) or, more commonly, as getting a green card (the card isn't actually green). Most people accomplish it through sponsorship by relatives, who are already US citizens, or through their employer. Spouses of American citizens are immediately recognised as relatives, but the government is quite specific about other relationships that qualify people to be sponsors.

The waiting time for a green card can be just a few months or run into years. It allows the holder free access to some (but not all) social security benefits, and must be renewed every ten years.

Applications

Many visa forms can be downloaded online. Up to date information is provided by the US Citizenship and Immigration Service or USCIS (www.uscis.gov), a division of the Department of Homeland Security (DHS). Other useful websites include United States Immigration Support (www.usimmigrationsupport.org) and the US State Department (www.state.gov). If you need help, there are immigration agencies which can assist with applications – and, inevitably, there are lawyers. For a reliable source of information about American lawyers, check out the Martindale-Hubbell list,

which includes ratings of individual lawyers (www.lawyers.com).

The Green Card Lottery

Each year the US government issues up to 50,000 residents' permits through the Diversity Immigrant Visa (DV) program, which is often referred to as the Green Card Lottery. To ensure that diversity really **does** mean diversity, nationals of any country which has sent more than 50,000 immigrants to the US in the preceding five years cannot apply – in 2009, citizens of Canada, Russia and the United Kingdom (although not Northern Ireland) are unable to take part. Nor does selection guarantee a green card, as candidates are expected to have achieved a certain level of education and work experience.

The lucky applicants whose 'tickets' are drawn don't receive an immediate green card. There are several more stages of red tape to go through, but if they're successful, residency is also extended to their spouse and all unmarried children under 21.

If you're feeling lucky, the Diversity Lottery website is www.dvlottery.state.gov. There are a number of advertisements, especially on the internet, promising to increase your chances of selection in the Green Card Lottery – for a fee! Don't be fooled. These are fraudulent scams which have no connection to the lottery, and will simply relieve you of up to $250.

Citizenship

A (big) step on from gaining your green card is becoming a naturalised US citizen. This gives you the same rights as anyone born in the US, allowing you to vote, perform jury duty, hold an American passport and even stand for public office – although you cannot become president, as this office is reserved for natural-born Americans!

'Any American who is prepared to run for president should automatically, by definition, be disqualified from ever doing so.'

Gore Vidal (American novelist)

Becoming an American Citizen

Any immigrant aged 18 or older is eligible to become a US citizen under a process called naturalisation. This requires that you live in the US for a minimum of five years – or three if you're married to an American. Assessment includes a criminal background check, fingerprinting and an interview.

In addition, you must pass a citizenship test, similar to the British 'Life in the UK' test, which is a series of questions about the US government and history, e.g. 'Who drafted the Declaration of Independence?' and 'What is the 4th of July?' In order to understand the test, applicants must be able to read, write and speak simple English.

Citizenship is conferred by a judge in a naturalisation ceremony at which candidates take an oath of citizenship. Except in extremely rare cases, it's impossible to become a naturalised US citizen without first obtaining a green card.

US law permits dual nationality for naturalised citizens, so 'new' citizens can keep their original nationality, as long as their country allows it – some, such as Japan, don't. America insists that its citizens travel in and out of the country on a US passport.

Becoming a citizen isn't compulsory for green card holders, who are free to live in the US for as long as they wish, renewing their residency every ten years, provided they abide by the laws of the land, file their tax return and don't 'abandon' the US for more than a year.

Citizenship is less popular than it used to be: it's thought that only a tenth of immigrants now go through the naturalisation process.

BUREAUCRACY

For a nation which is inordinately fond of documentation, American bureaucracy is surprisingly easy to cope with. Even the simplest forms are accompanied by a pamphlet, guide or contact details to assist you in completing it. Assistance is available in several languages, and others can be catered to on request. Some offices have translators – and all can supply someone who speaks Spanish.

One of the first things you must do on arrival in the US is obtain a social security number, as you'll need it to open a bank account, apply for a driver's licence and do a million other bureaucratic tasks. You may receive your number with your visa. If not, information about how to apply, and which documents you need, are on the US Social Security Administration's website (www.socialsecurity.gov).

Civil Servants

In America, a civil servant is anyone who works for the government, except for those in the uniformed services. The civil service operates on all levels from federal (national) to state and local government agencies, and is one of the largest employers across the US.

Your initial experience of America's civil service will be on arrival, when you're 'processed' by immigration and customs officers, who aren't generally known for their warm welcome. This can be a lengthy and tedious procedure, all the more so if you aren't white, English-speaking and reasonably well-dressed – people from countries thought to harbour terrorists or droves of illegal immigrants usually have a harder time. It pays to be as polite and courteous as possible, and treat all questions with the utmost seriousness.

Unlike people in some European countries, Americans don't deal with bureaucrats on a daily basis – contact is often via an intermediary, such as a real estate agent. For some, their only contact with City Hall may be to obtain a licence for their dog. However, when you do come face to face with American bureaucrats, you'll find (most of) them naturally helpful and, provided you know what you want and can communicate clearly and concisely, you'll receive accurate and clear information and be dealt with politely and efficiently.

Getting Round Bureaucracy

The simple answer to this is: you can't! And there's no reason to. America isn't a country noted for its red tape and obstructive bureaucracy, which will come as a relief to anyone who's travelled in parts of Europe or the Middle East. Generally, Americans are service-orientated, and the service they offer is detailed and efficient. There's a system, but it's been designed to help you, so make the most of it.

ACCOMMODATION

Like the British, most Americans prefer to own their own homes, and some 70 per cent of households are owner-occupiers, while the remainder rent. On arrival, you'll probably start by renting a home, at least in the short term, until you're able to put down more permanent roots.

Rented Property

Your first few nights will probably be spent in a hotel. For a stay of more than a few nights, look for 'corporate' hotels or aparthotels, which are self-catering serviced apartments available on a

weekly basis. Many hotel chains, such as Marriott, offer long-term stays in 'suites', often comprising of a kitchen, bathroom, living area and a bedroom. There are also specialist 'suites hotels' such as Homestead Suites and Amerisuites – the cheaper ones consist of a room with a kitchenette.

Hotel accommodation is priced per room (not per person) and ranges from over $500 a night for five-star luxury to $30 a night for a basic motel room – townhouses, suites and serviced apartments are somewhere in between.

You can search for accommodation (American say 'accommodations') on the internet. All the major chains have a website, and offer better deals to online bookers. Reputable websites include 🖳 www.expedia.com and www. travelocity.com. Ensure any price you're quoted includes local taxes.

The next step is a longer-term rental property, your best option if you're only staying in the US for one or two years. Cost depends upon size, facilities and, especially, the location; not surprisingly, accommodation in uptown New York costs a great deal more than in downtown Boise, Idaho.

Most city accommodation consists of apartments and condominiums (both are flats in British English). If you want a house with a garden (yard), head for the suburbs where rents may be cheaper, but remember to 'cost in' the commute to your place of work. As a rough guide, expect to pay from $500 a month for a small one-bedroom or from $750 for a two-bed apartment, although you can pay **much** more in some states and cities.

Properties are generally let unfurnished, although most have white goods such as a fridge-freezer, cooker and dishwasher. 'Condos' may be furnished – some are let as holiday homes – and may have access to communal facilities such as a laundry room, pool or gym.

In New York, and other major cities, there's a shortage of good accommodation, which is why many people live in studios (one room plus kitchenette and shower room) or 'walk ups' (no lift). Most people pay high rents for a tiny apartment – the equivalent of renting an entire house in a provincial town – for the privilege of living in Manhattan.

There are numerous ways to apartment hunt. Friends, relatives and work colleagues are often the best scouts, although there are also advertisements in local newspapers and magazines – be prepared to view on the day of publishing. Estate agents also manage rental properties, whereby the landlord usually pays their commission, so be wary of an agent who tries to charge you an upfront fee for 'registration' or any other service. Good web sites for rental properties across the US include 🖳 www.forrent.com and www.homes.com

Landlords & Contracts

Most landlords have only a handful of properties for rent. Their 'ideal' tenant pays the maximum rent, keeps the property in good order, and rarely contacts the landlord. There are laws protecting tenants' rights, and many cities have 'rent control' laws to prevent excessive rents, and to control the percentage by which the landlord can raise the rent between contracts.

Some landlords will only accept rental payments directly from your bank account to theirs; many will want to see proof that you have a job and can pay the rent. It's normal to pay a deposit or holding fee, which is paid back in full at the end of the agreement, provided there's no 'undue' wear and tear. The amount of the holding fee varies, depending on the size of the property and whether or not it's furnished. They will also expect you to pay a deposit or two month's rent in advance, so that you don't do a midnight flit and leave them out of pocket!

Tenancy agreements are drawn up by the landlord, although the documents are usually standard. However, be sure to read the agreement carefully before signing it, and if anything seems odd, ask for an explanation. Honest landlords have nothing to hide.

If English isn't your first language or you suspect the legal speak is hiding something, consult a lawyer with particular expertise in tenancy agreements. You can find one on recommendation (the best course of action), in the telephone directory or at your local library. A consultation costs about $60.

If your rent is inclusive of utilities, make sure that there's not a clause in the contract allowing the landlord to impose an increase to cover a rise in the price of, say, electricity. You shouldn't accept a re-negotiation of utility rates until the rent agreement has expired.

Buying a Home

Buying makes more sense than renting if you're staying long term. Even if you've owned property before, in the US you're effectively a first-time buyer, and not being in a chain gives you a bargaining advantage. The process begins with the real estate agents (realtors or realtists) who will fall over themselves to help you – but there are some aspects of the American property buying system which you should be aware of:

● Lawyers aren't strictly necessary – most states have mandatory title insurance to protect against future claims on a property's title.

● Real estate agents handle everything. The vendor uses an agent to sell, and the buyer may also contract an agent to handle the purchase. Pick your agents' brains about schools, public transport, utilities and council services. Make them earn their fee!

> **Use a real estate agent who's a member of a professional organisation, such as the National Association of Realtors (NAR). A 'rating' of agents by experience and commission rate can be found on Home Gain's website (🖥 www. homegain.com).**

● Contracts, once signed, are conditional but binding. If you pull out without a good reason, you may lose your deposit or can even be forced to buy the property.

- In some states, all funds must be placed with a neutral third party, the 'escrow agent', approved by both parties. He's responsible for checking all documents and disbursing the funds on closure.

- Surveys are a good idea, especially on older properties – America has many wood-boring insects!

- If you need a mortgage, the interest rate will depend on your 'credit score'; the higher it is, the lower the rate. You'll need to build up a decent credit score in the US before you can make major purchases, such as a house or car, unless you can put down a large deposit.

- When budgeting for a house purchase, allow around 5 per cent of the purchase price for closing (settlement) costs.

Almost everything you do in the US is determined by your credit score. The higher your score, the better the interest rate you'll be offered on a loan or mortgage; you may also be offered a cheaper insurance policy. Many employers also run credit checks on prospective employees, so having a bad score can lose you a job. As a new resident, you're unlikely to have a credit history, so your score will be low. A good way to start establishing a credit score is to apply for a credit card, use it, and pay off the whole amount each month. Debts have a negative effect on your credit score, so ensure you pay all utility bills on time.

The phrases 'subprime' and 'credit crunch' have been synonymous with the US property market since the 2007/8 recession, which saw banks founder, house values plunge and thousands lose their homes. In the simplest terms, subprime lending is providing loans at higher interest rates to borrowers less able to make the repayments. It's this uncontrolled lending – and the subsequent defaulting by borrowers – which sparked the 'credit crunch' and subsequent recession. The end result for the buyer is more and cheaper properties for sale (particularly foreclosures), although for those who need finance, home loans are harder to obtain.

BUYING OR HIRING A CAR

America has the highest ratio of vehicles to drivers on the planet, and unless you live in a big city with reasonable public transport, it's likely you, too, will be driving everywhere. The good news is that cars are relatively cheap to buy and rent, and petrol (gas) is cheaper than almost anywhere else in the western world.

Driving Licence

As a tourist, you can drive for up to a year with your national licence (this applies to most nationals, but not all), although if it isn't a photo-licence it's advisable to have an International Driver's Permit (IDP).

If you're staying on in the US, you must

acquire an American driver's licence within the first 12 months – sooner if you're a student or taking up work – which requires passing both a written and road test. It makes sense to tackle this as soon as possible, particularly as a US driver's licence is a useful piece of ID. Note that licences are issued by individual states, and drivers must exchange their licence if they relocate to a different state.

All documentation allowing you to drive in the US – your licence, insurance, identity papers, etc – must, by law, be carried at all times when driving.

Car Hire/Rental

Renting a car (Americans don't hire) is a popular way of travelling from one part of the US to another. Car rental companies may offer good deals on 'returns' – the renter delivers the car to another city – while 'driveaways' are a unique American concept, whereby you get free use of a car or truck in return for delivering it to a certain destination.

Renting a car for local use is less economical, especially in New York where the rental fees can be five times higher than in, say, Florida. Expect to pay between $30 and $150 a day, and make sure it includes sufficient liability insurance. To rent a car, you must be 21 or older, and have held a licence for at least one year.

Buying a Car

Most Americans buy a car for private use, whereas they may lease one for business use. Your budget will dictate if you buy a new or used model. Finance is available in the form of a hire purchase agreement or loan, provided you have a decent credit score (see

Buying A Home, above). There are always taxes to pay, which vary from state to state. There are also 'lemon' laws, which protect buyers against being saddled with a severely defective car.

> **'People can have the Model T in any colour, so long as it's black.'**
>
> Henry Ford (US car manufacturer)

New Cars

Americans love their cars – the bigger the better – and if you're a foreigner from a country where fuel costs are high and drivers more environmentally aware, you may struggle with their love of monster 4WD gas-guzzlers. The most desirable vehicle – before the gas price went through the roof in 2008 – was the sports utility vehicle (SUV) – a posh version of the pick-up truck which used to account for around half of all vehicles on American roads. A largish Mercedes saloon is described as 'compact'; a Ford Focus is 'sub-compact'. Many Americans won't even entertain the idea of driving a European or Japanese 'mini' car, any more than they would a car with manual gears (stick shift) or without air conditioning (AC).

Buying a new car is a simple process, provided you don't let the dealer get the better of you. Focus on the base sticker price (this includes the warranty but not the optional extras, many of which are standard anyway) and be prepared to haggle. Don't be rushed, take your time and as many test drives of as many vehicles as you want. A car is the second-largest purchase most people make (after a home), so it pays to have every base covered. Find out how long

(in time and/or mileage) your parts and labour warranties will last.

If you need a loan or hire purchase to buy the car, don't just accept an agreement from the dealer. Try every lender (including your bank) and double-check whether there are penalties incurred for late or missed payments.

Used Cars

Ensuring you aren't ripped off when buying a used vehicle is more difficult. If your knowledge of vehicles is limited, take along an expert or have the car checked out at a garage – especially if it's a private sale. Nearly-new used cars can be excellent value for money. You can pick up a classic 'junker' for under $500 – this may be your only opportunity to drive an elderly Cadillac with fins and a gas-guzzling V-8 engine!

The Unofficial Department of Motor Vehicles website has plenty of useful advice (💻 www.dmv.org). Good sources for checking prices include the National Automobile Dealers Association's (NADA) Used Car Price Guide (💻 www.nadaguides.com) and Kelley Blue Book's website (💻 www. kbb.com).

Registration

All vehicles must be registered, which is done at the Department of Motor Vehicles – where waiting lines are the stuff of legends. The required documents differ from state to state, but officials will want to see proof of your identity and ownership of the car (such as a notarised bill of sale) – check exactly what documentation is required in advance.

Fees vary widely, depending on the state and the condition and age of your vehicle. A full list of the requirements can be found in our sister publication, *Living and Working in America*, while 💻 www.dmv.org (see above) offers a state-by-state breakdown of the documentation required to keep you legal on America's roads.

EMERGENCY SERVICES

America's emergency services telephone number is 911. This is the number to call for an ambulance, the fire service or police. It can be dialled from any phone, including mobiles.

Once through to an operator, state clearly and concisely which service(s) you require, plus your address or precise location, and give a brief explanation of the situation. Nobody expects you to know medical terminology; however, descriptions such as 'hurt head', 'broken arm' or 'unconscious' will help the operator to assess the situation. Stay on the line and follow the operator's instructions – they've dealt with most situations countless times.

There's sometimes a long wait for a city (public) ambulance, although a private ambulance will turn up immediately – look up 'Ambulance Service' in your Yellow Pages, and keep the number by the phone. There are other numbers to contact your local police and fire service, and you should use these numbers for less urgent problems, such as a lost wallet or if your cat is stuck up a tree. **Only dial 911 in a genuine emergency.**

HEALTH SERVICES

> '**America is the country where you [can] buy a lifetime supply of aspirin for one dollar and use it up in two weeks.**'
>
> John Barrymore (American actor)

Americans are obsessed by their health. The faddiest diets, most punishing exercise regimes and truly bizarre treatments all have their roots in the US. Attitudes are often contradictory. Thinness is highly desirable, but food is cheap and abundant, and a great many Americans are overweight. Physical fitness is a universal goal, but most people go everywhere by car. The nation suffers from all the typical 21st-century ailments, brought about by poor diet, dependence on drugs and alcohol, and stress – stress suffered by expatriates is an acknowledged medical condition in the US

Most illogical of all, America leads the world in medical innovation, and spends 16 per cent of its gross domestic product (GDP) on health – but it's almost impossible to get free treatment unless you're destitute.

State Healthcare

The US is the only major developed country that doesn't have a national healthcare system. Whether you visit America for a day or a lifetime, you must have medical insurance. There's state healthcare, but it's a small safety net with large holes, and designed to look after only a small proportion of the population. Everyone else is expected to have insurance (either personal or through their employer), or enough money to cover their medical bills. Many don't. Over 40mnAmericans are uninsured, while a further 60mn have inadequate insurance. Crippling medical bills are the most common reason why Americans file for personal bankruptcy.

Medicare is a government-funded social insurance programme targeting senior citizens, while Medicaid is a social protection programme, partly state-funded, which covers certain categories of low-income people (including mothers, children and those with disabilities). Between them, the two schemes provided healthcare to just fewer than 80mn people in 2006. As a foreign immigrant, it's highly unlikely that you'll qualify for either system.

Private Healthcare

The lack of universal public healthcare raises many negatives – but there's one positive point. For those who can afford private treatment, the service is second to none. The private service sees you as a paying customer and (as is the case everywhere in America) the customer is always right. Americans have more control over their treatment than patients anywhere else in the world.

> **'Attention to health is life's greatest hindrance.'**
>
> Plato (Greek mathematician & philosopher)

Registering with a Doctor

Registering with a doctor is one of the first things you should do on arriving in the US. Americans consult specialists for everything, but you'll still need a family practitioner (similar to a British GP) to deal with day-to-day problems. Ask your employer, work colleagues and neighbours for recommendations, but bear in mind that your choice of a doctor may be influenced by your health insurance package, which may limit your options or require you to pay more for visiting a doctor outside the network. Over half of employers provide medical care through Health Maintenance Organisations (HMOs),

some of which stipulate precisely where treatment can and cannot be obtained.

Visiting the Doctor

Visits are by appointment only. Arrive in good time, and bring your insurance card – it's the first thing staff will want to see. You'll only receive treatment once they're convinced that you can pay the bill. As a new patient and/or foreign resident, they may expect you to pay cash, as well as any co-payments. Fees are high – up to $150 to see a family practitioner, and twice as much to consult a specialist. Medicines, tests and treatments are extra, and many doctors over-prescribe or order unnecessary tests for fear that the patient may sue if they misdiagnose, all of which adds to the cost.

After any consultation, you receive an itemised list of charges – this isn't the actual bill, but check it carefully as mistakes do happen. Inform the doctor immediately if anything is wrong. Your insurance company usually pays a doctor or hospital directly, and if there's an outstanding amount that isn't covered by your policy, the doctor will bill you for it.

Emergency Treatment

Fewer than 10 per cent of doctors make house calls. If you fall ill before you can register with a doctor, you can go to an urgent care centre (sometimes called a 'doc-in-a-box'). These often open evenings and weekends, but you may wait several hours before you get to see a medic.

Private ambulances charge up to $200, so if possible get yourself to the nearest emergency room (ER) by car or public transport. Most are open 24 hours. Most are also under-staffed, oversubscribed and stretched to breaking point – the television series *ER* is close to the truth – but the care is good.

Contrary to the urban myth about uninsured patients being turned away, if your condition is critical (life-threatening), a private hospital is obliged to take care of you, regardless of your finances. If you're unable to pay, once stabilised you'll be transferred to a public hospital, but at least you'll be treated.

> Carry your health insurance card with you at all times. If you have an accident, are knocked unconscious or fall seriously ill, it pays to have your card some place where it can be found easily.

It has become common to put an ICE number – the person to call In Case of Emergency – on your mobile phone, and the emergency services may check your mobile for this number if you're involved in an accident.

Medicines

Prescriptions can be filled at a chemist, called a pharmacy or 'druggist' in the US – strangely, a 'drug store' is a general store. Costs may be covered by your medical insurance, but few provide complete coverage, and you might still be responsible for a co-payment of up to $20. Brand-name prescription medicines cost many times more than generics, as the US has no pricing regulations.

Some medicines are hard to find. Soluble aspirin is rarely available, and Americans treat headaches with drugs containing acetaminophen rather than paracetamol. Among the most frequently prescribed drugs are anti-depressants – it's estimated that 6.5mn people are taking them at any one time.

Hospitals

Most hospitals offer semi-private rooms for two patients. If available, you can have a room to yourself, although you pay extra for the privacy. A hospital bed costs more than a luxury hotel suite. The level of care is usually good, although the number of people treating you can be disconcerting. Never be afraid to ask what is happening. Despite the high number of medical lawsuits in the US, many hospitals still make mistakes, which are sometimes fatal. Many are caused by giving a patient the wrong medicine dosage or even the wrong medicine. If you have doubts about your treatment, speak up.

A hospital stay is followed by bills, and you may receive several from various departments – and doctors – at the same hospital, usually before you've been discharged. If you're sent a bill for which your insurance company is liable, don't pay it – but refer all requests for payment to your insurers. However, if you're picking up your own bill, check it thoroughly.

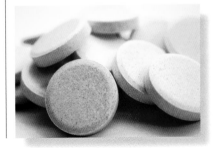

Audits have revealed that 95 per cent of hospital bills contain errors.

Nursing Care

Most American nurses take great pride in their work and do their utmost to ensure you receive the best possible care. However, there's a shortage of nurses in the US, therefore sometimes one nurse has to care for many patients at the same time, and standards can slip. Despite this, the custom in some European (e.g. Spain) and most African and Middle Eastern hospitals, where the patient's family moves in and takes over some of the care, isn't encouraged in US hospitals, where visitors are tolerated rather than encouraged.

Plastic Surgery

Americans love plastic surgery. In some parts of the US, people find it rather strange if you've reached a certain age and haven't resorted to a nip and tuck, and few people try to hide the fact that they've been aesthetically enhanced. On the contrary, there are even greetings cards you can send to congratulate someone on their liposuction or new nose. Breasts are always big – over 150,000 pairs of breast implants are slipped into place each year. However, men as well as women are increasingly going under the knife, with 700,000 American men a year opting for cosmetic procedures, such as having chest or buttock implants. Cosmetic surgery is yet another instant fix in a society where immediate gratification is one of the unwritten amendments to the constitution.

Childbirth

Although it's possible to have your baby at home, with a midwife in attendance, almost 90 per cent of births in the US are in hospital, with one in three by Caesarean section (C-section). Many don't need to be, and surveys reveal that the procedure is often performed at the mother's request or to speed up the birth process or even avoid lawsuits arising from complications. You may need to be firm to insist on a natural birth, and should shop around for an obstetrician-gynaecologist (OB-GYN) who supports your viewpoint. Note that once you've had a C-section, your next birth is automatically scheduled as a C-section in most hospitals.

Like everything else to do with health, childbirth is expensive. A hospital stay is about $4,000 and your obstetrician-gynaecologist (OB-GYN) charges a similar amount to deliver the baby. Your health insurance should cover part of the cost, but not if you were already pregnant when you took out the policy. Even newborns can't risk going uninsured in America – many parents add Junior to the family policy before he/she is even born.

INSURANCE

> 'I don't want to tell you how much insurance I carry with Prudential, but all I can says is, "When I go, they go too."
>
> Jack Benny (American comedian)

Certain insurances are compulsory in the US. These include liability (third party) insurance for vehicles – although not in every state – and home insurance, which is required by mortgage companies, who may also insist you have life insurance. Health insurance, although voluntary, is the most important of all. You should also consider travel insurance (for short stays), liability and pet insurance.

Insurance is a massive business and the choice of companies is endless. Shop around for as many quotes as possible. There are substantial discounts if you take out several different types of insurance with the same company, and this can work out cheaper than chasing different insurers for their best deals.

Read every document before signing it, and then read it again. There are independent advisors who can lead you through the insurance maze, and their services can save you money. They shouldn't be confused with brokers, whose job is to sell you a policy. Ask contacts and local expatriate groups for their recommendations – everyone in American has a story about insurance!

The Insurance Information Institute provides useful advice (💻 www.iii.org) as do state Departments of Insurance, which you can find via 💻 www. ican200.com/state.html.

Health Insurance

Health insurance isn't compulsory, although many people think it should be. The average family spends up to a fifth of their income on health, and coverage of less than $500,000 is considered woefully inadequate. You can save money by going through one of the Health Maintenance Organisations (HMOs) which cost, on average, 30 per cent less than conventional fee-for-service insurance, but limit your treatment options. On top of this you'll also need dental insurance. Americans have the best smiles in the world, and so they should when they spend thousands of dollars on fillings and crowns. American insurance companies are increasingly allowing Americans to save money by getting treatment abroad under the terms of their plan.

No health insurance policy pays all of your costs. Many have an annual 'deductible' (excess) which is the amount you have to pay each year before your cover kicks in. Co-payments are capped contributions which you pay every time you seek treatment, and are designed to put you off making 'frivolous' claims.

Car Insurance

The American love affair with the car means there are all manner of insurance policies to protect it, you and everyone else on the road. The choice is confusing, and legal requirements differ between states. With no driving record in the US, you could pay up to $2,000 a year in premiums, so it's vital to shop around – companies which operate solely online have cheaper deals. Others ways to save money include choosing a 'low profile' or older car, and dropping some of the extras, such as towing services and replacement rental cars. For more information, see 🖥 www. iii.org.

Liability & Legal Insurance

Americans are the most litigious people in the world. They will sue each other, organisations and authorities at the drop of a hat, sometimes for the most bizarre reasons. It's wise to have liability insurance, in case someone tries to sue you – and useful to have legal insurance, for when you need to sue. This eagerness to resort to law is one of the Americans' less endearing qualities, but it keeps the lawyers – and insurers – happy.

Household Insurance

The US is prone to many natural disasters, including hurricanes, tornados, earthquakes, wildfires and floods, yet it's been estimated that 80 per cent of households are under-insured. Household insurance is essential – mortgage companies insist on it. If you're renting, you can get insurance which covers your belongings and valuables against the usual risks.

If you need to make a claim for theft or burglary, you muse report the incident to the police and obtain a case number, which is required by insurance companies.

EDUCATION

There's no national education system in America, where each state runs its own. As a consequence, standards and requirements vary widely, depending on the state – or even the district – where you live. This may well have a bearing on where you decide to live.

Education is compulsory for about ten years (the ages vary from state to state, but most Americans study for an average of 12 years. State (public) education is free in primary and secondary schools – which are attended by about 90 per cent of students (even eight year olds are referred to a 'students'). The remainder attend private fee-paying schools, many of which are sponsored by religious groups, such as the Jewish community or Catholic Church; in the public system, religious tuition is forbidden by law. A growing number of children are educated at home.

To enrol your child in school, you need to produce proof of residence, a birth certificate and details of your child's medical history, including immunisations, plus their educational records.

American or International School?

Your choice of school depends upon several factors, including your child's ability to speak English, their career plans, the length of time you're likely to be staying in America, and your finances.

International & Private Schools

There are a number of private schools, including 'prep' schools which 'prepare' students for the top universities, and foreign schools which teach entirely in a foreign language, such as Korean, preparing students for further education abroad.

International schools are fee-paying schools which cater to students for whom English is a second language. They follow the American curriculum and accept students of all nationalities, offering intensive English language tuition where necessary. They tend to promote a more balanced 'world view', which is less relentlessly pro-American than state schools.

Many teach the International Baccalaureate (IB), a diploma which is a recognised standard of entry to universities worldwide. This is of particular importance if your child wants to study outside the US, as an American high school diploma isn't enough to get a student into university in some countries, including many European countries.

Private school fees are high: a year's teaching costs from between $1,000 and $2,000 for secondary schools, but can be as high as $15,000. Fees tend to increase by up to 10 per cent annually. The National Association of Independent Schools website (www. nais.org) has a search facility for finding a private school in your area.

> '**By the age of six the average child will have completed the basic American education... From television, the child will have learned how to pick a lock, commit a fairly elaborate bank hold-up, prevent wetness all day long, get the laundry twice as white, and kill people with a variety of sophisticated armaments.**'
>
> Anon

State Schools

American high-school education is about two years behind that of most other industrialised nations for children of a comparable age. Students lag behind in mathematics and sciences, in particular. Americans don't learn for the sake of learning, but see it as a means to an end. State education is locally funded (by property taxes), therefore schools in wealthy areas have more money than schools in inner-city areas and rural farming communities.

Younger expatriate children will find it easier to fit into the state system

than teenagers who've experienced a very different type of education structure. Lack of English doesn't bar a child from state education. Around one child in 20 enrolled in public schools cannot speak English adequately. In California, public high schools routinely teach a range of languages, including Arabic, Cantonese, Russian and Spanish – in cities with a major Hispanic population, Spanish may be the main language of instruction. If English isn't your first language, you may need to live in one of these areas or where English as a Second Language (ESL) classes are available.

The American Education System

Most of us are familiar with American schools from films and television. High school is portrayed as a microcosm of life, populated by 'jocks', prom queens and drop-outs, where 'fitting in' is at least as important as learning. There are similarities with other western education models, but also ways in which the US school system is different:

● There are three levels of education. Elementary (primary) school is from ages five to 11; middle school (junior high) from 12 to 14; high (senior high) from 15 to 18. These stages are also referred to as grades, from 'K' to 12, so a high-school student aged 15 is in grade 10.

● A student in the first year of high school is known as a 'freshman'. Second-year students are 'sophomores'. Confusingly, third-year students are 'juniors' and in the final year they become 'seniors'.

● The school year runs from early September until May or June (nine months) and is divided into two 'semesters', which are known as fall (September to December) and spring (January to May). A different system uses 'quarters': three are terms, while the fourth quarter is the long summer break.

● The school day in elementary schools is usually from 8.30am to 3pm or 3.30pm, with an hour for lunch. High schools start and finish one hour earlier. Extra-curricular activities and sports take place after school hours and there are no lessons on Saturdays or Sundays.

● American children have a ten-week holiday from June through to September. Many are packed off to summer camp, considered to be an important stage of a child's development, where he learns self-sufficiency, responsibility and friendship. Some 8mn children attend over 10,000 camps each year.

● Discipline isn't a strong suit in US schools, which tend to be more relaxed than their European equivalents (as is the whole country). Absenteeism and tardiness is a huge problem in some inner-city schools, where violence arising from drugs and gang culture are depressingly familiar.

In a few tough areas, students may be frisked for weapons or checked with metal detectors on arrival at school. There's even a law which automatically suspends students for a year if they bring a gun to school!

● Teaching standards vary from state to state. All teachers must have a licence or certificate to teach in public elementary and secondary schools, while a few states demand a master's degree. The status of teachers isn't especially high.

● Grades relate to a particular school, so it's difficult to compare education in different states. Marks are dependent on general school work, periodic testing, class participation, homework assignments, and independent projects. There are commercially prepared tests in some areas – students in New York state sit state-wide exams. On graduation from 12th grade, a student receives a high-school diploma. Graduation ceremonies are a rite of passage ('life cycle event'), and are sometimes referred to as 'commencement', as the student commences a new stage in life.

● Top-scoring students compete to be the 'valedictorian', who gives the oration or farewell speech at the graduation ceremony.

● A student can legally leave (quit) school at 16. This is known as 'dropping out' and is not recommended, as jobs are scarce for anyone without a high school diploma. Most students stay on until 18.

● Would-be university students are evaluated using a range of tests, such as the Scholastic Aptitude Test (SAT). A maximum SAT score is 1,600 (800 mathematical and 800 verbal skills), and students need a combined score of over 1,300 to gain entry to a top university.

Parents should encourage their children to get involved in extra-curricular activities. As well as helping them to integrate, it's also an investment in their future. Universities and employers place great value on students' achievements in activities such as working on the school newspaper or organising social activities, e.g. the school 'prom'. Proficiency at team sports is almost as important as good grades – some universities overlook mediocre grades if a student is good at baseball or football!

University

There are about 3,500 accredited colleges and universities in the US, catering to a college population of some 15mn students, of which around 500,000 are overseas students. Many American students expect to attend college or university as a matter of course, and more than half of high-school graduates go on to some sort of higher education. As a result, the academic standards required to earn a

bachelor's degree in the US are lower than in many other countries.

As well as universities, students can attend a two-year community or junior college or a four-year liberal arts college, which offer vocational training as well as a springboard to the four-year universities. In many states, only the top 10 to 15 per cent of graduating high school students go directly to a four-year university. It's four years because this is the average time it takes a student to complete a bachelor's degree requirement of 120 credits – many students take a good deal longer. Those with the highest grade point averages (GPAs) 'are graduated' Summa cum Laude, which is the equivalent of a British double first.

Higher education isn't free. It's paid for by a complex combination of government loans, scholarships and grants – and parental contributions. Average tuition fees for public (state) four-year colleges and universities are about $3,500 per year, and for private institutions $15,000 per year. Add on the costs of registration, room and board, health insurance, books and supplies, transportation and parking, and other expenses, and some parents pay up to $100,000 to put a child through college. Many begin saving for college before their child has spoken a word. Students often fund their college education with a variety of part-time jobs. It's difficult – although not impossible – for a foreign resident to obtain a partial scholarship.

Many of the most prestigious universities are private foundations and receive no federal or state funds. The most famous universities include the Ivy League universities (so called because they're so long established, they have ivy growing on the walls),

which include Harvard, Princeton and Yale. Other world-renowned American higher education institutions include the Massachusetts Institute of Technology (MIT) in Cambridge (Massachusetts), and Stanford University in California.

> **'Everyone has a right to a university degree in America, even if it's in Hamburger Technology.'**
> Clive James (Australian writer & broadcaster)

COUNCIL SERVICES

Refuse Collection

Americans generate a phenomenal amount of refuse (trash). There are gadgets which dispose of or reduce it (many homes have a waste disposal unit, some have a compactor), but the bulk is collected one or two times a week. Houses have their own dustbin (trash can), while apartment blocks have a communal bin. Rules and regulations differ between states, but most require your rubbish to be put in a bin or tied up in (intact) trash bags. Make sure that you know where, when and how your trash is collected, as putting it out too early, in the wrong place or leaving it on the street, can attract a fine of up to $500.

Usually, the city authority is responsible for rubbish collection, although in some states it's put out to private contractors. Payment is included in your property taxes or billed monthly.

Recycling

The US lags behind Europe when it comes to recycling, and some states such as New Jersey and California, are more 'green' than others. However, most have introduced the concept of recycling, and provide containers for glass, metal, plastic, paper, clothes, etc – these can also be taken to neighbourhood collection points. Contact your local library or information centre, or check council websites for details about local recycling facilities and requirements.

Other Rubbish

Larger items, such as furniture, are collected on specific days, either free or for a small fee. A few neighbourhoods organise their own community recycling projects, but the vast bulk of America's trash ends up in landfill sites.

Fresh Kills Landfill site in Staten Island, New York City, opened in 1948, and by 2000, was the largest refuse dump in history. At its peak of operations, it covered 2,200 acres (890 hectares), and could even be seen from outer space! It's now being transformed into a city park.

UTILITIES

Electricity, gas and water companies in the US are called utility companies. Some are government or state-run, but increasingly they're private companies, which means more competition, better service and, hopefully, cheaper bills. It's possible to arrange connection by telephone, although there's usually a connection or start up fee. Some utility companies also require a deposit, which is held for an agreed period or until you've proved that you pay your bills on time.

Most utilities are metered, and bills are sent out every one, two or three months. Check them, especially if they're based on an estimated reading. You have around two weeks to pay, after which a penalty is added. Further failure to pay attracts a 'notice of discontinuation of service' and a black mark against your credit score.

Electricity

A huge 70 per cent of America's electricity is produced from fossil fuels, such as coal – in 2005, the US was the world's largest emitter of carbon dioxide from the burning of fossil fuels.

The electricity supply is 110/120 volts AC, with a frequency of 60 Hertz (Hz) or cycles, so few European devices will work, unless they're dual voltage and designed for 60Hz operation. In addition, sockets take two-pin plugs. Adapters are available, but it's easier to buy new appliances.

American plugs have two flat pins (live and neutral) plus an optional third pin (earth). Most appliances come with a moulded plug, but if you need to fit a plug, the colour coding is usually white (neutral), black (live) and green (earth).

Gas

Natural gas is piped to all but the most remote corners of the US. It's charged by the cubic foot (therm), and prices have been rising steadily since 2000. Gas and electricity is often supplied by the same company, and depending on where you live, it may be more economical to opt for one fuel.

Supply Problems

Power cuts do happen. In August 2003, a blackout occurred throughout parts of the Northeast and Midwest US (and Canada), leaving about one-seventh of Americans without power, some for more than 24 hours. Fortunately, such incidences are rare. All utility companies supply a contact number for emergencies, and if it's a regional problem, there'll be a recorded information line. If it's just your house affected, a service engineer will visit.

> **Always ask for identification and check it before admitting any strangers into your home.**

Over 40 states have 'utility consumer advocates' who deal with consumers' problems with utilities. Contact the National Association of State Utility Consumer Advocates, 8380 Colesville Road, Suite 101, Silver Spring, MD 20910 (☎ 1-301-589 6313, 💻 www.nasuca.org).

Water

Water is cheap, though not necessarily plentiful. The supply is managed at state level, and in areas with low rainfall and long, hot summers, i.e. the west and southwest, there are restrictions during summer. You may not be able to wash your car or (perish the thought) fill your swimming pool.

Water is usually controlled by the local municipality, which either makes a standard charge or provides a meter. It's charged by the unit, and even the cleanest American would be hard-pushed to use over $100 worth in a year.

Quality

Tap water is safe, but chemical treatment can make it taste unpleasant; many people prefer the bottled water. This has created a water-cooler culture in US offices, where workers gather to gossip and discuss sports and television soaps. Water is usually drunk teeth-numbingly chilled and loaded with ice – Americans don't like lukewarm drinks, and an ice machine is a feature of even the seediest motel.

Drinking water from rivers or streams isn't advisable, as there are high levels of pollution.

Telephone & Internet

Americans love to communicate, so it isn't surprising that the US has the highest number of internet users in the world, or that only 2 per cent of Americans can survive without a telephone. Fortunately, the telephone system is cheap and efficient, with plenty of choice for the consumer.

Installation

Many US homes have a telephone point in every room, although you must supply the phones. A line can be installed in a few days. As with other utilities, depending on your credit score, a deposit may be required, although it may be waived if someone (e.g. your employer) acts as guarantor. Bills are sent out monthly.

States or regions are served by local telephone companies, such as Verizon or SBC, which are regulated by state and federal agencies. For long-distance, e.g. interstate and international calls, there are independent companies, such as AT&T and Sprint. Some offer incentives if you put all your calls through them, but it may pay to use different providers for different calls. Shop around for the best deals, and forget about loyalty; some 40,000 people a day switch carriers, and many do so several times in a year.

To help you through the phone maze, there are a number of websites that compare offers and rates for telephone services (e.g. 🖳 www.telecombeacon. com or www.bettertelephonerates.com).

Making Calls

American phone numbers consist of a three-digit area code (e.g. 111), followed by a three-digit exchange code (234) and then a four-digit number (5678) – you dial 1 for long distance, so the number is usually written 1-111-234-5678. Area codes may cover part or all of a city, or an entire state, so there's no need to dial it when calling within the same area.

If you're dialling abroad from the US, you first call the international operator code, which is 011, and then add the code of the country you're calling (the UK is 44), the area code and the subscriber's number. Calling the US from another country, you need to dial America's country code which is (not surprisingly) 1.

It's likely you'll make a lot of international calls, so look for a plan which cuts the price for the countries you call regularly. Check out calling cards, which allow you to call abroad, from any phone, at cheaper rates; and get online so that you can take advantage of cheap or free internet calls with VoIP or Skype.

> Toll-free (no charge) numbers begin with 800, 866, 877 or 888 and are used by businesses and organisations. Don't confuse them with premium-rate 700 or 900 numbers. Other numbers to be wary of include 550 (for group conversations), 940 (adult content) and 976. Many phone companies allow you to block these numbers.

Mobile Phones

Roughly half of the US population has a mobile phone (cell phone), which are offered by the main telephone companies as well as by specialist companies such as T-Mobile and Virgin Mobile. If your credit score is a problem, sign up for 'pay as you talk'; but be aware that, unlike in Europe and many other countries, you'll be charged for incoming as well as outgoing calls. Another oddity is that mobile phone numbers cannot be distinguished from landline numbers (they have no special code), so you can't tell which you're dialling.

Directory Enquiries

In most areas, you dial a local number, e.g. 411, for local enquiries. A residential contract includes a number of free directory assistance calls each month, but directory enquiry calls are almost always free from payphones.

Internet

More than half of all Americans have access to a high-speed internet connection (broadband), which is rapidly replacing dial-up as the standard form of access. They also enjoy the world's lowest internet access charges, thanks to intense competition between the many internet service providers (ISPs). Internet connection is provided by local telephone companies as well as independent ISPs, such as America Online (AOL). Cable television companies also offer it as an add on. You'll need to get online, not just to stay in touch with friends, but because almost all information is now supplied via the internet.

Many places offer Wi-Fi (wireless) internet access: if your laptop is configured

for Wi-Fi, you can surf for free in many hotels, airport lounges and coffee shops

Faults & Problems

Check that there's nothing wrong with your telephone equipment before reporting a fault. Take the phone from the room where the fault was first identified and try it in another room, or your neighbour's house. Then try plugging a different phone into the offending socket. Only call the engineer if you're sure there's a fault, otherwise you'll be billed for the call out.

STAYING INFORMED

Television

Television invades life at every level, 24-hours a day. American TV is all about quantity, not quality – there are 100s of channels but very few worth watching! Many Americans admit this, referring to their TV as a 'boob tube' and worrying about its effect on their families, but it doesn't stop them watching an average of three hours a day. About 85mn tune in during 'prime time' (7-11pm).

Most foreigners' knowledge of American life is gleaned from television. Fortunately, those programmes which sell around the world are the cream of the crop. For every *Cheers*, *CSI* and *Ally McBeal*, there are thousands of banal talk shows, trashy soaps, bizarre game-shows and cheap reality TV programmes. If these were screened worldwide, America might be a less desirable designation for emigrants.

US television won't keep you informed about life back home – TV news is high on shock and low on analysis, and pays scant attention to events outside America – but knowledge of the top-rating TV shows, such as *Desperate Housewives*, *Grey's Anatomy*, *House*, *The Oprah Winfrey Show* and *The View*, plus televised sporting events, is invaluable when you're getting to know Americans.

There's no escape from television and most homes have one in every room. TV features in the cheapest motel room and in every bar, diner, store and waiting room, and you can even watch it while you have a filling at the dentist.

Broadcasters

There are five 'national' networks: the American Broadcasting Company (ABC), the Columbia Broadcasting Service (CBS), and the National Broadcasting Company (NBC), known as the big three, plus Warner (Brothers) TV and Fox TV. In addition to these, there are over 800 commercial and 400 public channels. Not all are available across the nation, but most viewers can zap into 20 or so channels, plus umpteen cable and/or satellite channels. One of the most interesting networks is the Public Broadcasting Service (PBS), which shows a lot of foreign (especially British) imports, documentaries, live music and theatre.

> **'Nobody ever went broke underestimating the taste of the American public.'**
>
> Henry Louis Mencken (American journalist & critic)

Advertisers

There's no television licence; programming is paid for by advertising. Some advertisers spend over $500mn a year on plugging their products, and have a great deal of control over content, one reason why there's very little sex, nudity or swearing on US TV. Adverts interrupt every show, cutting in (loudly!) without warning and taking up almost 50 per cent of airtime; increasingly, they're designed to join as seamlessly as possible with the programme, to prevent viewers 'hopping' to another channel.

Getting Connected

America uses National Television Standards Committee (NTSC) transmission; Europe uses PAL. This means that European equipment won't work in the US. Many people still watch TV via a rooftop aerial, and reception can be poor. Most cities have cable – which has its own bonanza of specialist and often unwatchable channels alongside the network favourites – and people in more remote areas use satellite.

A basic cable service costs $10 to $15 per month; a premium service with a range of film channels up to $75 per month. For information on satellite TV, contact DIRECTV (☎ 1-888-238 7177, 🖳 www.directv.com) and Dish Network (☎ 1-800-333 DISH, 🖳 www. dishnetwork.com).

Videos & DVDs

Four out of five American homes have a video or DVD player (or both), and most neighbourhoods have rental shops, such as Blockbusters, which also sell/rent video games in various formats, plus popcorn, candy, ice-cream, chips and all the other essentials of a couch potato's life. Libraries offer a selection of classic (i.e. 'old') movies for rent. Both videos and DVDs are also inexpensive to buy, costing from around $10.

An increasingly popular way of renting DVDs is by post, through companies like Netflix (☎ 1-800-585 8131, 🖳 www.netflix.com) which sends you up to three DVDs for as long as you like for a fixed fee.

Radio

There are over 10,000 local radio stations, some of which are divisions of national broadcasting networks, while others are a man in a shed with a pile of CDs. The audience for radio is growing, maybe because it's less intrusive and has fewer advertisements. Because it's so localised – you may change stations every hour as you drive through the US – it's a great way to learn about local areas.

The AM band is home to news and talk radio, while a staggering range of music goes out on FM stations – from rock and reggae to bluegrass, gospel, country and classical. Stations classify themselves as either AM or FM following their own three or four-letter call sign; those located east of the Mississippi are prefixed with a 'W' and those to the west with a 'K'.

The radio version of PBS is National Public Radio (NPR), which is non-commercial and financed by grants and donations. It broadcasts news and public affairs – some of its content is taken from the British Broadcasting Corporation (BBC). For the real thing, the BBC World Service is broadcast on short wave on several frequencies simultaneously, and is now switching to satellite radio. It's also possible to tune in to this, and many other foreign radio stations, via the internet. For more information on World Service, see 🖳 www.bbc.co.uk/worldservice.

The Press

Perhaps because of its vast size, the US has no national press. Although there are over 9,000 newspapers – including dailies, evening, weekly and free papers – all are regional. Readership has been in decline for years. The closest America comes to a national newspaper is *USA Today*, a tabloid which majors on pictures and sports. The *Wall Street Journal* is also distributed nationally, and the *New York Times* and *Washington Post* have national influence.

Few American newspapers contain much foreign news. The best way to get your news fix is through online editions of your favourite national newspapers. Some require you to subscribe for privileged access, which is cheaper than buying foreign newspapers, which are expensive, and often a few days late. However, you can also buy weekly editions of a number of British newspapers, such as the *Daily Express* and the *Daily Telegraph*, which are a great way to catch up on news from home.

There are good quality magazines, such as *Newsweek* and *Time*, which provide a digest of American and international news. At the other end of the spectrum, you can read all about celebrity sex lives and alien invasions in the weekly gossip tabloids, such as the *National Enquirer* and *Weekly World News*.

The newspapers in the US with the highest daily circulations are:

USA Today – 2,284,219

Wall Street Journal – 2,069,046

New York Times – 1,077,256

Los Angeles Times – 773,884

(figures from the Audit Bureau of Circulations)

BANKING

Banks are down there with lawyers and politicians in the American popularity stakes. Many people regard them as a necessary evil: necessary because most workers' wages are paid by cheque or directly into their bank account, evil because of the many charges they impose. It's thought that some 15 per cent of Americans don't have a bank account.

US Money

American money can be confusing. All denominations of dollar notes are small, similar looking and feature a dead president; while the coinage has only the official names and value in words stamped upon it, not the value in numerical terms. It's advisable to take the time to familiarise yourself with the different notes and coins, to save holding up queues in shops and banks.

There are six coins and seven banknotes, although some, such as the $1 coin and $2 note, are rarely used. The dollar is divided into 100 cents, and almost every amount has an official and slang term. The table opposite is a guide to the most common US coins and notes.

Choosing a Bank

There are thousands of banks to choose from in the US, some of which may have branches nationwide, while others operate in just one state or city. The biggest banks, such as Bank of America, aren't always the most user-friendly, and you may be better off with a smaller bank or credit union. Alternatives include online banking, or an overseas branch of one of your home country's banks. When choosing a bank, always check the charges and fees, and ensure that a bank is a member of the Federal Deposit Insurance Corporation (www.fdic.gov), which guarantees your money up to $250,000 in the event of the bank collapsing.

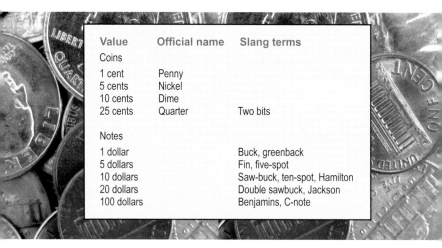

Value	Official name	Slang terms
Coins		
1 cent	Penny	
5 cents	Nickel	
10 cents	Dime	
25 cents	Quarter	Two bits
Notes		
1 dollar		Buck, greenback
5 dollars		Fin, five-spot
10 dollars		Saw-buck, ten-spot, Hamilton
20 dollars		Double sawbuck, Jackson
100 dollars		Benjamins, C-note

Banking in America is a complex subject, but the following are some of the more important points:

- **Bank account** – Start with a current (checking) account for daily transactions. To open it, you need to show proof of address and a social security number, and may be asked for extra ID, such as a passport.

- **Bank charges** – Banks make a service charge as well as charging for cheques and transactions. Some will waive charges if you keep an agreed minimum balance in your account.

- **Cash machines** – Known as Automatic Teller machines (ATMs), these allow you to deposit or withdraw funds, 24 hours a day. There's no charge for using one affiliated to your bank. ATM cards can also be used as debit cards to pay for purchases without the need for cheques.

- **Cheques** – There are no cheque guarantee cards, but a lot of cheque theft, so many businesses won't accept them. You'll need to write your name and address on the back, and support it with some ID. If a cheque bounces, the penalties can be high.

- **Credit cards** – The average American has eight credit/charge cards, and it may harm your credit score not to have one. You don't have to use a card from your bank – shop around for those with the lowest interest rates and no annual fee. Note that charge cards, e.g. American Express, must be paid off in full at the end of each month.

- **Foreign currency** – Many businesses won't accept sterling, Euros or other foreign currency, nor will they accept foreign-currency travellers' cheques.

- **Opening hours** – Most banks are open from 9am to 5pm and rarely close for lunch. Some open on Saturday mornings. Drive-in banks open longer hours, but check out the procedure before using one, otherwise you could hold up a lot of impatient customers!

● **Overdrafts & borrowing** – You should always agree an overdraft or loan in advance. Unauthorised overdrafts are expensive, and even illegal in certain states.

● **Security** – Identity theft is a growing problem. Keep your social security number separate from your bank cards, and never use the former to guarantee a cheque.

TAXES

American taxes are complicated, diverse and largely unavoidable – and far beyond the scope of these few pages. You'll find plenty of useful information on tax and other financial matters in *Living and Working in America*.

'Read my lips – no new taxes.'

George Bush Sr (the former President) during his 1988 presidential campaign – two years later, taxes went up.

Income Tax

There are three levels of income tax: federal (government), state and local. You may not pay tax to all these authorities, but you'll certainly pay it to some, and what you pay is largely dependent on where you live.

Federal tax takes the biggest chunk, although America's income tax rates are among the lowest in the industrial world. Tax filing day is April 15th, when everyone must complete a tax return. Even if you aren't liable to pay taxes (yet), you should still submit the relevant documentation to prove

it. Expert advice is available, either from a tax advisor or from the Internal Revenue Service (IRS), which has local offices across the US, as well as a comprehensive website (www.irs. gov).

State income tax varies considerably; California's is the highest at 10 per cent, while Texas and Florida have no state tax at all. A few states also allow individual cities to tax their population. State income tax can sometimes be off-set against federal taxes.

Social Security

Social security contributions are called taxes, and go towards retirement, disability and health benefits. They're paid by employers, employees and the self-employed, and range between 7 and 15 per cent of gross salary. Employees have their payments deducted at source; the self-employed pay them along with

their tax. For more information, see the Social Security Administration's website (⌨ www.ssa.gov).

Sales Tax

Most states impose a sales tax on various goods. This is America's version of Value Added Tax (VAT), and is by far the most diverse and confusing levy. Rates and taxable goods vary wildly. The tax ranges from zero to 8 per cent, and it isn't included in the purchase price of the item, so can come as a nasty shock when you reach the till. For more information, see **Chapter 9 (Retail Therapy)**.

Other Taxes

● **Property tax** – This is an annual duty on property, to pay for local services such as education, police and transport.

● **Capital gains tax (CGT)** – Applied to any asset you sell or otherwise dispose of. This includes stocks, bonds, vehicles, jewellery, etc. It doesn't penalise homeowners, as a portion of a gain made on the sale of your principal home is excluded from CGT, provided you've owned and occupied the property for at least two of the five years prior to the sale.

● **Estate tax** – The equivalent of inheritance tax or death duty, in other countries, so it isn't something you're likely to encounter, being newly resident in the country (and it's in the process of being phased out).

Tax Fraud

Americans are obsessed with reducing their taxes, but avoiding them altogether is a criminal offence. As everyone is responsible for declaring and

paying their own taxes, the system is open to fraudulent claims. The IRS is particularly strict, even for a tax department, and prosecutes anyone they find cheating with their taxes. Don't imagine that the IRS won't bother with individuals, as it's easier to find smaller offenders – and tax fraud adds up to a substantial sum which justifies the government's actions. Anyone found making fraudulent claims can expect to be charged and, depending upon the severity, may face a fine, prison or even deportation.

> **'I'm proud to be paying taxes in the US. The only thing is, I could be just as proud for half the money.'**
> Arthur Godfrey (American broadcaster)

COST OF LIVING

America isn't an expensive country when compared with many European and Far Eastern countries. The Mercer Cost of Living Survey for 2008 ranked New York as the most expensive city in the US – but at 22nd in the survey (and the only US city in the top 50), it was well behind Moscow, Tokyo and London, which occupied the top three places. If you judge America against Europe, certain items are clearly cheaper, such as fuel, food and clothing. Other expenses, such as healthcare and insurance, are frighteningly high. The most important factor is people's standard of living, which for most Americans is high, particularly for the 'middle' classes. However, the rise in world food prices and oil, and the credit crunch of 2007-8, created huge problems for almost everyone in the US – which was exacerbated (at least for exporters) by the acute rise in the value of the greenback.

For immigrants, one of the biggest factors is deciding where in America to begin a new life. If you already have a job, your choice of home will be limited. However, unless it's a really well-paid job, you should consider living in the suburbs and commuting to work by car or public transport. When job hunting in the US, the cost of living and commuting are factors you should consider when applying for or accepting a position. An indication of comparative rates of pay and living costs between US cities is available from ⌨ www.salary.com.

Big cities are significantly more expensive than small-town America, and the east and west coasts are harder on your pocket than the south central states. For example, Richmond, Virginia is a middle-of-the-road city, where a reasonable salary of $50,000 would provide a comfortable living standard for the average family. However, move that family to New York, and to maintain the same standard of living, they'd need an income of over $100,000, whereas the most they could expect to earn would be an extra $10,000 to $20,000. Then again, most New Yorkers would say that a smaller apartment, cheaper groceries and no car is a fair price to pay for the thrill of living in the city which never sleeps.

Whitefish Point Lighthouse, Lake Superior, Michigan

4.
BREAKING THE ICE

One of the best ways of getting over culture shock, and to feel more at home in the US, is meeting and getting acquainted with Americans. Making new friends anywhere is never easy, and the language and cultural barriers in the US can make it even harder. This chapter offers information about important aspects of American society and family as well as the expatriate community. It gives advice on how to meet people and how to behave in social situations, as well as topics to steer clear of in conversation, plus guidance on dealing with confrontations and officials.

> 'The most important trip you may take in life is meeting people halfway.'
>
> Henry Boye (writer & publisher)

COMMUNITY LIFE

Small-town America has always been associated with friendliness – on television at least. From *Peyton Place* to *Desperate Housewives*, it's a place where people leave their doors open for their neighbours to drop in, and newcomers are greeted with smiles and cherry pie. Big-city America, meanwhile, is often portrayed as a lonely place, where singles eat cold pizza behind locked doors while the street outside echoes with the sound of police sirens. However, in real life, you're just as likely to be warmly welcomed in a Chicago apartment block as you are to be ignored in a Midwestern suburb.

Most Americans have a sense of community spirit, which surfaces at holiday times, such as the 4th of July or during Halloween trick-or-treating.

But they're also self-sufficient and for many, the family is enough. They may greet neighbours politely, but never really feel the need to get to know them beyond the occasional backyard barbecue. Americans don't live in each other's houses in the way that, say, Irish or Turkish people do.

Most have an almost primeval need to be self-sufficient, which may date back to the days of the pioneers, when a settler's nearest neighbours were 100 miles away across the prairie. For an American, the idea of being a nuisance to his neighbour is almost as bad as his neighbour being a nuisance to him. Just as an Englishman's home is his castle, an American's home is his 100-acre ranch.

Community Regulations

Apartment blocks and condominiums usually have a written set of rules and regulations, which can cover everything from where to hang your laundry to how loud you can play your stereo. A few even interfere in your private life, and there are some upmarket apartment co-ops which interview prospective buyers and tenants.

> In the film *Green Card*, Andie MacDowell's character wants to live in a flat in a block which only accepts married couples, so she makes a marriage of convenience to an illegal alien, played by Gerard Depardieu, who is desperate to stay in the US. Neither gets exactly what they want.

Being a newcomer in any neighbourhood or community is unsettling. As well as official regulations, there are also unwritten rules.

After a heavy snowfall, it's expected that the entire able-bodied male population of a street will join forces to clear the road and pavements (sidewalks). If you're unprepared and don't have a snow shovel, your neighbours may think you're lazy. They will come to the same conclusion if you don't keep your lawn immaculate throughout summer. In areas mainly occupied by families with young children, late-night parties and loud music are frowned upon before a school day, while in suburbs with an older population, people may grumble about your noisy kids.

Generally speaking, American neighbours make an effort to assimilate newcomers into the community – or at least they make the gesture. Use this initial contact to try to find out some of

the neighbourhood 'do's and don'ts'. Stay friendly and open with your new neighbours, but don't expect to become their friends – at least not for some time. And never invade their privacy.

SEXUAL ATTITUDES

There are few sexual taboos in the US. It is, after all, the country which unleashed on the world women's liberation, free love and gay rights. Men and women really do appear to be equal, and they interact on an equal basis without any loss of honour or virtue. American girls don't have chaperones; American boys usually know just how far they can go.

It wasn't always this way. The founding fathers of the US came from Puritan stock, where sex before marriage was unthinkable, and this moralising streak is still a characteristic of some communities. In the Bible Belt (the

term used to describe a large wedge of the US which stretches from Virginia to Texas), conservative Christianity has a big influence over people's lives.

Despite the number of 'adult' channels, movies are highly edited for sexual content when they're shown on mainstream television. Bad language is either beeped out, or actors voice over the swear words with less offensive ones. If nude scenes do make it onto the screen, people's 'private parts' are blurred out.

Americans appear ambivalent towards sex. Since the '60s, they've championed their right to have sex whenever, wherever and with whomsoever they want, but they can still be priggish about extra-marital sex, especially if the offender is a politician or religious leader.

Many feel that a too-open attitude to sex is having a detrimental effect on the nation's morality. Despite easy accessibility to contraception, the number of unmarried and/or teenage mothers in the US is among the highest in the developed world, and the rate of sexually transmitted diseases is increasing. Paradoxically, sexual abstinence is also becoming fashionable as more teenagers take a 'virginity pledge', vowing to save themselves for their wedding night.

> **In spite of their liberal lifestyles, many people feel short-changed by sex. In a recent Durex Global Sex Survey, 45 per cent of Americans said that they weren't getting enough, although only 17 per cent would admit to having had an affair.**

The Role of Men & Women

The roles of men and women in society have changed beyond recognition in the last few decades. The man is no longer the bread-winner on whom the family rely; the woman has moved far from the stay-at-home Stepford Wife she was in the '50s. Financial pressures, female emancipation and the high cost of child care, mean that if the woman's potential income is higher than her husband's, he may stay at home and look after the children while she goes out to work. In a large number of married couples, both partners work, which has helped to reinforce equality at home and in the workplace.

Men

Marlboro Man or Homer Simpson? The foreign stereotype of the American male as an aloof explorer of the high plains has been largely replaced by a loud, Hawaiian-shirted, Budweiser-drinking, sport-fixated family man. It isn't so far from the truth. American men love their beer and their sport, almost as much as they love their families.

In such a huge country, it's difficult to pinpoint a typical male, but it's fair to say that most US men are confident, self-sufficient and adaptable. They're comfortable with the opposite sex, but they enjoy bonding with 'the boys': an all-male excursion to go fishing and hunting – or just watch sport on television with a six-pack or three – is a strong part of the culture.

Men still climb higher up the corporate ladder than women, and they earn higher salaries. However, thanks to technology, women are catching up and invading previously all-male domains. In the days before power steering, it was physically difficult or impossible for most women to be truck drivers, but nowadays there are female truckers on highways across the US.

Women

American women enjoy more freedom than most females in the world. They're free to wear as little as they want, although foreign men should be aware that revealing clothing is a personal statement and not an invitation for sex.

For years the woman's role was a domestic one, and for many it still is. Studies have shown that even when a couple both work, it's still the woman who takes on the lioness's share of the housework and childcare. But few would describe themselves as a 'housewife'. Not many women make it all the way to the top in business or politics – Hillary Clinton is the exception rather than the rule – and their pay still lags behind their male peers, but women now identify themselves by their careers. Many are having children later; and some are leaving it too late to embark on motherhood at all.

The pressure to be a Superwoman reached its peak in the '80s, when many women realised that 'having it all' came at a high price. But many have no choice. The high rate of divorce – about half of all marriages end in the lawyer's office – has left many families divided, and the vast majority of single-parent families are headed by the mother.

> **'America is a land where men govern, but women rule.'**
>
> John Mason Brown (American Abolitionist)

Abuse of Women

Domestic violence in the US is nowhere near the problem that it is in less developed countries, although it's still a big issue. According to the American Institute on Domestic Violence, up to 95 per cent of all domestic violence victims are female, and over 5mn women are abused each year. Moreover, it's the leading cause of injury to women. A recent government survey found that, on average, at least three women are murdered by their husbands or boyfriends in America every day.

Fortunately, in such an information-friendly country, there are plenty of resources to help women in violent situations, from telephone help-lines to shelters (the National Domestic Violence Hotline is ☏ 1-800-799-7233).

Some believe that the ability of women to stand up for themselves has increased confrontations between the sexes. Studies have shown that every year in the US, over 3mn men are the victims of an assault by an intimate partner. Men are far less likely than women to report these attacks or seek help, therefore the real figures are likely to be considerably higher.

Homosexuals

Gay-rights campaigners have moved mountains to make homosexuality acceptable in the US, although the advent of AIDS and the gay community's courageous reaction to the disease, has done much to win them respect among heterosexuals.

It's illegal to discriminate against someone because of their sexual preferences, and there are gay people in prominent positions across all fields – not just in entertainment but also in industry and government. Laws have been relaxed in many states to recognise same-sex relationships, but this doesn't give gays equal rights across the board. Only Connecticut and Massachusetts allows same-sex couples to marry, and thereby enjoy those social and financial benefits only available to married couples. A few other states allow same-sex unions, but in a large swathe of the Midwest, where Christianity still has huge influence, marriage and similar unions are only recognised between men and women.

MEETING PEOPLE

In the US, attitudes to friendship are very different from many other countries. People can overwhelm you with their welcome, but then it trails off, and it takes time before they decide to accept you as a friend.

America appears to be a classless society, but wealth and education are still essential barometers. It's fairly unusual – although not impossible

– for a white lawyer to be buddies with a black or Hispanic street sweeper. But America's 'class system' is fluid. White and blue-collar workers can easily share the same status, and can move up or down the rungs of the ladder, depending on their personal success. If the lawyer files for bankruptcy, and the street-sweeper wins the state lottery, their roles will be reversed.

Wealth and education are the 'values' which confirm your status with your friends, colleagues and neighbours and, initially, you may have to deal with a certain amount of distrust until people have established where you 'fit in'.

Among the many ways to make friends and meet people in America are:

● **At work** – Your work colleagues may be the first Americans you really get to know. People are always keen to extend friendship over a coffee or beer after work, so always accept invitations. Even if they don't lead to a lasting friendship, socialising will improve your understanding of your workmates.

● **Expatriate groups and clubs** – There are expat networks all over the US, with activities ranging from

social clubs to support groups.
Contact them through the expatriate
press, websites, forums or your
country's consulate or embassy.

- **Local clubs** – Shared interests
  bring people together, whether
  it's cooking, local history or golf.
  Check out any interesting groups or
  societies (try your local library for
  ideas), and join one or two. If you're
  sporty, you'll have an advantage, as
  many Americans' social lives revolve
  around their tennis, golf or country
  club. People also like to 'contribute
  to society', therefore joining a
  volunteer group will increase your
  social standing.

Many neighbourhoods have what's
known as National Night Out, which
is usually held in May or June,
and sometimes involves a picnic
or barbecue in a local park or in
the street. This began as a way for
people to get to know their neighbours
and to help prevent crime in the
neighbourhood, but has evolved into
a genuine social event, and is an
excellent way to meet local people who
you would otherwise drive by with a
cheery wave.

- **At school** – Your children's school
  is a social hub where you can get
  to know other parents. People
  like to get involved with their
  kids' education, and there are
  always parent-teacher associations
  (PTAs) and other groups. Again,
  volunteering makes you stand out
  from the crowd.

Friendship

This is important to Americans, who
often rate their friends as being as
important as their family. Young people
living away from home will share
accommodation with friends made at
college or work – often referred to as
roommates or 'roomies' – and these
friendships can endure over many years.
The hit US comedy *Friends* is a good
illustration.

But just because friendship is
important, it doesn't mean that people
make friends easily, nor that friendship
implies the same ties and obligations
as it does in other societies. Americans
don't make excessive demands on their
friends; nor do they drop everything and
rally round in times of crisis, which will
be when you discover who your friends
really are!

Friendships are sometimes
compartmentalised – he's the friend I
work with, she's the friend I go to the
gym with – with certain people filling
different roles in each others' lives.
They can work across the sexes and
in the same couple: a man may have a
female tennis partner, while his wife
goes shopping with a gay male friend,
and it's entirely possible that the two
'friends' will never meet.

'We must meet for lunch some time'
can mean just that. It can also mean,
'It was nice to meet you but I'm really

not bothered if I never see you again'. Don't take new acquaintances' words at face value. Americans often say what they think you want to hear, not what they really want to say.

Dating

Dating means many things to many people. It might be two people sharing a meal or going to the movies in order to fill a free evening, a long-standing physical relationship or anything in between. However, just because two people date, it doesn't mean they're heading for a lifetime of commitment. Contrary to the inference by the US media that no American is happy until he or she is in a relationship – or the number of books written on the subject – dating isn't just a means to a happy ending. People still aspire to meet Mr or Ms Right, but if they don't, then they're in good company: US government statistics reveal that half of all households consisted of just one person.

The formality of dating is not what it was. Time was when the man made all the moves. Today it's just as likely to be the women who suggests a venue and picks up the bill – or, at the very least, offers to share it. The concept of speed-dating, where couples have a few minutes in which to impress their partner, and the huge growth in internet dating, where relationships develop at a distance online, without the couple ever meeting, has completely changed the American attitude to dating.

Don't expect a date to lead to marriage – it's often a one-time meeting. For some people, it's more like a sport, as they move from one partner to another like social butterflies. Sex is optional, but if you get that far, then you should be prepared to practise safe sex (using condoms) and be aware of your own personal safety.

The American dating scene is especially daunting if you come from a culture of introductions, arranged marriages and chaperones. Where on earth do you begin? There are umpteen books on the rules of dating (including a best-selling book called simply, *The Rules*), and the subject is covered to exhaustion by the US media, from TV situation comedies (sitcoms) to dating movies – often called 'rom coms' or 'chick flicks'. Other sources of information (and vicarious entertainment) are the real-life talk shows, such as those hosted by Oprah Winfrey or Jerry Springer, where people reveal the most intensely personal details of their lives. There's plenty of research material out there before you take the plunge.

Sexual attitudes are markedly different according to age and religious beliefs. Location is also a factor. As a (very loose) generalisation, people tend to be more sexually open in cities than in rural areas, or in the more laid-back coastal states as opposed to those in the God-fearing Bible Belt.

> **'I think the most un-American thing you can say is, "You can't say that."**
> Garrison Keillor (writer & broadcaster)

Where & When to Meet

It depends on who you're meeting and for what purpose. Men may choose to bond in a bar, whereas women might prefer a shopping trip. Most Americans will prefer to meet on neutral territory.

Don't invite someone to your house if you don't know them well, and never expect to be invited to theirs. It takes a long time for Americans to drop their drawbridge to comparative strangers.

If you're going to the cinema, theatre, concert or similar event, arrange to meet in a nearby bar or coffee shop. Most women will be more comfortable sipping a coffee than standing on a street corner. Always take into account the comfort and safety of the other person, and never arrange to meet a woman late in the evening on a deserted street or parking lot. Consider your own safety also. If you're going on a date with someone you don't know very well, tell a friend your plans and let them know where you're going and what time you expect to be home.

What to Talk About

Newcomers are often surprised by the American propensity for revealing quite personal information to strangers in general conversation. Even more surprising is the realisation that having opened up to you, he or she doesn't consider you a life-long friend. Be careful how you respond to initial advances, as faced with such openness it may be tempting to demur and not give too much away – in the US, being frank and open about oneself is a way of demonstrating honesty, and if you're too coy, people may think that you're aloof or that you have something to hide.

If you're stuck for conversation, television, sport and health are fairly safe areas for both sexes, while politics is a little more risky, and international relations should be

avoided. Americans don't share the British fascination with the weather.

> **'Americans adore me and will go on adoring me until I say something nice about them.'**
>
> George Bernard Shaw (Irish playwright)

Paying the Bill

This depends on the nature of the date or meeting. If it's just two people filling in time, then it's normal to split the bill (this is known as 'going Dutch'). If it's a romantic date, or one which may lead to a relationship, then either may pay. If you aren't sure, then offer to pay your share; this gives the other person the chance to accept or not. Be warned, however, that American women may consider a male date rather mean if he appears keen on going Dutch on a first date.

INVITATIONS

Sooner or later, you'll be invited to attend a social gathering. Luckily, there's no long list of rituals, and most of the do's and don'ts are basic common sense. But there are one or two nuances which can make all the difference.

In a land which champions diversity, the little things which make you stand out from the crowd can be nurtured – and can actually help break the ice. Your accent can be an excellent prop. People tend to be fascinated by accents different from their own, especially the British accent. Comments like 'I love your accent' are frequently made by Americans, many of whom believe that they have no discernable accent at all.

Receiving Invitations

If you receive an invitation, acknowledge it immediately – in writing, by email or by phone. It's impolite not to. You can accept or decline, although as a newcomer, it's better to accept as many invitations as possible. If you aren't sure whether you can attend, let your host know why (Americans love detail), and tell them when you'll be able to give a definite answer. If you say yes, and something happens which will prevent you from attending, let them know at the earliest opportunity.

Most cultures have a way of declining an invitation without appearing rude. In America, if you cannot accept an invitation but might like to do so another time, you can take a 'rain check' as in, 'I'll take a rain check on that, if you don't mind'. The idiom comes from the practice of issuing a ticket for future use after an event has been postponed or interrupted by rain.

If you're unsure what the event is about, ask. You won't be invited unless the host knows you, either personally or through someone else, and they won't be offended if you ask them to explain what's happening. Often, they'll be delighted to introduce you to a new custom. Sometimes an invitation will have been sent to someone else who has asked you to be their 'date', in which case ask them. They will be only too happy to explain what to expect, as this means that you're less likely to embarrass them!

If you're a vegetarian, say so as soon as you receive your invitation. Nobody will be offended; people are normally happy to cater for others' food whims (most Americans have a long list of what they can and cannot eat). Don't accept an invitation to a barbecue and then eat nothing but salad, as this may embarrass your hosts.

Dress Code

An overly-formal dress code is regarded as undemocratic in the 'classless' US. There will be times when you must dress up – if the invitation states 'black

tie', it means evening dress or dinner jackets (tuxedos) for the men, elegant gowns for the women – but these are few and far between. Smart casual dress is sufficient for a party or meal, and even that may be over the top at a backyard barbecue when everyone is wearing shorts (Bermuda shorts to Americans). Fortunately, invitations tend to be specific about the type of gathering. If you're still unsure, ask someone else who has been invited if wearing, for example, jeans, will be acceptable. This will produce a more specific response than 'What shall I wear?'

> If you come from a European country where people take pride in dressing up, with matching accessories and not a hair out of place, you may spend a lot of time in the US feeling distinctly overdressed.

Gifts

An invitation to dinner, or to anything which involves visiting someone's home, requires a gift. Flowers (not carnations), chocolates or a bottle of wine are fine, although not if your hosts are teetotallers. On occasions, you may be invited as a house guest, and should take along a gift to present to the hostess when you leave. Give a small ornament, book or CD, if you know the hostess's tastes; or something unostentatious and representative of your own country.

The Meal

The main event at most social events is the meal. Your hosts will have spent a lot of time planning, buying, preparing and cooking the food on offer. The last thing they want is someone ruining their timing. You must turn up within 15 minutes of the stated time, but on no account arrive too early. America pioneered the concept of the potluck supper, where everyone brings along a dish, so it's a nice idea to ask if you can contribute something, such as the salad or a side dish.

Americans enjoy sampling cuisine from around the world and may offer well-rehearsed dishes to guests, but they always eat like Americans. A lot of food is designed to be eaten with the fingers and a napkin is always at hand.

Parties

If you're invited to a party, don't arrive too early or you'll appear rather desperate. The invitation will probably state a time, e.g. 7pm to 11pm, in which case it's fine to arrive at 9pm, but not at 10.30pm, as this suggests you had better things to do. Only celebrities, who do have better things to do, can get away with arriving fashionably late.

Parties are an excellent opportunity to meet a lot of people in a short space of time, and an excellent chance to observe Americans at play. The sexes are never segregated at a social gathering, unless by choice. Women tend to back away from a discussion about sport or automobiles, while a man's contribution to a debate about make-up or shopping may single him out as gay.

Most Americans will show you over their house if you're invited to a meal or a party, and will expect you to pay them some compliments (and you should be prepared to show visitors around your home).

> **The acronym BYOB means 'bring your own bottle' – you'll see this on invitations, and it means you're expected to turn up with some alcohol. On occasion, during barbecue season, the 'B' may stand for beef (as in steaks).**

Extending Invitations

For every favour or good deed done, no matter how small, you're expected to return it, and one day you'll be required to invite friends and acquaintances to dine at your home. Don't panic. With a little planning this can be less stressful than in your previous homeland.

The informal nature of American entertaining means you can avoid a sit-down meal and instead lay on a cold buffet or barbecue (if it's the latter, remember than in America it's men who rule the grill). A detailed invitation will make your guests feel more comfortable by helping them to know what to

expect, so include as much information as possible, such as arrival times, what to wear and what to bring.

Accept any gifts graciously. If people bring wine or beer, and it's chilled, then they will expect you to serve it. Lay on some soft drinks for those who are driving or are teetotallers (a surprising number of Americans don't drink).

Your guests will expect to try something from your culture's cuisine. This doesn't mean roasting a sheep or serving up a Chinese banquet; just a taste will suffice. There's no need to be overly sophisticated or lavish. In fact, this should be avoided, as your guests may not be especially sophisticated and may think you're poking fun at them. Stick with what you know, don't be pretentious or outlandish, and extend a warm welcome. That way, your reputation as a host will be a good one.

Dining Out

On occasion, you might be invited, or invite friends to a restaurant meal. Who pays? Unlike in some cultures, where the host is expected to provide all food, drink and entertainment, Americans are usually happy to split the bill (which they call a check). If the meal is a thank you to friends who've been especially generous with their hospitality or time, then it's a nice gesture to take care of the bill, when it's best to do so discreetly before it arrives at the table.

RESPECTING PRIVACY

When you first arrive in America, it seems that everyone wants to be your best friend. This is misleading. Many Americans are private people. While their outer appearance is warm and fluffy, their inner shell is a tough nut to crack. In conversation, they will let slip personal information which they wouldn't reveal in response to a direct question, e.g. a woman might bemoan the expense of hiring a lawyer for her divorce but may be offended if asked by a stranger, 'Are you divorced?' Never push for information. It's unlikely that anyone will ask you intimate questions unless they, too, are foreign and therefore know no better.

Privacy extends to the home, the car and anywhere else where an American can hide from the outside world. You may know someone a long time before you receive an invitation to their home, and should be aware that this confers exceptional trust and honour. Conversely, people may find you strange – and very forward – if you issue invitations to people you've only just met.

It's a bad idea to drop in at an American 'friend's' house unannounced when you could telephone, and it isn't advisable to phone late in the evening – use email! Should you wish to offer help, try to do so in a way which avoids suggesting that the recipient needs it, or that you'll ever expect their help in return. Self sufficiency must be preserved at all costs, even at the expense of loneliness.

TABOOS

Americans accept that foreigners make mistakes. However, there are a few unforgivable gaffes and taboo subjects of conversation which you should be aware of. This section is a brief guide to potentially embarrassing actions and words.

- Avoid physical contact, especially in crowded situations, with people you don't know well. Make sure you respect their personal space.

- Be aware of the level of your voice. Speak too loudly and you'll offend people; too quietly and you'll irritate them (especially on the phone).

- Don't stare at people, even when you're in conversation with them. You should make eye contact, so as to appear trustworthy, but glance away occasionally so they don't feel as if you're staring.

- Never spit, even if you see others doing so.

- Some Americans seem to be constantly chewing gum; if you do it, try to do so quietly and with your mouth closed.

- Cover your mouth when you yawn, sneeze or cough – anything else is regarded as gross bad manners. If someone sneezes it's customary to say 'bless you'; the correct response is 'thank you'.

- If you're a man who wears a hat, remove it when you're indoors. Gentlemen always remove their hats as they cross the threshold.

> 'It is, I think, an indisputable fact that Americans are... the most self-conscious people in the world, and the most addicted to the belief that the other nations of the earth are in a conspiracy to under-value them.'
>
> Henry James (American author)

Conversation

Americans are the most obviously patriotic nation on the planet, and any criticism of their nation – or their patriotic attitude – will not be appreciated. The same goes for their symbols. You may find it rather ridiculous that the national anthem is sung before every sporting event, or that schoolchildren renew their allegiance as part of the school day – but you should never say so. Don't attempt to dent the Americans' belief in their country, as they will always stand their ground.

There are several topics of conversation which you should steer clear of, and these include

- **Iraq & Afghanistan** – A lot of Americans are against the country's presence in these countries, while others feel it's their job to keep the world a safer place. None like to be told by an outsider that America routinely interferes in other nation's affairs, even if it's true.

- **Presidential bloopers** – US comedians have great fun relating the slips of various politicians' tongues, for example, George Bush has been a great source of mirth. However, they're American and can say what they like. You shouldn't, unless you're sure of your colleagues' political persuasion.

- **Racism, sexism or any other –ism** – Any subject which even hints at a division in US society is best left alone. Americans can be touchy about past 'mistakes', such as slavery, the treatment of Native Americans or Vietnam. Even the American Civil War, which ended nearly 150 years ago, can still bring out ill feeling in the southern states. Be as politically correct as you can bear to be.

- **Cultural stereotypes** – Some Americans are comfortable making jokes about rednecks, Poles, women drivers or blondes, but you shouldn't unless you know your audience well. Try to avoid any disparaging remarks about US culture – or the lack of it. It's all been said before.

- **Abortion** – This is a subject which polarises many people. Some advocate women's right to choose whether or not they have a baby; others are strongly pro-life. Doctors who perform abortions have been murdered, while clinics have been bombed. It's a contentious subject.

- **Religion** – The US is a secular country where religion and politics aren't allowed to meet – at least theoretically. Americans can worship whoever or whatever they want, but many are evangelical Protestants who believe firmly that God was a heterosexual, church-going Christian, just like them. Get into an argument with one of these people and you'll be there 'til kingdom come (particularly if you get into a discussion with a creationist).

- **Weight** – Americans are extremely touchy about their weight. 'You've put on a few pounds' is the last thing they want to hear. So if you come from a culture where you speak as you find, rein in your tongue. Conversely, it's OK to discuss health or even plastic surgery – most people will happily elaborate on their surgical enhancement.

- **Sex** – However liberal people seem to be, most are reluctant to talk about sex, at least in mixed company.

- **Money** – As long as you don't ask personal questions, e.g. 'How much do you earn?', you'll find people open to discussing money, investments and the state of the US economy.

Dress & Behaviour

Think about the way you dress. Women can get away with low cut tops and short skirts, but wearing both at the same time may mark you out as 'trailer trash'. Nudity is unacceptable, except in naturist camps – Americans don't have the relaxed attitude to their bodies as do, say, the French or Germans. Ironically, being overdressed can be almost as bad, as it intimates that your fellow guests haven't made much of an effort.

Outward displays of affection between a man and a woman are acceptable in America, provided it doesn't go much further than kissing and you don't do it in front of dignitaries at an official function. If it becomes too passionate, you'll doubtless hear the cry, 'Hey you two, get a room!' from someone nearby.

> **'The statistics on sanity are that one out of every four Americans is suffering from some form of mental illness. Think of your three best friends; if they're okay, then it's you.'**
>
> Rita Mae Brown (American feminist writer)

EXPAT COMMUNITY

With such a disparate population, there's bound to be someone somewhere from your home country – or even your home town. Locating them is the challenge. Much depends on your point of origin. The areas of large cities where Puerto Ricans or Chinese predominate are virtually a home from home for these nationalities. The situation is very different for the lone Madagascan trying to make his way without a fellow national for thousands of miles in any direction.

In most large cities, virtually every nation on earth will have some representation and there may be a club or group for each. The nature of these clubs depends very much on the number of people involved and how often they meet. They exist to try to make the newcomer's arrival in the US as smooth as possible and, as such, should be among the first contacts you make – possibly even before you arrive. Their knowledge and experience will be invaluable, and they in turn will welcome a fresh outlook on news from 'home'. At the other extreme, in rural areas, the chances of finding a fellow expat are greatly diminished. Again, it makes sense to do some research before you arrive.

Don't be discouraged if there are no groups representing your home country. There are also groups set up to assist non-nationals in general, rather than those hailing from specific countries. There's also the option of joining an expatriates' group online, such as 💻 www.britishexpat.com, www.expatboards.com, www.expatexchange.com and www.expatfocus.com.

Advantages & Disadvantages

There are both advantages and disadvantages to mixing with your fellow country folk in the US. Expats provide an instant support system of people who speak your language and know how to get things done. They understand your culture and culture shock, and it's good to have people you can talk to when you're frustrated, confused or just plain homesick.

However, while lots of expats are fascinating people – writers, artists, genuine adventurers – many come with a lot of 'baggage'. You may end up socialising with people whom you'd avoid in your home country. Some expats spend their entire time complaining about America and the Americans, and too much of this negative vibe is unsettling. Worse, some are predatory and possessive, and there are many stories of new arrivals being ripped off by their fellow countrymen. And, last but not least, the more time you spend with

expats, the less time you'll spend with Americans.

CONFRONTATION

Inevitably, you'll encounter some conflict. Whilst confrontation is best avoided, Americans don't usually hold a grudge. They will leave you in no doubt as to their feelings, and will voice their opinions loudly but, having made their feelings known and received a response, they will simmer down as quickly as they fired up in the first place. This seemingly volatile exchange is the American's way of communicating his or her honesty, and demanding a frank and candid exchange of views, rather than an act of aggression. Of course, their reaction depends on the subject. Where issues of patriotic pride are at stake, the debate will likely continue until you back down or one of you drops through sheer exhaustion.

You're more likely to encounter conflict in cities than in smaller towns or rural areas, not simply because there are more people. The faster pace of life in the northern and eastern states tends to keep people on a shorter fuse than in the more laid-back west and south.

Gun Culture

Whenever you're on the end of an argument with an American you don't know, remember that people carry guns in real life and not just on TV. The Second Amendment of the US Constitution allows people the right to bear arms. Gun control is a hot topic – some people fiercely guard their constitutional right to carry a gun, while others are totally against it. There's also a growing concern about the number of shootings in US schools.

Handguns account for only one-third of all firearms owned in the US, but they're the weapons used in over two-thirds of all firearm-related deaths each year. While many people think guns are only carried by thieves and gangsters, a lot of victims are shot during arguments over trivial things. Make sure that you don't become a statistic.

DEALING WITH OFFICIALS

Civil Servants

You may be surprised by the efficiency of civil servants, especially if you come from Italy or France. Treat them with respect from the outset and you'll receive excellent service.

Police

The US police force commands respect. As long as they receive it, they respond with courtesy and extreme politeness; disrespect them and you may end up spread-eagled over the bonnet (hood) of your car. Address the police by their rank (if you know it) or simply as 'officer'. If you feel you're being treated unfairly, don't argue the point there and then as this will gain you nothing but trouble. Make a note of their details and raise your complaint afterwards.

> **If you're stopped by the police, stay calm and do as they say. Don't make any sudden moves such as reaching into your glove box for a driver's licence. Remember that in America police carry guns – and are prepared to use them!**

Teachers

Although teachers don't always get the respect they deserve, most are proud of their skills and successes and will be pleased to help you. Teachers are usually happy to speak at length about themselves, their school, and the state's education system. Schools set aside times for parents to meet with teachers, but if you need to discuss your child's education outside these times, a telephone call will get you a quick response if the problem is urgent, otherwise an email or letter will suffice. It's rarely necessary for you to attend in person.

Workers

You're the customer, which means you're always right. Be polite but firm and don't accept any work you're unhappy with. If you seek out reliable tradesmen with a good reputation they will do a good job at a fair price – but they're not servants. Treat them badly and you'll end up with leaky plumbing, a dirty pool and a garden full of weeds.

city mansions

Elementary
Intermediate
Advanced
PROFICIENCY
WELL DONE!
A

5.

THE LANGUAGE BARRIER

Being able to communicate with Americans, and knowing what to do and say when you meet them, are priorities when you move to the US, especially when you first arrive. If you're from part of the English-speaking world, this isn't such a problem – over 80 per cent of Americans speak English as their primary language – otherwise, you'll have to learn the language.

> 'A different language is a different vision of life.'
> Federico Fellini
> (Italian film maker)

Learning a foreign language is never easy, and is full of potential pitfalls. Even if English is your mother tongue, you'll find that Americans speak their own, unique version of the language. There's a new vocabulary to learn, as well as slang and dialects to comprehend. You may also struggle to understand some of the regional accents, from the twang of New York's Brooklyn dwellers to the southerners' laid-back drawl.

All expatriates have stories to tell of when they said the wrong thing at the wrong time, often with embarrassing consequences. To help keep your own collection of anecdotes as small as possible, this chapter offers tips on learning American English. It also looks at other languages spoken in the US, plus its regional languages and dialects, and an explanation of body and sign language (and their importance in communication). Finally, it offers useful advice on correct forms of address and greetings, as well as telephone and written etiquette.

LEARNING AMERICAN ENGLISH

When you first arrival on American soil, your ability to speak at least some English will be critical unless, that is, you speak Spanish and live in certain areas, such as California and Florida, where Spanish is almost as widely spoken as English.

Like the English, most Americans speak no language other than their own, and there are few allowances made for non-English speaking residents. Almost every piece of written information you encounter – road-signs, newspapers, contracts, utility bills, instruction manuals, billboards, notice boards, timetables, menus and so forth – is in English. All entertainment on television, radio and in cinema is in English (although there are foreign-language films and films with foreign subtitles,

with a private tutor gives the best guarantee of success, although you must be prepared to put in the hours in both lessons and practise. The advantages are that you'll learn at your own pace, while the tutor can concentrate on your areas of weakness. Fees will be much higher than for group lessons at a language school, although this often acts as an incentive to study.

The alternatives are either joining a class at a language school or signing up for an online learning course. Classes are more sociable and supportive, and there's always the chance (albeit remote) that someone else in the class is relocating to the same place in the US. Online courses can fit around a busy lifestyle, and some allow you to communicate with a teacher by email or internet phone such as Skype, but they require more self-discipline.

Ensure that your course, classroom or online, teaches American English and not British English. Courses in European countries tend to teach the latter, whereas those in the Far East teach the American version of the language.

Once in America

Don't stop studying, even with all the distractions of a new country. Now, more than ever, you need to understand English, and the incentive to learn will be that much greater. Either carry on with your online learning or look for a new language class. There are schools in most large towns, but those specialising in intensive courses are found mainly in the major cities.

Most language schools offer a choice of classes. These take into account your ability, time, available funds and how fast you need to learn. Courses vary in length from a week to six months and

and also cable TV stations showing programmes in a variety of languages). The main exceptions are Spanish-speaking areas, where information is given in both languages, and in immigrant enclaves of big cities, where people still communicate in their mother tongue.

Without English, you'll struggle in the most fundamental areas of American life, such as crossing the road (where the signs instruct you to 'WALK'/'DON'T WALK') or using public transport. Certainly, you'll find it almost impossible to secure a job, or make any progress in mainstream US society.

Know Before You Go

Don't believe people who tell you that you'll learn English more easily by immersing yourself in the language once you arrive. With all the other stresses of relocation, immersion will feel more like drowning. There's no substitute for gaining a good grounding in English before you get to the US.

To give yourself the best possible chance, start learning at least six months before departure. A one-to-one course cater for all ages, and some are available as part-time or evening classes. Expect to study for up to 20 hours a week on a standard course, or over 40 hours on a total immersion course. Fees vary from a few hundred dollars to thousands for a full-on intensive executive language course.

Never commit to any course unless you're sure it's right for you, especially one which requires payment up front. A reputable school should assess your ability, and offer an introductory lesson.

As well as language schools, adult and further education institutions also have classes in English. Colleges and universities often run an American Language Program, which is a pre-academic English-as-a-Second-Language (ESL) course for students whose native language isn't English. Some states, such as California, provide government-mandated ESL programs for residents, free of charge.

If you prefer private lessons, there are plenty of tutors in the US, who advertise in local newspapers, at libraries and on school notice-boards – or you can place your own advertisement. Ask friends and neighbours, as well as your (or your spouse's) employer. Other foreigners will have been in your situation and be better placed to help you find a suitable teacher.

There are many language schools across the US offering ESL and other language courses. Berlitz is an international brand with over 60 schools in America (🖥 www.berlitz.com) and 🖥 www.englishinusa.com is a good resource.

Children

Depending on their age and how far along they are in their home country's education system, most children find it easier to adapt than adults. Certainly, small children pick up new languages in a fraction of the time it takes their parents, and they will probably end up teaching you. All children are more receptive to the evolution of language than adults – most are sponges when it comes to learning slang. A few, usually older, children may need to take language classes, especially if they have no experience of English. If they're at an important stage in their education, they may be more comfortable being educated in an international school, although in some state schools, such as those in parts of California, classes are available in many different languages, besides English (and Spanish). For more information, see **Education** in **Chapter 3**.

Your children may need a recognised qualification in English, or to pass a Test of English as a Foreign Language (TOEFL) in order to be accepted at a college or university. Information is available from the Educational Testing Service (ETS, Rosedale Road, Princeton, NJ 08541, 🖥 www.ets.org/toefl). You may also need to prove your English skills to prospective employers, therefore you should ensure that any course you take provides a certificate at the end.

THE ENGLISH LANGUAGE

The US has no 'official' language. However, the language of business and education is English – or, to be precise, Standard American English. This is similar to but not the same as the English spoken in the UK or other parts of the English-speaking world. There are distinct differences between the English spoken on either side of the Atlantic. Unless it's your mother tongue, you may not even notice these differences.

Ironically, if you speak British English fluently, you may encounter more problems. Your familiarity with the language could lead you to pay less attention to small but important differences, and, as you appear to speak 'their' language, Americans may be less tolerant of your mistakes.

Apart from differences in spelling, there are variations in grammar and also in the way that certain words are used. Some of these have the capacity to leave egg on your face – for example, when the English say 'rubber', they mean a pencil eraser, whereas Americans use the same word to refer to a condom. There are more **False Friends** listed in **Appendix D**, along with other examples of American terminology.

> **'You say eether and I say eyether,**
> **You say neither and I say nyther;**
> **Eether, eyether, neether, nyther,**
> **Let's call the whole thing off!**
> **You like potato and I like potahto,**
> **You like tomato and I like tomahto;**
> **Potato, potahto, tomato, tomahto!**
> **Let's call the whole thing off!'**
>
> Lyrics from *Let's Call the Whole Thing Off*, George & Ira Gershwin (American composers)

Although foreigners speak a variety of American and British English (among others), the world learns most of its English from films and television shows, the vast majority of which are American made. A Chinese child will pick up words and accents from TV, so he will know the word 'Coca- Cola' but probably not the word 'tea'.

Most Americans cannot differentiate between 'other' English accents and lump together Brits, Antipodeans, South Africans and all other English speakers. They won't be able to tell if you're from Crewe, Canberra or Cape Town. However, at the same time, you shouldn't have too much trouble understanding their accents. Some take a little getting used to (especially in remote corners of Texas) but none is as incomprehensible as Glaswegian (Glasgow) or Geordie (Newcastle) in the UK.

Standard American English has many unique characteristics which set it aside from British English, enough to fill a book of its own, including the following:

● The letter 'T' is often dropped altogether in speech, e.g. inneresting innerview (interesting interview). The 'h' may also be dropped, e.g. herbs (erbs).

- Acronyms are popular – for example ASAP (as soon as possible, often pronounced eh-sap), DOA (dead on arrival or hopeless) and GSOH (good sense of humour). Many are derived from the language of the US military.

- Nouns are often used as verbs. Managers will 'Google' for information and then 'cascade' it down to their staff; if they're old-fashioned, they may 'fax' it instead.

- The emphasis on vowels can be very different. 'Hostile Iraqis' may be described in a US newscast as 'hostel Eye-rackies'.

- The stress in words is often placed on different syllables, as in advertisement and oregano. Pronunciation can also be quite different, e.g. Americans pronounce vase as 'vais', while the British say 'vars'.

- Americans are always coming up with new and bizarre words, which the British reluctantly later adopt – such as boondoggle (a pointless time-wasting plan), doohickey (something unknown like a 'thingy') and discombobulate (to confuse).

OTHER LANGUAGES

In addition to Standard American English, there are over 300 other languages which are spoken, written (and signed) by Americans. More than half of these are Native American languages, which you're unlikely to encounter. However, one language does challenge and, in places, overwhelm the supremacy of English – Spanish.

Hispanic and Latino Americans are the fastest growing ethnic group in America, and can hardly be ranked as a minority. US Census figures for 2007 reveal a population of just over 45m, or 15 per cent of all Americans – the fifth-largest Spanish-speaking community in the world.

According to the US Census, the top five languages spoken by Americans aged over five in 2000 were as follows:

English – 215mn
Spanish – 28mn
Chinese (Cantonese and Mandarin) – 2mn plus
French – 1.6mn
German – 1.4mn

Spanish

Spanish is the second most widely spoken language in the US, after English. Most government agencies have staff who can speak Spanish. Many states, such as California, where 35 per cent of the population are Spanish speaking, require legislated notices and official documents to be printed in Spanish alongside English. In addition, many manufacturers of cosmetics and household cleaning products now list ingredients and instructions in Spanish as well as English.

Meanwhile, companies are sending supervisors and managers to school to learn to speak Spanish so that they can converse with Hispanic workers, some of whom refuse to learn English. Depending on where you live, it may be necessary for you to do this in order to improve your job prospects or deal with potential clients. There are neighbourhoods in New York and Miami where Spanish is the predominant language: it's spoken by over half the population of Miami, and you won't get far in this city if you can't speak it.

The language even influences the entertainment industry. There are Spanish language channels throughout the US, and even some Spanish networks, such as Telemundo, which broadcast news, variety and game shows 24 hours a day, exclusively to the Hispanic community.

Chinese

The next most frequently spoken language is Chinese, spoken by at least 2mn Americans. Within the Chinese communities the language is usually Cantonese, especially in California. However, many young Americans who aren't of Chinese descent are learning Standard Mandarin, the official language of China. This may have more to do with business and trade than with culture.

French

Spoken by people of French, Cajun-Haitian and French-Canadian descent, French is the fourth most widely spoken language in the US. You should expect to hear French spoken occasionally, or more frequently if you move to the north-eastern states of Maine or New Hampshire, or to Louisiana, where it's is the 'official' second language.

Other European Languages

Large communities of immigrants from Italy, Poland, Greece and the former Soviet Union made the US their new home during the 19th and 20th centuries. It was once common to hear them speaking in their native tongues, but this is slowly dying out as the older generation dwindles. Similarly, little is now heard of Dutch, Gaelic, Welsh, Swedish, Finnish and Portuguese, as their speakers have been almost totally assimilated into the American language.

Some European languages live on in closed communities such as the Amish, who are an Anabaptist Christian sect living a 19th-century life without cars, phones or electricity in parts of the eastern states. Many Amish live in Pennsylvania, and as well as English, they speak a German dialect known as 'Pennsylvania Dutch'.

Indigenous Languages

A common myth is that there was only one Native American tongue. There were, in fact, thousands of dialects in the Americas before the European settlers arrived. Of the 176 which have been categorised as languages, almost one-third are now extinct, and the rest are slowly disappearing.

There are eight indigenous languages still spoken, mostly by older people: Apache, Blackfoot, Cherokee, Choctaw, Cree, Dakota, Navajo and Ojibwe. By far the most widely spoken is Navajo with some 175,000 speakers, as many as all the other Native American languages put together.

Other indigenous languages include the Hawaiian, Samoan, Chamorro and Carolinian tongues still used to varying degrees in the regions of the Pacific under US control.

Minority Languages

There are natives of just about every nation in the world somewhere within America's borders so, in theory, it should be possible to hear every language on the planet. However, because the different races are spread so thinly, and the numbers of speakers aren't great, their

languages are rarely heard. There are speakers of Japanese, Korean, Arabic, Yiddish, Hindi, Gujarati, Armenian, Vietnamese and others, but such is the influence of English that they're unlikely to retain much of their mother tongue for more than a couple of generations.

> The large number of Filipino immigrants in the US means that speakers of Tagalog and Ilocano are well represented – over 1mn Filipino Americans speak Tagalog, although even this language is changing as younger people adopt Taglish, a hybrid Tagalog and English.

'New' Languages

Considering the sheer size of the US, the languages spoken are remarkably uniform. There are local idiosyncrasies, many of which include words in everyday use – for example, what's called a convenience store in the southern states is known as a party store in the north. There's also a wide range of accents. However, the number of new languages which have evolved in the US is limited:

- **African-American Vernacular English** (AAVE) – This language is spoken by many, but not all, African Americans throughout the US, and even by some white Americans. AAVE is also known as Ebonics (ebony and phonics) or as Black English. It may provide a link between Creole languages of African origin and those of European settlers, and sounds like the language of slaves in the old south, as portrayed in Hollywood films such as *Gone with the Wind*. Speakers miss out the verb 'to be', saying 'he workin' rather than 'he is working'. 'T's are turned into 'D's (he been had dat job) and isn't loses out to ain't as a negative indicator ('it ain't necessarily so'). AAVE is an influential language which has contributed many words to Standard American English – such as banjo, hip (as in fashionable) and bling (ostentatious jewellery). A few educators claim that in areas where AAVE is a strong part of local tradition, English should be taught as a 'second dialect'.

- **Cajun French** – This is one of several variations on the French language, and is limited to southern Louisiana. It's thought to have been brought to the region by settlers from the Acadia colony in Canada and Maine.

- **Gullah** – An English-African Creole language with strong West African influences, common to the islands of South Carolina and Georgia.

Education in Bi-lingual Regions

In Florida, California, Texas, Arizona, Nevada, Colorado, New York, New Jersey and Illinois, at least one in seven people use Spanish as their first language. The language sections of the state schools reflect this, with both English and Spanish being used in classrooms. Spanish is also taught in many states as a second language, and some schools, even at kindergarten level, are offering immersion classes where children as young as five can learn the language.

When ethnic populations are sufficient to make the teaching of another language or culture necessary or viable, local government will almost always cater to this need. In public schools in most states, children are taught in a variety of languages (in addition to English), including Armenian, Cantonese, Japanese, Korean, Russian, Spanish and Tagalog (Filipino).

Dialects & Accents

English may be a uniform language across the US, but there are still many dialects and accents. The American equivalent of Home Counties English – the 'accent-less' accent spoken by television announcers – is known as General American.

There are clear differences between the accents of people from the north and south, and also quite marked variations between different cities, although this may only be apparent when you hear people speaking together. Certain accents, such as those spoken by people from Georgia, Boston or New York City are recognisable in much of the English-speaking world.

Accents and phrases you'll encounter in the US include:

- Mid-Atlantic – This describes a version of English which is neither predominantly American or British, and is used to describe various forms of North American speech that have assimilated some British pronunciations. Orson Welles notably spoke in a mid-Atlantic accent in the 1941 film, *Citizen Kane*, as did many of his co-stars.

- **Boston** – Also heard around eastern New England, it's noted for speakers clipping the 'r' out of words such as car and park and lengthening the 'a' sound. Speakers include Senator Ted Kennedy (all of the Kennedy clan, in fact) and UK TV presenter Loyd Grossman, who built his career on his distinctive accent.

- **New York** – This is the accent of gangsters in '40s Mafia films, and among the most recognisable in the US. Woody Allen and Joan Rivers are typical exponents, or, for a more extreme example, Joe Pesci in the movie *Goodfellas*.

- **Southern states** – Southern American English is the widest accent group, stretching from Virginia to Texas and the Gulf coast. It's best described as a lazy drawl in which speakers substitute 'them' for those, 'don't' for doesn't and, most famously, 'y'all' for 'you all'. There are many regional variations. Jimmy Carter speaks with a coastal (Georgia) accent, while Bill Clinton's is midland south from Arkansas.

- **California** – This state is well known for its lexicon rather than its accent, having graced America's vocabulary with such words and phrases as 'awesome' (wonderful), 'dude' (male individual) and 'gag me with a spoon' (how disgusting!). California-speak also, like, uses the word 'like' as a conversational filler. Hear it from the lips of actor Jack Black, and in the film *Fast Times at Ridgemont High*.

> To hear some US accents, go to the Audio File (💻 www.alt-usage-english.org/audio_archive.shtml) which has a range of spoken samples.

SLANG & SWEARING

American English has an especially rich vocabulary of colloquialisms, slang and swearwords – far more than British English. The majority of new English words, especially slang, are invented in the US and then exported to the rest of the world.

It's easy to pick up colloquial terms – the more bizarre they are, the simpler it is to remember them – and tempting to use them. But choosing the right context is difficult. Use slang sparingly or not at all, unless you're certain of the meaning, and sure that you won't upset or confuse your audience or end up sounding stupid.

Swearing is even more risky. It's easy to offend unintentionally by swearing at the wrong time, in the wrong place or too harshly. Some Americans appear to use strong swearwords like adjectives, but leave it to them – swearing is often the last resort of inarticulate people!

In today's politically-correct America, it's far worse to use racist or sexist expressions than it is to use sexual or scatological terminology. The word 'nigger' is far more insulting than the 'F' word – unless you're African-American, in which case 'nigga' can be a casual reference to black people. Similarly, calling a homosexual a faggot or a fag is extreme offensive, unless you, too, are gay. Such is the confusion caused by PC – and another reason for leaving swearwords well alone.

You need to be aware of slang and swearwords, especially if you're a parent. There are plenty of websites which list 'American idioms, oaths and slang' – a good place to start is English Daily (www. englishdaily626.com/slang.php), which has a comprehensive page on American slang. There are many dictionaries and books on the subject, including McGraw-Hill's *Dictionary of American Slang and Colloquial Expressions* and *American Slang* by Robert L. Chapman & Barbara Ann Kipfer (Collins).

A list of American sayings and slang is included in **Appendix D.**

BODY & SIGN LANGUAGE

Your body language has a key affect on how other people perceive you. Often, it's far more subtle than words, although this isn't the case in the US, where words always speak louder than actions.

Gestures

Americans aren't like Mediterranean or Latin people. They don't gesticulate or throw their bodies around to make a point – unless, that is, they come from

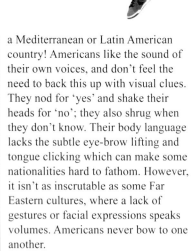

a Mediterranean or Latin American country! Americans like the sound of their own voices, and don't feel the need to back this up with visual clues. They nod for 'yes' and shake their heads for 'no'; they also shrug when they don't know. Their body language lacks the subtle eye-brow lifting and tongue clicking which can make some nationalities hard to fathom. However, it isn't as inscrutable as some Far Eastern cultures, where a lack of gestures or facial expressions speaks volumes. Americans never bow to one another.

If you come from a culture where gestures speak louder than words, try to keep them to a minimum when conversing with Americans, so that your actions aren't misinterpreted. It's advisable not to copy any American gestures until you're sure of your interpretation and your audience.

Some of the more popular gestures in the US include:

- **The High Five** – A greeting in which two people slap each other's raised hand. It can offer congratulations or show agreement. The phrase 'gimme five' is an invitation to the gesture; but if one person raises their hand and no one reciprocates, they've been 'left hanging'. No one knows where the gesture got its origins, but one theory is that it was first seen in the '50s in a television comedy, *The Phil Silvers Show*. During that era, it was a common gesture among NASA test pilots. Today, at sports events, team members often 'high five' one another after a goal's been scored or the game's been won. They also do the 'sky five', where both jump into the air while giving a 'high five'.

- Thumbs up – Everything's OK. It was first given by pilots during the Second World War to tell deck crews they were ready for take off.

This sign can be offensive in other cultures. Making a circle with thumb and forefinger also says 'OK', but can also mean zero and be an insult.

- Punching the air – Yes! Look at me! Making a fist and punching the air, shows you're psyched up or excited about something, e.g. a sportsman winning a point in a game. Players also pound their chest in celebration.

- Fist to fist – Connecting your fists with someone else is a way of saying, 'What's up? What's happening? I haven't seen you for a while.' It's a more physical version of a handshake.

- **Striking your forehead with your palm** – Silly me! This suggests you've forgotten something.

- Hand on my heart – The majority of Americans put their right hand over their heart during the playing of the National Anthem. This conveys sincerity and emotion.

- Holding an imaginary phone to your ear – You're asking someone to call you.

> Sticking your middle finger in the air – Known as 'giving someone the finger', 'flipping the birdie' or even the 'New York hello', this gesture is sure to cause offence. Do it while driving and you invite road rage. Thumbing your nose at someone is almost as bad.

- **The 'V' sign** – Made with your index and middle fingers, this means

'Victory' or 'Peace'. If you do it with your palm facing towards you, you risk insulting the British – but Americans won't mind.

Personal Space

Americans cherish their privacy, and this means lots of personal space – at least a metre and preferably more. They're aware of their own space and everyone else's, and will say 'Sorry' if they intrude into yours. Even an accidental nudge is followed by profuse apologies. They expect you to do the same. You'll know if you're getting too close during a conversation, as your companion will start backing away. The average American speaks loudly enough for you to converse at a 'civilised' distance.

Physical greetings consist of a handshake, neither too firm nor too limp and certainly not prolonged, which is acceptable to either sex.

(However, bear in mind that a strong firm handshake and good eye contact is much more likely to land you a job.) Two women will sometimes hug and kiss, although there may be little body contact, and the kiss will be a brush of the cheeks and a 'mwah' sound. Men, too, may hug, or rather grasp each others' shoulders. Texans like to slap each other on the back!

It's rare for two Americans of the opposite sex to greet each other with a kiss, unless they're in a romantic relationship. Touching a stranger's arm or shoulder during conversation can be construed as too personal. Americans rarely touch other people's children – or even their own.

FORMS OF ADDRESS

America is a young nation which cast off its notions of nobility at the end of the War of Independence. In a country where everyone is equal, everyone addresses everyone else in the same way – or, at least, most do.

Formal & Informal

American English has no formal/informal mode of address, as exists in French, Spanish and many other languages. 'You' is just 'you'. Formality, when it does occur, is based on whether you address someone by their title and surname, their first name or even their nickname. Most Americans are more formal in their approach to older people, those in authority and those they've only just met.

> **'If you'll be my bodyguard, I can be your long lost pal**
>
> **I can call you Betty, and Betty when you call me, you can call me Al.'**
>
> *You Can Call Me Al*, Paul Simon
> (American singer & songwriter)

Surnames & Titles

Titles include Mr for a man, Mrs for a married woman and Miss or Ms for an unmarried woman. Ms (pronounced 'mizz') is an alternative, and politically correct, title which doesn't give away a woman's marital status. Ms sounds odd but is almost always used in formal letters, i.e. those where a title is included.

Americans dislike formality, but they do show respect where it's due – to doctors, professors and other people with titles. These titles have, of course, been earned rather than inherited. You should always use titles when addressing anyone from the military profession, religious figures, doctors, politicians and so forth.

How can you tell? Whoever introduces you will almost certainly include any title, and if there's no third party, the addressee will tell you which title he or she prefers you to use with their name. If the title isn't included with their name, you aren't expected to use one, and if they introduce themselves by their first name, you can call them by that name.

If in doubt, start with the surname, e.g. Mr Jones. It's odds on that its owner will correct you. Americans like to get things clear and straight from the outset, so they will often say, 'Hi, I'm Robert Jones but you

can call me Bob.' Diminutives are popular in the US, which is why there are ex-presidents called Jack, Jimmy and Bill – politicians want to be everyone's best friend. (Incidentally, politicians are usually addressed by their title, such as Mr President or Governor, Senator or Congressman, even after they have retired.) You should introduce yourself in the same way, taking care to speak slowly and clearly if you have a 'foreign' name, or even offering to spell it.

Nicknames are another confusing aspect of American nomenclature. Bob Jones may well be known to his buddies as Beano, for mysterious reasons which go right back to his college days. You don't have to call him that – unless he asks you to. If you have a nickname which you're happy to use, let people know. They'll be more than happy to use it.

Children

The relaxed attitude towards formality means that American children frequently address adults   by the first

name; many adults don't object and some even encourage it. Even parents get the first-name treatment in lieu of Mom and Pop. However, you should play safe, and ensure that your children address adults as Mr, Mrs, Miss or Ms, plus their surname, unless they're expressly asked by the adult to use their first name.

The same applies to teachers and anyone in authority, for whom a title might also be required. Other acceptable titles are 'Sir' or 'Ma'am'. In many states, both children and adults may address someone as Mister or Miss and the person's first name, e.g. Miss Daisy, as in the film *Driving Miss Daisy*.

Youngsters address each other in the strange and often incomprehensible ways that children do everywhere. Just as with adults, a series of nicknames (some mystifying, others clever) are used. When speaking to children, they will enjoy it if you call them by the same name their friends use – just make sure the nickname isn't an insulting one!

GREETINGS

In rural America, even total strangers greet each other with a casual 'Hi'. In cities, the greeting may be slightly more formal: 'Good morning/afternoon/evening', depending on the time of day. Most will also ask, 'How are you?' Always respond that you're 'Fine, thanks', even if you're fighting off a cold or deeply depressed. Americans like to look on the bright side, and expect you to do the same. A breezy, 'And how are you?' keeps everything suitably upbeat.

Good Manners

'Please' and 'thank you' are important to Americans, who rate manners highly – these are never implied, and must be verbalised. Some people say 'sure' or 'OK' when they mean please; others may respond 'no problem' instead of saying thank you. But the meaning is the same. If you need someone to repeat something, say 'Excuse me?' 'Sorry?' is for when you invade someone's personal space.

Americans say 'We'll talk to you later' in lieu of 'goodbye'. This doesn't mean they're going to call later that day, or even that week – for many, it's just a way of ending the conversation, and they may have no desire to talk or see you ever again.

Any time you thank someone for a service or kind word or just stepping out of your way (and you should thank everyone for everything), they will probably respond with 'You're welcome' (or maybe just 'uh-huh'). This standard rejoinder is less common among younger people, some of whom find it insincere and patronising.

TELEPHONE, LETTERS & EMAIL

As elsewhere in the western world, the telephone has largely killed off the art of letter writing, while email and text messages are now doing the same thing to the telephone. All these forms of communication have their own etiquette.

Telephone

Answer the telephone with a cheery 'Hello', whether you're making or answering a call. If you're making a business call, introduce yourself as you wish to be addressed. If answering, use the caller's name as they introduce themselves, e.g. 'Hello Bob (Jones), how are you?' If you don't know the name of the person on the end of the line, 'Sir' or 'Ma'am' is fine.

Always be polite, even if you have a complaint to make; many businesses routinely tape their calls. Maintain a degree of formality, but not too much, as Americans are quite relaxed in this respect.

No one in America answers the phone by reciting their telephone number. When answering a phone at work, they will answer with the name of the company and/or department, plus their name, e.g.

'This is the XYZ Company, sales, Bob speaking.'

Even if English is your mother tongue, many Americans will still think you have an accent. Any accent needs to be 'tuned into', particularly when speaking on the telephone. Speak slowly and distinctly. Saying, 'Good morning, my name is Jane Smith. May I speak to Bob Jones?' gives the listener some time to tune in. If you do this, they won't have to ask you to repeat everything, creating less embarrassment or potential confusion. Americans from states with a great mix of immigrant populations are more adept at understanding accents. However, even people who speak British English may have a tough time being understood in more isolated rural areas.

Letters

Starting

Formal: Begin a business letter with the salutation 'Dear Sir or Madam' if you don't know the name of the person you're writing to. If you know their name, write their title and

Recipient	Mr A President
House name/apartment and/or number	The White House
Street name and number	1600 Pennsylvania Avenue NW
Town or city	Washington DC
State (can be abbreviated) and zip code	DC 20500

surname, e.g. Dear Mr Jones. If you aren't sure whether a female contact is married or not, use 'Ms' (see **Surnames & Titles** above).

Informal: As long as you're on first name terms with the recipient, start your letter with 'Dear Bob' or even (if you're on nickname terms) 'Dear Beano'.

Addresses

American addresses are written in the format shown above.

When writing to a person in a large building, state the building, floor, and the number of the specific property in the second line. You can include the recipient's address on the left-hand side of the letter, stacked above the date and the salutation. If desired, you can include your address on the left beneath your signature.

On forms, the date is input numerically as 'mm-dd-yyyy' (i.e. month-date-year), although government offices may use the 'dd-mm-yyyy' format which is used in other countries (just to confuse you). Write the date as 'August 14th 2007' rather than '08-14-2007'. The date goes above the salutation in a letter.

Signing off

Formal: A letter written to a specific person should be signed off with 'Yours sincerely'; if you know the person well, it's OK to use a more informal ending, such as 'Kind regards'. If you're writing

to Sir or Madam, end your letter with 'Yours faithfully'.

Informal: Your sign off is entirely dependent on how well you know the person you're writing to. 'Best wishes', 'Love from' or even 'Big hugs from' are all acceptable in the ever-informal US.

Emails & Texts

Email is almost as instantaneous as a telephone call, and has the advantage – or disadvantage – of being permanent. The same goes for text messaging. Think hard before you hit the 'send' button, as your mistakes can go down on record.

Americans are generally less formal in emails than they would be in letters. Emails to friends are chatty and informal, and may be littered with contractions such as 'u' (you), 'ne' (any), 'b4' (before) and so forth. If you aren't 100 per cent sure about the meaning of a contraction, then don't use it – and never use them in business emails.

Formal emails should be as polite as a letter. Use the recipient's title, and end the communication with a formal sign off. Never put anything in capital letters, even if you want to make things clear – to an American, it's the equivalent of shouting in their face. Although you're less likely to use them in business, the same rules apply to text messages.

6.
THE AMERICANS AT WORK

One of the most common mistakes foreigners make when coming to America to work or start a business, is to assume that they can continue working in the way they did in their home country, particularly if they had a successful business there. Many expatriates underestimate the differences in business culture between the Americans and Asians, Europeans or even the British. Working in the US usually involves a fairly steep learning curve for a foreigner – professionally, linguistically and culturally.

This chapter provides information about the cultural differences you can expect to experience when working for or with Americans, setting up a business, and in business etiquette.

> 'My father taught me to work, he did not teach me to love it.'
>
> Abraham Lincoln (16th US President)

WORK ETHIC

Americans are among the hardest working people in the world. Surveys consistently show that people in the US work longer hours and have less time for leisure and family, than in almost any other nation except for Korea and Japan. They work more overtime, take fewer holidays – less than half the amount taken by Italians – and are more likely to snatch a sandwich lunch at their desks.

The Protestant work ethic, brought to the US by the Pilgrim Fathers, equated hard work with Godliness, moral strength and material gain, and it still infects many Americans today. As a nation of immigrants, many have had to work hard to make their mark in a new land. From the early settlers who forged a trail across the badlands to 20th-century Asian immigrants who imported their culture of hard work along with their business acumen, all have been motivated by the 'can do, must do' mentality that still spurs on so many people to success.

Figures from the Organisation for Economic Cooperation and Development (OECD) reveal that Americans worked, on average, almost 1,800 hours a year, compared with, for example, just under 1,350 hours clocked by the French. However, today's workers have it easy compared to their forefathers – in mid-19th century America, people laboured for over 3,000 hours each year.

Wherever you go in the US, one aspect of business never varies, and this is the belief that the customer is always right. Whether you're an employee of a well-established company or setting up your own venture, the basic rules are the same: be efficient, be respectful and always give your customers what they want, when they want it. Most importantly, do it with a smile!

> **American children learn the work ethic early. This may involve a paper round or babysitting a neighbour's kids, or just doing jobs (chores) around the house in exchange for pocket money (allowance).They must fit this around social and sporting activities, homework and family commitments. In the US, it's never too soon to learn the skills of multi-tasking.**

PERMITS & PAPERWORK

Finding a job in America is straightforward in comparison with obtaining a visa that will allow you to work in the US. Which visa you need depends on several factors, such as the type of work you're seeking, how long you need a visa for, your country of origin, and your skills and experience.

There are several different types of work visa, for example:

● H-1B Work Visa – These are issued to professionals who can 'make a valuable contribution' to the American economy. The H-1B visa is valid for up to three years and can be extended for a further three years, during which time holders can apply for permanent residency (green card). There's an annual quota of 65,000 H-1Bs, which is inadequate for the

number of applicants (a much larger number was issued up to 2003).

● **H-2B Work Visa** – This is the most common work visa. It was created to help the US fill jobs where workers were in short supply, and is issued to people seeking temporary, mainly non-agricultural, employment in industries such as construction, manufacturing and leisure. Up to 66,000 are issued annually.

● **E-3 Work Visa** – This is currently available only to Australians, and includes the right of spouses to work in the US (unlike many other visas). It can be renewed indefinitely in two-year increments, but doesn't allow permanent settlement in the US.

● **TN NAFTA Work Visa** – This visa may be issued to citizens of Mexico and Canada as part of the North American Free Trade Agreement (NAFTA).

US visas are an incredibly complex subject. There are over 60 different visas allowing work, residency or visiting rights, and it's essential that you and your family obtain the correct ones. This is one area in which legal assistance isn't just desirable, but essential. For more information on visas, see **Chapter 3**.

FINDING A JOB

Ideally, you'll arrive in the US with a job already lined up, allowing your employer to deal with all the red tape. If you have specific skills or good qualifications, contact international recruitment agencies who act for US companies, who are often on the look-out for high-quality prospective employees. Writing to companies in the area where you'll be living can also bring dividends. Pay particular attention to multi-nationals who could be seeking someone with experience or good contacts in your homeland. Company websites often list vacancies.

If you arrive in America without a job, especially if you lack a degree or other professional qualification, then your search for work will be much tougher. Employers aren't against hiring a foreigner over an American, but many are biased against applicants with poor qualifications or an incomplete employment history or those aged over 45 – discrimination on the grounds of sex or colour may be illegal, but ageism isn't and is rife.

Employers prefer to hire people already in work, so it pays to have a job (any job) as soon as possible. You may need to target jobs for which you consider yourself over-qualified – or even dumb down your CV – just to get a foothold in the job market. Once you've demonstrated your skills and proven your reliability, you'll then have a reference. No matter how many glowing references you bring with you from abroad, American employers always prefer to see those written by fellow Americans.

'Early to bed, early to rise, makes a man healthy, wealthy and wise.'

Poor Richard's Almanac by Benjamin Franklin (from a series of 'best-selling' pamphlets published in the first half of the 18th century)

Job Market

As in Western Europe, flexibility is the key to survival in an increasingly tough job market. Few Americans have, or even want, a job for life. Many change jobs or careers several times in their lifetime, and most will take a menial or unskilled job, such as waiting tables, rather than be unemployed. 'Safe' full-time employment is slowly but surely being replaced by fixed-term contracts and freelance work, or 'telecommuting' (working from home by computer), all of which provide fewer benefits and virtually no security.

Contract or freelance work is available across the board. Rates of pay may be better than for those in full-time employment, but you're responsible for your own social security payments. Note that you may be penalised if you opt out of a contract early.

Part-time work rarely leads to a full-time opportunity, employees have little legal protection, and the work is often poorly paid. One exception is job-sharing, where you split a full-time job (including benefits and holidays) with another worker.

At the bottom of the job pile are tedious, temporary cash-in-hand jobs such as washing up, fruit picking, cleaning and mowing lawns – the kind of work which, supposedly, Mexicans cross the US border for. Many of these workers are employed illegally, and have no legal protection whatsoever.

The best place for facts and figures on the US job market is the Bureau of Labor Statistics (☎ 1-202-691 5200, 🖳 www.bls.gov). It publishes a wealth of information on employment trends and job prospects in the US, as well as number of guides for job seekers that provide information about employment practices in the US.

Speaking English

As discussed in chapter 5, it's difficult to find a job if you don't speak fluent English. If, however, you speak a second language, such as Spanish, Mandarin Chinese or even Tagalog, you can use this to your advantage. Some employment agencies deal in bi-lingual staff, and many international companies need multi-lingual people to communicate with overseas contacts. Such positions can be difficult to fill, and usually offer a good salary. The public sector can also be lucrative for foreigners who are able to interpret or translate between English and their mother tongue.

Qualifications

Americans put a lot of emphasis on achieving educational goals, as they open doors to employment. Any qualifications you have from your homeland should stand you in good stead, provided they're recognised and sought by employers. Ensure that you list all your qualifications on your curriculum vitae (CV) and have any important documents translated into English (if applicable).

Curriculum Vitae (CV)

A CV is known as a résumé in America, where it's a hugely important piece of paper. Make sure you state every skill and achievement and make it sound like a gold medal-winning performance – Americans aren't backward when it comes to selling themselves. Ensure you can back up any claims with references and qualifications. Potential employers may not understand qualifications

gained in a foreign country, therefore you should state the approximate US equivalent in brackets.

> **'Work is the refuge of people who have nothing better to do.'**
> Oscar Wilde (Irish playwright & wit)

Employment Agencies

Government

Employment Service Centers are the equivalent of a UK Jobcentre. There are over 2,000 across the US, and their main role is to get job seekers into work and help employers locate qualified staff. They operate 'job banks' – lists of vacancies, local, state-wide and national – and can arrange interviews, while some have counsellors who can test your skills and advise on training and careers.

Employment Service Centers are listed in telephone directories under 'Employment Services' or 'Job Service' in the 'State Government' listings section.

Private

Agencies are the major source of employees for many large companies: a few employers deal solely with recruitment agencies to save the hassle of head-hunting executive staff. Some agencies specialise in a particular field, such as medical recruitment, office staff or banking. It's advisable to sign on with a number of agencies, as they will have far better contacts that you can hope to build up in months of job hunting.

Some agencies employ workers directly, and hire them out to other employers. The work is often temporary to begin with, but it gets your foot in the door, and if you're a good worker can lead to a permanent position.

Employers don't pay agencies until they supply a suitable candidate, so it's in their interests to ensure you have every chance of landing a job, and they will assist you as much as possible. Some offer free classes on CV writing and interview skills.

A reputable employment agency is paid by the employer, and should never ask a job seeker to pay a fee.

Job Hunting

Don't just leave it to the agencies. You can also seek work through the following:

● **Newspapers** – most have a 'Jobs' section, and some have 'Work wanted' sections where you can advertise your skills. Many newspapers also have a website where job vacancies are posted. The best day for job ads is Sunday.

● **Libraries** – most large branches operate job research resources with internet access. There are also free copies of local newspapers.

● **Internet** – start your job hunt before arriving in the US. There are many websites dedicated to employment, such as Monster (🖳 www.monster.com) or Yahoo (🖳 www.hotjobs.yahoo.com) or even the federal government's site (🖳 www.usajobs.gov). It's worth posting your résumé on 'hosting' sites, such as 🖳 www.resumenet.com, which are often browsed by employers.

● **Networking** – use every contact you have to put out the word that you're looking for work. Expatriate groups and websites can be a great source of help.

Selection Process

This usually involves an initial job application, followed by one or more interviews. Some employers attempt to sift would-be staff by using psychometric or aptitude testing. Whatever the procedure, resist the temptation to be modest or to understate your abilities. In the US, you're expected to sell yourself; the challenge is to fit in with the system, but still stand out from the crowd.

Interviews

Attend the interview dressed smartly, even if you're applying to wash dogs or stack shelves. Preparation is everything. Find out as much as you can about the company – use the library or internet – and be ready to answer any questions about your life and career. You're sure to be asked about your reasons for relocating to the US. Prepare some interesting questions, too, for when you're asked, "Is there anything you'd like to know about the job or company?" You'll have to provide evidence of passport and/or work visas, as well as the contact details for three personal or professional referees. Increasingly, candidates are also asked to sign a credit-check consent form, as many employers don't want to hire staff with bad debts.

After the interview, write a letter to the person(s) who interviewed you, thanking them for their hospitality and confirming that the job is what you're looking for – which serves as a reminder to prospective employers.

> '**About the time we think we can make ends meet, somebody moves the ends.**'
>
> Herbert Hoover (31st US President)

Salary

Your salary and its rate – which will be hourly, weekly, monthly or yearly – should be stated at the interview. By accepting a job offer, you're also agreeing to the rate of pay. If you get the chance to negotiate your salary, bear in mind that your holidays will be shorter and working hours longer than in your home country. You'll also need to top up your health insurance – employers' schemes never offer 100 per cent cover – so you should haggle for the best wage you can get.

An increase in salary is usually arbitrary, i.e. a reward for good work, rather than an increase based on inflation (the annual rise in the cost of living), unless this is made clear

in your contract (see below). In recent years, some employers have frozen workers' wages or even implemented pay cuts. It's unwise to discuss your salary with anyone, particularly your co-workers.

The Rate for the Job

American workers aren't highly paid, particularly considering their long hours and lack of job security, and many unskilled workers need two jobs to make ends meet. The average household income in 2007 was around $45,000 a year for men and $35,000 for women. The federal minimum wage was $6.55 an hour in 2008, although it's higher in many cities (who may set their own minimum wage) and states, particularly Washington, Massachusetts and Oregon.

Salary Payments

Virtually no one is paid by cash in 21st-century America (unless it's black money). Most workers receive their salary as a bank deposit or a 'pay cheque'. Cheques can be cashed directly, with identification such as a driving licence, at almost any bank, grocery store, gas station, or other retail outlet. Your employer must supply an itemised pay slip (pay stub) detailing your deductions.

Deductions

Your social security contributions are usually deducted at source from your wages by your employer, but as a newcomer to the country, your liability for registration and/or making social security payments depends upon your circumstances. You're responsible for declaring and paying income tax. For more information, see **Chapter 3**.

> '**A survey says that American workers work the first three hours every day just to pay their taxes. So that's why we can't get anything done in the morning – we're government workers.'**
> Jay Leno (American chat-show host, comedian & writer)

Discrimination

In the land which gave birth to political correctness, discrimination on grounds of race, colour, sex, nationality, age or religion is illegal. Nor can employers refuse to employ someone who is pregnant or overweight – or both! Federal law also protects ex-servicemen and disabled people. Gender-neutral job titles such as fire-fighter and salesperson ensure that no one can take offence, and some employers even operate positive discrimination (affirmative action) to assist young blacks and Hispanics into work. However, in spite of all efforts towards racial equality, minorities still lag behind in the job market.

Discrimination is difficult to prove, although there's always a lawyer ready and willing to try. If you think you've been passed over for employment because of your nationality or any other reason, the Equal Employment Opportunity Commission (EEOC) website (⌨ www.eeoc.gov) is a good place to start.

Pensions & Retirement

The state pension fund is the Social Security program, which provides benefits to workers who retire at 65 or older. Like many western countries, America faces the dilemma of too many ageing baby boomers, and many retirees find that their social security income falls far short of expectations. About half of all people working for a private employer, as well as most public sector employees, are covered by a pension plan which tops up the state retirement fund. There are tax incentives to encourage employer contributions, but many workers put in 100 per cent of the funding.

Employees cannot be forced to retire at 65, and, provided they're fit and healthy, they can carry on working, although frustrated employers have been known to fire workers who refuse to retire.

CONTRACTS

As soon as you accept your employer's terms and conditions, they become binding on both sides. However, not every employee receives a written contract. Your offer of employment letter often serves the same purpose, especially if your terms and conditions

are included – and it should be kept safe.

Your employer may require you to undergo a medical examination, and some also require a drug-screening test and/or a criminal background check, which depends on the type of work you're applying for. The offer letter may also be conditional on you receiving a visa.

Never sign a contract unless you fully understand it, and query anything that's unclear – and. if necessary, have it translated into your mother tongue before you sign or agree to it.

> **'Lisa, if you don't like your job you don't strike, you just go in every day and do it really half assed. That's the American Way.'**
>
> Homer Simpson (American cartoon character)

Collective Agreements

The law allows union membership and collective bargaining on wages, hours and other terms and conditions of employment. However, in private-sector businesses, such as retail and banking, union power is weak or even non-existent, and you'll have to negotiate your own terms, conditions and remuneration. Some employees, such as farm and domestic workers, have no rights to collective bargaining (and very few rights at all, particularly if they're illegal workers!).

STARTING OR BUYING A BUSINESS

Working for yourself is part of the American dream, and entrepreneurship is highly respected in the US. If businesses fail, their founders simply pick themselves up and start again – there's no stigma to this.

As regular, well-paid jobs become harder to find, more and more people are turning to self-employment through necessity as much as desire. Meanwhile, the trend by bigger companies to contract out and use short-term solutions has offered more opportunities to enterprising individuals.

If you're self-employed, you must take care of your own social security payments and provide your own health and pension plans – and you won't qualify for unemployment insurance or workers' compensation. Moreover, you must ensure that you have adequate liability insurance, in case a client trips over your cat on the way out of your door, and you may also need malpractice insurance.

For support and information, contact the National Association of Self-Employed (☎ 1-800-232 6273 ⌨ www. nase.org), the US Small Businesses Administration (⌨ www.sbaonline.sba. gov) and the Internal Revenue Service (⌨ www.irs.gov).

Starting a Business

There's more to self-employment than just having an excellent idea and the talent and energy to follow it through. Many entrepreneurs underestimate the investment and sheer hard work required to keep a new enterprise on track, and nearly two-thirds of new businesses fail within the first five years. Your location and local competition will have a direct bearing on your success – or failure – and you can never do enough research or take sufficient expert advice.

Before starting up, you need to decide on the business organisation. These range from joint-venture and corporation businesses, to sole traders (proprietors) and partnerships (limited or general). It's reckoned that the latter two small business structures comprise around two-fifths of the US's gross national product (GNP).

Complicated tax laws affect your choice of business set up, while national and state laws and regulations can tie you up in knots before you even start. You'll find it pays to hire a business and investment consultant, as well as a tax adviser.

> **If you aren't willing to pay for expert advice in a tough market like the US, it's odds on your business will fail.**

Buying a Business

Investing in a successful business is an easier option than starting from scratch, although much of the above advice applies. There are many owners of failed businesses just waiting for a hapless foreigner like you, so that they can offload their car lot/sandwich bar/poodle parlour and run! Don't invest without the same due diligence and expert advice you would employ for a business start up.

When buying an established business, you must make the purchase conditional on obtaining a visa (see below) and licences, and the vendor proving their financial status and business value. Add a licensed business broker and an accountant to your army of experts, as you'll need someone to negotiate the deal and go through the books with a fine-tooth comb. If there are any doubts, walk away.

Franchising

This is a popular and sensible choice, as franchises enjoy a higher success rate than independent start ups – although you may pay a premium to obtain one. With a franchise, you open a branch of an established business, with all the groundwork done for you, training available and a job that's the same all over the world. It's no coincidence that many convenience stores are franchises run by non-nationals. Many large organisations are, in fact, franchises, from McDonalds to Radio Shack. There are details of opportunities in the *Franchise Opportunities Guide*, available from the International Franchise Association (💻 www. franchise.org). Many magazines and books are published for prospective franchisees.

Business Visas

Just as you need a visa for employment, so you need one to run a business. The most popular is the E-2 Treaty Investor visa. Although it's a non-immigrant visa, holders can use it to apply for a green card once they're in the US. More people are 'buying' their way into America with an E-2 visa nowadays, rather than going the route of the H-1B/H-2B visa, especially those from European countries such as Britain and Germany.

Buying an existing business, especially a franchise, is seen as a quick route to obtaining an E-2 visa, although it isn't a guarantee. Your investment must be 'substantial', and it must generate 'more than enough income to provide a minimal living' for you and your family. **A business purchase or franchise agreement must contain a clause that releases you from the deal if you fail to obtain your visa.**

Loans

Unless you're extremely wealthy, you'll need a loan or grant (or both) to finance your venture. Loans are difficult to obtain for newcomers who've not yet built up a credit rating, and may only be possible if you've managed to transfer to a US-based branch of the bank you worked with in your home country. Financing is regulated in the US, and is usually limited to no more than 25 per cent of the value of the business.

You may be offered loans with very high interest rates – which should be avoided like the plague! Provided you have a viable business proposition, and have put together a good business plan, you should find a reputable and honest backer – eventually.

Grants

Federal (government) grants are available to non-nationals, which, unlike loans, don't need to be repaid. There are some 1,400 different grants available, ranging in value from $500 to $50,000, which along with the almost unlimited number of possible business ventures, makes grant qualification a long and complex procedure. The subject is covered in the government grants website (💻 www. grants.gov). Grants are also available from local and state bodies, although non-US nationals don't usually qualify.

> **'A real entrepreneur is somebody who has no safety net underneath them.'**
>
> Henry Kravis (American businessman & entrepreneur)

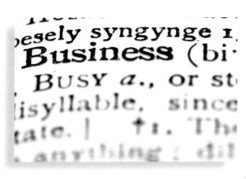

Business Premises

Where you locate your business is as important as what that business offers. Again, in-depth research is the key, so that you can discover where your ideal customer base is located, and/or what services are needed in the areas under consideration. Examine the history of similar businesses; for example, are there a lot of failures, and if so, is the location to blame? A sushi delivery service could be risky in rural Nebraska, for example, where locals may prefer more traditional fare; or a landscape business in downtown Manhattan.

You should also find out if there are any restrictions regarding, say, pollutants, or problems sourcing supplies. Only with all these boxes ticked should you start to look at premises.

Leasing

Few people can afford to buy business premises outright – and unless you're planning to build a huge manufacturing plant, you won't need to. A leasing agreement is the most sensible option, and gives you a fixed expenditure over a reasonable period of time and is almost as secure as owning the premises. Unless you break the terms of the leasing agreement, the property is yours to do with as you wish for the duration of the term.

If you abide by the rules and regulations and keep the premises in good order, you'll most likely be able to renew the lease at the end of the term, and you may even be in a position to negotiate a more favourable leasing term. Good, trustworthy lessees are always in demand.

Renting

This isn't as long term as leasing, and doesn't give tenants the same legal rights, but the same principles apply and good tenants can be hard to find. Remember, too, that if your business is thriving, you won't want to abandon a prime location.

> **'My son is now an 'entrepreneur'. That's what you're called when you don't have a job.'**
> Ted Turner (American media mogul)

Working from Home

Many service industries require no premises. However, you must check whether you're permitted to run a business from your home, or whether this infringes the terms of your rental agreement. If you're planning to run a home-based business, check it out before you sign a tenancy agreement; and if the idea comes up later, talk to your landlord. Most service industries are unobtrusive and, provided you don't erect advertising hoardings around the property or disturb other tenants, your landlord may not object.

Marketing

Selling yourself and your ideas is a very American skill. One of your most effective tools is the internet. Make use of the free business listings on 🖳 www.yell.com, which enables your clients to search businesses by location and type. There are also business guides available at libraries, where you may wish to be listed. Advertising in the local press may be necessary, while having your own website is almost mandatory in the current competitive climate. However, the most effective marketing is personal recommendations – if you've satisfied customers, ask them to pass on your name to family, friends and clients.

View every gathering as an opportunity to advertise your skills. Always carry cards (virtually every American has them, even if they aren't in business) and if, at a party, you're introduced to someone who might be a good contact, ask them directly and concisely if they're interested. If you receive a positive answer, make an appointment to get in touch and then drop the subject. Don't discuss business there and then, or you'll appear too pushy (even to Americans).

BLACK ECONOMY

The black economy operates on all levels in the US, where under-declaring income, accepting cash-in-hand payments and employing casual, often illegal, labour is commonplace. It's said that if all the illegal workers in the US were rounded up and deported, then food service would cease, houses would disappear under dust, gardens be choked by weeds

and produce would rot in the fields – such is people's dependence on poorly paid and unprotected (usually foreign) workers. (This is why the authorities only pay lip service to getting rid of illegal immigrants – the economy would collapse without them!)

You may even find yourself part of the black economy, albeit unwittingly, but should do your best to avoid it. Anyone employing an illegal worker (i.e. any non-national lacking the appropriate visa to live and work in the US) risks a $20,000 fine, and even imprisonment. Anyone working illegally risks deportation, and a five-year ban from the US.

WORKING WOMEN

For many years, a woman's role in the workplace was clearly defined, with entire areas off limits. Nowadays, women can, and do, compete on equal terms with men – at least, that's the official stance. In practice, there's still inequality, most notably in salaries; research has shown that on average, women earn only 80 per cent as much as their male colleagues, and few earn more.

Women find it difficult to reach the top in business, but they don't

find it impossible, even though they have to work twice as hard (and be twice as smart) as men to get there. Employers are painfully aware of their responsibility to make positions available to women, and if a man is in competition with a woman for a plum job, he will often lose, as some bosses are unwilling to risk an accusation of discrimination.

> You'll come across women in positions of power. If you're a macho man from the Mediterranean or South America, this may come as a shock. When meeting a group of Americans, never assume that the woman is the secretary – she may well be the boss. If she wants to pay for dinner, let her – and never ever suggest a cosy drink, after hours!

BUSINESS ETIQUETTE

Polite but not too formal, efficient but still friendly, Americans' attitude to doing business makes this a fairly routine affair. That said, if you're from the Middle or Far East or even southern Europe, you may find them overly confident and assertive to the point of rudeness. Americans don't feel the need to build a relationship before doing a deal – the deal is everything, and they prefer to get straight to the point.

Business Cards

Every American has a contact card, but business cards don't have the importance they do in more formal parts of the world. They're just something which explains who you are and what you do for a living. Choose a simple design, and include all relevant information, such as your website, email and mobile number, as well as your office details.

Business Gifts

In the US, there's a danger that any business gift can be construed as bribery, particularly cash or anything too valuable. Public sector (federal) workers may be prohibited from accepting gifts of any kind. If you must give a token of appreciation, then a small gift at Christmas is OK, but anything which even slightly hints of being an inducement will make you and your company appear dishonest.

Business Hours

White collar and office workers typically work from 8am to 5pm, with breaks totalling around one hour throughout the day. Lunch is rarely more than 30 minutes, and coffee and lunch are frequently taken at the desk – so 'break' is an arbitrary term. Indeed, working late is almost a way of life in some businesses, such as law, where workers feel that the only way to hold onto their job is to be seen to be at their desk longer than the next man (or woman). If you have a business meeting scheduled, it may well take place during 'lunch' or, if the company is really keen on saving time, at a breakfast meeting ('power breakfasts' are increasingly common).

> **'Lunch is for wimps.'**
> Gordon Gekko (American actor Michael Douglas in the movie, *Wall Street*)

Business Lunches

Many Americans don't 'do lunch' – at least, not in the sense of a long leisurely repast with wine and liqueurs, so beloved by the French and Italians. Therefore, it follows that business lunches tend to be hurried affairs, and are often no more than a hasty sandwich in the boardroom while watching a presentation. If you can persuade clients to join you for lunch, you'll find that business takes precedence over the food or any social aspect of the gathering. It's also highly unlikely that they will drink alcohol. In which case, it's probably best that you also stick to mineral water.

Dress

Despite their love of informality, Americans still conform when it comes to office attire. Men wear a suit – subtle, discreet and definitely not shiny – with a plain white shirt and understated tie. Women have more freedom, but those with their eye on promotion will wear a skirt or pants suit. Low cut tops and short skirts aren't serious office attire. There are, of course, exceptions, and Texans may well appear in the boardroom in cowboy boots and hat – like JR in *Dallas* – while Californians can get away with chairing a meeting wearing a Hawaiian shirt. However, if you do the same, they may think you're poking fun at them. Many offices have dress-down Fridays, when you can wear casual attire rather than a suit and tie.

Meetings

From mega-corporations to small-town companies, America is obsessed with meetings. No excuse is needed: some organisations schedule meetings over lunch, so employees can eat their sub (sandwich) while listening to the CEO talk about sales figures. Many times you'll phone someone at a company only to get the response, 'They're in a meeting right now.'

Always ensure you're on time and well prepared for meetings, however unimportant you think they are. Everyone is encouraged, even expected, to contribute, and Americans will (politely) jostle to be heard. It's rude to interrupt, but equally bad to sit on the sidelines and say nothing. It is, of course, bad form to answer your mobile or walk out during a meeting. If you're hosting the meeting, you should have all your charts, graphs and projections ready – your 'audience' will be expecting a performance!

Agenda

The agenda should include all points to be brought up at a meeting – and it's important that you stick to it. You should also include a list of those who will be attending the meeting, along with their position or job title, even if everyone knows who they are and what they do.

Language

Keep business language formal and simple, and avoid jokes and jargon unless you're sure they'll be understood and appreciated. However, be aware that in some industries, such as information technology (IT), it's unacceptable not to use the appropriate jargon. If you're attending a meeting in a language other than your own, you must take an interpreter, as no one will allow for your lack of English – or Spanish.

Negotiating

Americans aren't subtle negotiators, and they leave you in no doubt as to where they stand on a subject. They appear aggressive, but there's usually room for negotiation. They like to lay all their cards out on the table, so get yours out in the open, also – this is seen as forthright honesty, rather than aggression, and will often prove successful.

There are a few points to bear in mind when negotiating with Americans:

● First impressions count. If you appear sloppy, untidy or disorganised, you can sink your deal before you even float your ideas.

● Don't waste time on social niceties. Americans don't want to sit around sipping tea and talking about families when they could be off closing another, perhaps more important, deal.

● Be energetic, upbeat and assertive – both physically and verbally. Avoid self deprecation and irony. To Americans, it just sounds negative.

● Sell, sell, sell – you are your product, and if you can't sell yourself, then no one will buy your merchandise. If you're the buyer, don't be offended by the 'hard sell', as it isn't designed to make you feel uncomfortable.

● Never string people along. If you don't have the necessary authority to close a deal, be upfront about it from the start.

● Americans like to have the first word – and the last. They will state their position and wait for a reaction. They can be persuasive, so stand your ground.

● Silence is golden. If you really want to make an American uncomfortable, especially on the cusp of a big deal, then say nothing. Most cannot cope with silence, and will say something, anything, to move the conversation along. This is your best opportunity to trip them up and gain the upper hand

Regional Differences

In New York and other fast-paced east coast cities, employees demonstrate their loyalty to the firm by conspicuously putting in extra hours – this is known as 'face time'. Their Californian cousins prefer to make it look effortless, sometimes appearing to do nothing at all – although those in the money markets are at their desks by 6am to catch the opening of the New York stock market (America straddles several time zones). People in the south do everything at a slower pace, but it doesn't mean their brains work any slower. Your working life may well be affected by where you settle, but the basic business ethic doesn't differ much from one region to another. **Wherever you are, it's all about closing the deal and making (lots of) money.**

Timekeeping

To a working American, killing time is almost as bad as killing a sale. They hate to be unproductive, even for a minute. Circumstances which waste time – from broadband breakdowns to delayed trains – are stress inducers. This is why they view countries where things aren't fixed immediately as hopelessly uncivilised.

Don't ever waste their time. Always arrive exactly when you should – if you're going to be late, then phone (with a really good excuse). Conversely, arriving too early suggests you're over-eager. Be American: obey the clock!

EMPLOYING PEOPLE

US employment law is complicated and full of pitfalls for the unwary foreign boss. While it's easier to hire and fire workers than it is in other countries, such as Britain, the rules on discrimination and the American penchant for resorting to law make employment a risky area. Always take expert advice. The US Department of Labor's guide to employment law is a good place to start (www.dol.gov/compliance/guide). Bear in mind that if you hire a worker, even someone to mow your lawn, you're responsible for ensuring their taxes and social security are paid. You must also ensure that you're adequately insured against workers seeking compensation for accidents or illness suffered in the workplace (or in your home).

Contracts

There's no legal requirement to draw up a contract of employment between employer and employee, but a written job offer, stipulating working parameters and including rates of pay, working hours, holiday entitlement and so forth, will help avoid any misunderstandings or unpleasantness later on.

Domestic Help

Domestic workers, whether cleaners, gardeners, au pairs or even the pool 'boy', are all considered employees if they work for you on a regular basis. Many Americans pay their 'hired help' cash in hand, but this is technically illegal.

Social Security

As an employer in the US, you're liable to pay a total of 7.65 per cent of every employee's wage in social security contributions, up to a maximum of

$102,000 (2008). The employee then pays a contribution based on their wages. Self-employed workers must pay 15.3 per cent of their income to the social security plan. For more information, contact the Social Security Administration (☎ 1-800-772 1213, 🖥 www.ssa.gov).

Tax

As well as withholding income tax from employees and paying personal income tax, business owners may be liable for a wide range of taxes, such as unemployment tax, which is paid on behalf of employees, and excise tax, which is payable on certain commodities. The whole picture is diverse and utterly bewildering – even for Americans. Fortunately, you can get help from the Internal Revenue Service (☎ 1-800-829 4933, 🖥 www.irs.gov), which has offices across the US.

TRADE UNIONS

Back in the '50s, over a third of American workers were unionised and unions, such as the Teamsters, had a great deal of power. Today the figure is around 15 per cent (less than 10 per cent in the private sector). Unions have lost much of their influence, and Americans don't strike at the drop of a *chapeau*, as

workers do in France. Unions have more power in the northern industrial states such as Michigan (motor manufacturing) and Pennsylvania (mining), where state laws favour, protect and support the unions against the huge conglomerates. In southern states such as Florida, Mississippi and Texas, which have no tradition of big industry, union power is limited.

Joining a Union

No employer can refuse to employ a union member, nor can they dismiss someone for joining a union. However, depending on where you're employed, your collective bargaining power may be negligible. It may come as a surprise to find that US law permits the hire of permanent replacements for striking workers.

Joining a union means paying a subscription. If you don't want to join a union, make sure there isn't a closed-shop policy, whereby the company allows and recognises just one union which all employees must join. Almost half the states, all of which are in the south and west, have outlawed closed shops.

> **'By working faithfully eight hours a day, you may eventually get to be boss and work twelve hours a day.'**
>
> Robert Lee Frost (American poet)

WORKING WEEK

There's no statutory maximum working week. Individuals negotiate their own hours, and these hours are often long. A report by the United Nations' International Labour Organisation in 2001 found that Americans worked an average 250 more hours (or six weeks) a year than British workers. Part of this is down to a more limited holiday allowance (see below).

The standard working week is 40 hours, but most professionals average 45 hours, and blue-collar workers 50 hours. Workers are legally entitled to a 30-minutes break for each five hours worked. In practice, most take a lunch period of up to 30 minutes – it's unusual for Americans to take longer, unless it's a working lunch.

Overtime is a complicated issue. In theory, it's payable at one and a half times the hourly rate for any extra hour worked over the standard 40, but there are so many complicated exemptions and state laws that even some bosses don't understand it.

Coffee Breaks

Aside from lunch, employees working an eight-hour day are entitled to a 15-minute coffee break, morning and afternoon.

Holidays

Newcomers are often shocked by the brevity of American holiday allowances. Most new employees receive just one

or two weeks paid holiday a year – only the Japanese get less. Your entitlement rises by a day or two with each year of service, but you'd have to stay with a company for 20 years or more to enjoy the 25 days which most Europeans take for granted. It's especially hard on teachers, who aren't paid through the summer break, and usually need to take a summer job.

Americans refer to personal breaks from work as 'vacation', while a 'holiday' is one of the federal days off (see opposite), mandated by the government. Strictly speaking, these apply only to government employees, although many businesses observe them as national holidays, and close. Federal days are taken off in addition to your paid holiday entitlement, although when you first start a job, you may even have to take the Fourth of July holiday as unpaid leave!

If you're starting a new job, check whether your employer will allow any planned holidays. White-collar workers must usually work for six months – and blue-collar workers for a year – before they're permitted to take a vacation. Even then, you must book holidays up to a year in advance. Unpaid leave is usually only allowed in exceptional circumstances, e.g. bereavement, or your house burning down.

Christmas & Easter

Christmas is a federal holiday (see below), and you should be paid for it – just as you should allow employees paid holiday on this day. Christmas is a one-day break. Some employers give staff a half-day off on Christmas Eve but everyone's back at work on Boxing Day (December 26th, and a holiday in the UK and most Commonwealth countries).

Easter isn't a paid holiday because it falls on a Sunday. Christians consider Good Friday to be the holiest day of the year, so this is often a holiday in the more religious parts of the US, but whether or not you're paid is at the discretion of your employer.

Public Holidays

The only days off that everyone is entitled to are New Year's Day, Memorial Day, Fourth of July, Labor Day, Thanksgiving Day and Christmas Day. Other days may only be granted as a holiday to government workers and teachers.

In addition, there are a number of floating days which employers grant for any number of reasons, e.g. New Year's Eve, Christmas Eve and other religious holidays. Service and retail workers are expected to work on at least some federal holidays, although overtime rates will be paid and/or they'll receive time off on another day. Similarly, when federal holidays fall on a Saturday or Sunday, a weekday is substituted 'in lieu'.

When federal holidays fall on a Tuesday or Thursday, it's common practice to close on the Monday or Friday respectively, so that the company is shut for four consecutive days. These extra days may or may not be taken from your holiday allowance.

Leave

There's no US law requiring employers to give their staff paid leave for holidays, sickness or any other reason – so anything you get is

---

Federal Holidays Observed by Most Businesses

Date	Holiday
1st January	New Year's Day
Third Monday in January	Martin Luther King Day
Third Monday in February	President's Day, also known as Washington-Lincoln Day
Last Monday in May	Memorial Day, also known as Decoration Day
Fourth of July	Independence Day
First Monday in September	Labor Day
Second Monday in October	Columbus Day, also known as Pioneers' or Farmers' Day
11th November	Veterans' Day
Fourth Thursday in Nov	Thanksgiving
25th December	Christmas Day

a bonus. Unless you've worked for some years for a company, taking a sick day off may mean no pay, which is one of the reasons Americans go into work, even though they're sneezing and coughing all over their co-workers. Where sick leave is permitted, employees usually have a quota of days they can take each year – the average taken is seven days. You should notify your employer of sickness or an accident as soon as possible, i.e.

within a few hours. Some bosses require a doctor's certificate.

Compassionate leave and time off for jury duty is allowed, but may not be paid. The same goes for maternity and paternity leave, or for time off to care for a sick family member. Most employees are allowed by law to take up to 12 weeks unpaid leave for personal or family health needs – any more, and they may lose their job.

beach house, Maine, New England

New York City

7.
ON THE MOVE

Americans are deeply attached to their motor cars, and will not walk or use public transport, unless there's absolutely no alternative. Although the US has a good network of airlines, trains and long-distance buses, local public transport is unreliable in all but the largest cities; away from major population centres, it can be non-existent (even getting a taxi can be difficult, particularly when it's raining). Add to this the comparatively cheap cost of petrol (gas), and there's little incentive for people to leave their cars at home.

> 'A tree never hits an automobile except in self defense.'
> American proverb

It's been estimated that no more than 14mn people (or about 5 per cent of the population) use public transportation on a daily basis, while almost 90 per cent of all trips are made by car.

To help you travel around the US safely, reliably and cost-effectively, this chapter contains useful tips on motoring, road rules and driving etiquette, as well as information about public transport for those rare and unthinkable times when you cannot go by car.

DRIVING

Learning to drive is a rite of passage for American teenagers. Most get their learner's licence at age 16 – a few states allow this at just 14 – and so important is driving that it's even taught as part of the school curriculum. Not being able to drive is like not being able to read: it marks you out as a social misfit.

There are more cars in the US than drivers; some 240mn vehicles against 200mn licensed drivers, out of a population of around 300mn. Not surprisingly, families often have more than one car and many have a collection. America is the only country in the world where you can do your banking, drop off your dry cleaning, buy a hamburger and get married, all without getting out of the driving seat.

The safest US state for motorists is Massachusetts, where the road death rate is comparable to that of Switzerland; while the most dangerous state is Wyoming (see 🖳 www. driveandstayalive.com), where it's twice as high as that of Portugal, which has Western Europe's highest death toll.

Drivers

In the main, American drivers are courteous and careful, and more willing to give way to other drivers than European road users. The combination of big cars, wide roads and a strong police presence make for a more relaxed driving style. But American drivers have their faults. They often drive far too close to the vehicle in front of them (tailgating), and truck drivers may try to bully you into moving over by 'hugging' your rear bumper. Always leave a large gap between your vehicle and the one in front. You should also take care when approaching traffic lights, as running a red light is a common habit in cities.

Although the car is a status symbol, the sheer enjoyment of driving – so clearly exhibited by southern Europeans – is curiously lacking in the US, where skills are passed over in favour of convenience. A great many Americans cannot drive a car with manual gears (stick shift).

> 'Americans are broad-minded people. They'll accept the fact that a person can be an alcoholic, a dope fiend, a wife beater, and even a newspaperman, but if a man doesn't drive, there is something wrong with him.'
>
> Art Buchwald (American humorist and writer)

The road death rate is worryingly high, at over 40,000 a year, which is higher than in many European countries, including those inhabited by speed demons, such as Italy and Spain. Someone is injured every 15 seconds on US roads, and someone killed every 12 minutes.

Inexperience is a big factor in motor vehicle accidents, which are a leading cause of death in youngsters aged between 15 and 20. In 2006, almost 3,500 teenage drivers were killed and almost 275,000 injured in crashes, according to the National Highway Traffic Safety Administration. Mile for mile, teenagers are involved in three times as many fatal crashes as all other drivers. As a result, many states have placed restrictions on teenage drivers, such as increasing the amount of driver instruction, imposing night-time curfews and prohibiting them from carrying teenage passengers (and showing off to them after a few beers).

American Roads

There are 3.9mn miles (6.25mn km) of roads in America, including some 46,500mi (74,500km) of motorway (freeway). Rural-dwellers think nothing of driving several hundred miles to visit friends or eat pizza. Many interstate highways are long, straight and featureless – the sheer boredom of driving along them causes drivers to lose concentration (the technical term is 'highway hypnosis'). You may be tempted to speed on long stretches when there's no other car (i.e. police car) in sight.

Multi-lane highways are variously called freeways, expressways, speedways or thruways. Turnpikes are toll roads. Freeways are similar to motorways, therefore you cannot stop or park, and traffic is fast (as long as it isn't grid-locked).

The American road system is made up of:

● Interstate highways, e.g. I-55 from New Orleans to Chicago, are the fast transit routes which link states across the US. Those with even numbers run east-west, while those with odd numbers run north-south. Some divert around or act as spur roads into cities.

damaging road surfaces and creating almost legendary potholes – some are large enough to be described as craters. City streets, too, can be rough and uneven, which is one reason why American cars have such soft suspension.

Road Rules

Like many aspects of American law, these vary from state to state – the speed limit may change by as much as 10 mph as you cross a state border. However, there are many rules which apply more or less across the nation and which may differ from what you're used to in your home country.

These include the following:

- US highways or routes, e.g. US 14 which links Yellowstone National Park to Chicago, are the original interstate. They can carry less traffic than the interstate highways, and offer more scenic routes.

- State highways or routes (Rte) are local roads which vary from black top (tarmac or bitumen) to gravel tracks.

On a road with up to 12 lanes of traffic, it's advisable to know exactly where you're going, which lane to use, and where to exit safely. Don't attempt to drive on a busy freeway until you've practised on quieter roads and preferably been shown the route by a more experienced driver.

On a toll road or turnpike, you collect a toll ticket as you enter the road and pay as you leave. Your point and time of entry are recorded, and if you reach your exit point in a time which indicates you've been speeding, you may receive a fine.

With so many miles of highway, maintenance is a never-ending battle for national, state and local authorities. Extreme climates (especially in the north and midwest) add to the problem, with severe frosts and heat-waves

- Americans drive on the right-hand side of the road.

- It's legal to pass in the inside (right) lane. This means you can pass if the road is clear, or traffic is moving faster, but not that you can use the inside lane to deliberately overtake another driver.

- 'Stop' means stop, especially at junctions. If you carry on rolling, you may incur a fine.

- Flashing your headlights usually means, 'I have right of way!' Drivers also flash their lights to warn others of radar traps ahead.

- Some traffic lights flash from green to red and vice versa, with no amber in between.

- It's legal to turn right on a red light, unless the action is expressly forbidden (shown by a sign). You must stop first.

● School buses rule the road, and you must stop at least 25ft (7.6m) away from one with a red flashing light, as this means children will be crossing the road. Approach any school bus with extreme caution, flashing light or not. Passing one at the wrong time can result in a $1,000 fine.

All states publish road rules. Ask for information at your local Department of Motor Vehicles (DMV). The *Digest of Motor Laws*, published by the American Automobile Association (AAA), contains all state traffic regulations, including vehicle registration, taxes, driving licence, traffic rules, motorcycle and moped rules, and lots more. It's available from any AAA office, and is free to AAA members (☎ 1-888-859 5161, 🖥 www.aaa.com).

> **'The one thing that unites all human beings, regardless of age, gender, religion, economic status or ethnic background, is that, deep down inside, we ALL believe that we are above average drivers.'**
>
> Dave Barry (American writer & humorist)

Licence Points System

Driving offences are viewed as serious, not only by those who enforce the law but by the public in general. A lot of police time is spent warning drivers and issuing traffic tickets; a few states issue on-the-spot fines, but more usually you pay by post or at a local office. Never offer a police officer money to pay a fine, as this may be construed as a bribe!

As well as a fine, offenders may have points added to their licence – too many points and it's suspended for a period. In order to drive again, they may have to attend 'traffic school' or undergo counselling. Persistent and serious violations can lead to permanent disqualification and even imprisonment.

Speeding

Traffics cops are hot on speeding. There are patrols, radar speed traps and other speed monitors, so if you regularly flout the limit you'll eventually get caught. On average, the fine is around $50 for ten miles over the limit, plus a further $5 or $10 for each additional mile.

If you're stopped by traffic cops, stay in your car, stay calm and keep your hands in view – if you make any sudden moves, a police officer may go for his gun! He will want to see your licence, car registration document and insurance card, so carry these with you. Resist the temptation to joke. Apologies, delivered with a foreign accent, may get you off with a warning.

Seat Belts

Wearing a seatbelt is compulsory for drivers and front-seat passengers in all states except New Hampshire, where it only applies to under-18s. Some states insist that all passengers belt up. Fines range up to $50, but in some states you're only stopped if the police spot another violation, such as a broken brake light or erratic driving. The laws surrounding seatbelts are typical of the confusion created by having 50 states, each with their own traffic laws – the simplest (and safest) answer is to wear seatbelts front and back on every trip.

Drinking & Driving

Driving while intoxicated (DWI) or under the influence of alcohol (DUI) are serious offences. Drunk drivers account for two-fifths of all traffic fatalities, and over 1.8mn offenders are arrested each year. Even so, Americans can be blasé when it comes to drunk driving. It's illegal to carry open containers of booze in a vehicle, but in some rural areas, driving with an open six pack of beer on your lap is a way of life.

The legal limit is 80mg of alcohol to 100ml blood – the same as the UK and higher than many European countries – but state law varies. There are many ways for police to check your sobriety, including urine and breath tests. They can even ask you to close your eyes and touch the tip of your nose with an index finger! It sounds comical, but if you fail you could be looking at a 60-day jail term!

Finding Your Way

Most cities and large towns have straight streets laid out in grid formation, therefore provided you can tell your uptown from your downtown and differentiate east from west, you shouldn't get lost. Many new cars are sold complete with a satellite navigation system (Sat-Nav or GPS), or you can have one installed – by far the most popular is OnStar (for general information, see 💻 www.thetravelinsider.info/gps/gpsintroduction.htm).

In addition, there are websites which help you to plan a route, such as 💻 www.mapquest.com and maps.google.com – which are usually up to date. There's a street index (A to Z) to all

major urban areas, and road maps covering the entire US. If you get lost, most Americans are happy to give directions.

Drive Safe

There are dangers on American roads, but common sense will keep you out of most predicaments:

- **Be aware of your surroundings** – if an area looks rough then it probably is. Keep your car doors locked, windows shut and stay in your car until you're on familiar territory. Take locals' advice about no-go areas.

- **Know your route** – a decent map can keep you out of rough areas and save you some hairy moments trying to exit freeways.

- **Lock your car** – in the US, a car is stolen roughly every 20 seconds, but a decent anti-theft device will discourage thieves if there are easier targets nearby. Driving an old heap is an equally good deterrent.

- **Lock valuables out of sight** – or take them with you. Never leave car documents in a vehicle as this will make it easier for a thief to sell it.

● **Don't succumb to road rage** – the other driver may well have a gun!

● **Don't sleep in your car**.

● **Be careful who you stop for** – if stopped by police in an unmarked car, ask to see their ID before winding down the window. Thieves sometimes pose as police.

● **Trust your instincts** – if anything happens to make you suspicious, e.g. you've been shunted or 'tailgated', stay in your car. Be wary of stopping to help at the scene of an accident in a rough or deserted area, as these are sometimes staged to rob unsuspecting drivers. When in doubt, drive to a police station and report the incident.

Motorcyclists & Pedestrians

You can ride a bike up to 125cc on a full car licence, but must take a test for anything more powerful. Laws regarding the minimum ages, the wearing of helmets and other protective gear vary from state to state, and some are quite bizarre; for example in Arkansas, a 10-year-old can ride a moped, while in Rhode Island only the pillion passenger needs to wear

a helmet. Check local regulations with the local Department of Motor Vehicles (DMV). Note that a few Americans are hostile towards 'bikers', regarding them all as Hell's Angels.

Pedestrians are a long way down the 'food chain' on US roads. In rural areas – or parts of Los Angeles – walking isn't 'normal' behaviour, and people may stop to offer you a lift or just slow down and stare. Stay on the pavement (sidewalk) if there is one, and only cross at safe crossings such as pedestrian crossings with lights (they usually instruct you to 'WALK'/'DON'T WALK'). If you're unsure where or when to cross, follow the example of other pedestrians. In theory, there are fines for jaywalking, i.e. crossing the road at an unauthorised place, although in big cities, pedestrians can appear as fearless and foolhardy as drivers.

Roundabouts

Americans call these 'traffic islands' although many have never navigated one – they're rare in the US. Instead, there are confusing junctions (without traffic lights) called a 'four-way stop' where priority is given to the vehicle which stops first or you give way to the vehicle on your right. If you come across a roundabout, traffic already moving around the island has priority over those entering.

> 'Natives who beat drums to drive off evil spirits are objects of scorn to smart Americans who blow their horns to break up traffic jams.'
>
> Mary Ellen Kelly

Traffic Jams

Rush hours in big cities are generally a nightmare. The timing and length of the rush 'hour' is proportional to the size of the city, but usually lasts from around 7 to 9.30am and 4 to 6.30pm. Los Angeles is grid-locked for most of the day – or it seems like it – and some residents spend more than five hours a day commuting. Limitations on parking and lane use, as well as schemes to encourage car sharing (pooling) have done little to reduce congestion. Even high occupancy vehicle (HOV) lanes, which are reserved during rush hour for buses, taxis and cars carrying more than one passenger, have failed to solve the problem – it's possible to buy an inflatable passenger which occupies a seat and gets you into a HOV lane! The one thing which might help, i.e. decent public transport, has yet to be tried!

An additional factor is the weekend rush. Close of work on Friday sees traffic jams reach gargantuan proportions, and early Sunday evening is just as bad, as the tide of traffic flows back. The same problem occurs on the day before federal holidays (see **Chapter 6**).

Parking

Given the vast numbers of cars, parking is a priority in the US, where shopping malls have huge car parks which are well lit, accessible and usually free.

Most suburban areas have free parking, and there are always car parks and parking meters in town centres. Meter fees and times vary, but many are free in the evenings and on Sundays. Car parks cost between $10 and $25 a day in big cities and considerably less in smaller towns. It's worth the extra investment to park in a well-lit, attended car park, rather than on a patch of waste ground, especially if you plan to return to your car after dark.

You'll struggle to find somewhere to park in big cities such as New York, which is possibly the only US conurbation where it's best not to own a car. Many residents pay to rent a garage or underground parking space, which in Manhattan can cost the same as renting an apartment in a small Midwest town.

Parking is an acquired skill in a large American sedan. Luckily, car-parking spaces are usually diagonal to the kerb and require little steering. The US is also the originator of the parking valet, who will take your car from you at a restaurant or bar, park it and bring it back when you want to leave. Alternatively, you can eat or watch a movie without even getting out of the car!

Parking Illegally

There are many places where you cannot park. Anywhere with a sign saying 'No Stopping/Standing (Loading)/Parking' is pretty clear, but you must also steer clear of bus stops, taxi ranks and schools, or anywhere where the kerb is painted red. Watch out for 'snow streets' which must be kept clear for snow ploughs during winter and stay several metres away from fire hydrants, which must be accessible to the fire service at all times. In cities, some streets (or a particular side of the street) must be kept clear for street cleaning on certain days.

You cannot park and stay on the side of the road in rural areas or you'll have traffic cops knocking on your window. Park in the wrong place at the wrong time and you'll inevitably get a parking ticket, or may even be clamped or towed away. (The wheel clamp is also known as the 'boot' or the 'Denver boot' in the US, as it was first inflicted on motorists in this Colorado city.)

Petrol Stations

Petrol (gas) is cheap in the US; at least, it is in comparison with most other countries. Even as the surge in the world oil price has pushed up prices at the pump, taxes remain low. Petrol is sold by the US gallon (equal to around 3.8litres), which in 2008 cost around $4 for a gallon of regular unleaded – it's around double the price in the UK and many European countries. If a state governor attempted to raise petrol taxes to European levels, he'd soon be looking for another job!

You can buy three grades of unleaded, as well as diesel – few cars use diesel. In many areas, an attendant will fill your tank, check your oil and tyres and clean your windscreen; this is called 'full serve' as opposed to self service or 'U serve'. There are some fairly rundown gas stations in rural America, where it can be difficult to find one open after dark or on Sundays, so take care to keep your tank topped up (in some states you can be 'ticketed' for running out of gas). At late-night or 24-hour gas stations, you need to pay before you fill up in the evening or at night.

PUBLIC TRANSPORT

To many Americans, using public transport means flying (or taking a taxi) – long-distance trains and buses cannot compete with the cheap and comprehensive airline network. In cities, the most reliable option is usually the subway or other rail system, although in suburbs and rural areas, there may be no choice but to travel by car. In spite of its sheer size and mobile population, America has no national transport policy, and spends little money on public transport (mass transit) systems. If you have the time, taking a long-distance bus or train is an excellent way to see America, although if you're in a hurry it won't cost you much more to fly.

American timetables don't use the 24-hour clock but instead display times using am and pm. Am is sometimes shown as 'A' and pm as 'P'. All pm times (from noon to midnight) are usually printed in bold. Note that midnight is shown as 12 am (or 12 A), while midday is 12pm (12 P).

> **'Too bad all the people who know how to run the country are busy driving taxi cabs and cutting hair.'**
>
> George F. Burns (American comedian)

Taxis

Taxis (cabs) are inexpensive, plentiful and easily spotted on US streets, where they're usually bright yellow. You hail one by raising your arm (don't yell 'Taxi!' as they probably can't hear you). Those with a light on the roof are 'on call', i.e. available.

A licensed cab driver must, by law, take you anywhere within their official area, but don't state your destination until you're inside the vehicle. Drivers may refuse to take you to an area which they consider dangerous – they know the area better than you. Passengers always travel in the back, which is for the cabbie's protection, not yours, as drivers are frequently mugged by passengers.

Drivers are supposed to take tests in English and know the local geography, but many are recent immigrants who are still learning the roads – and the language. Over half of New York's legendary cabbies speak English as a second language, which can lead to 'misunderstandings' as you're taken the long way round to the wrong destination and then charged an excessive fare. Always make sure that the driver turns on the meter, and carry a map so that you can point out the destination and check the route if necessary. If you know the driver is going the wrong way, then say so. Most cabbies know when they have a switched-on passenger on board.

Fares vary according to your destination and the time of day, but there are federal standards for taxi meters, so if the meter's on, you shouldn't be swindled. Many drivers dislike changing large notes, and most have the capacity to turn nasty if you don't proffer a 15 per cent tip. If you want to complain about a driver, note his cab number, which is displayed on the dashboard, roof and/or the rear of the front seat, as well as the driver's licence number (usually on the dashboard, next to the driver) and the name of the taxi company. A reputable driver will provide a receipt containing this information.

Unregulated (rogue) taxis circle like sharks at places such as airports and train stations. These are known as 'pirate' taxis and are usually unlicensed, uninsured and drivers can be unpleasant should you challenge their fare. Airports and large bus and train stations usually have taxi dispatchers, whose job is to find you a licensed taxi and keep you out of the clutches of the bogus cab drivers.

Planes

Air travel in the US is cheaper per mile than travelling by car, and Americans use planes as routinely as Europeans hop on a bus or tram. More than 1mn passengers take a domestic flight every

day, and there are some 250 destinations to choose from.

With so much air traffic, delays are inevitable, and these tend to stack up through the day, with some travellers experiencing waits far longer than the actual flight time. America's weather (tornados in summer, blizzards in winter) adds to the unpredictability. Even so, Americans are casual about flying, and around 15 per cent of passengers fail to turn up for their flights. This means that domestic flights are routinely over-booked, and some passengers are 'bumped' off flights. This isn't necessarily a bad thing, as most airlines ask for volunteers, and offer bumped passengers upgrades and discount vouchers if there's more than an hour's wait until the next flight.

If you check in late (less than one hour before departure), you may be bumped regardless, especially if there's insufficient time to get you through the increasingly complicated security measures. These have been boosted beyond belief since the September 11th (9/11) attacks – all bags are X-rayed, as are shoes, while hand luggage and lap tops are carefully scrutinised. It's advisable not to lock your hold luggage, as locks may be cut off during security checks. Carry valuables in your hand luggage, and don't let it out of your sight.

For information about the latest security checks, see the Transportation Security Administration website (🖳 www.tsa.gov).

> **The busiest airport in the world is Hartsfield-Jackson Atlanta International Airport, which serves Atlanta, Georgia, and was used by almost 90mn passengers in 2007. Its closest rival is Chicago's O'Hare International – somewhat surprisingly, New York's JFK is a long way down the list at number 13.**

Fares

There are some excellent deals on flights, especially with 'no-frills' airlines whose fares can be up to 70 per cent cheaper than those of traditional carriers. You can also make savings if you fly out of smaller regional airports, travel on Saturdays or early in the morning, or take a 'red-eye' (overnight) flight or one that makes several stops en-route. There are better deals on popular routes such as those along the east or west coasts. With so many competing airlines, you can usually find a good deal, although promotional fares may need to be booked well in advance.

Use the internet to search for fares – good websites include Expedia (🖳 www.expedia.com) and Travelocity (🖳 www.travelocity.com). A reputable travel agent, preferably one who's a member of the

American Society of Travel Agents (ASTA), can also find you good deals.

You can save money on airport transfers by using a courtesy bus – many hotels will pick you up free of charge. There are also shuttle minibus services (which you share with other passengers) that are cheaper than taxis.

The busiest times to travel in the US are the days running up to Christmas or Thanksgiving, when it feels as if the whole of America is headed home for the holidays. Public transport is fully booked and roads are choked with traffic. Bad weather can create further disruptions – both holidays fall in early winter. If you want to know how difficult travelling can be at this time of the year, watch the amusing *Planes, Trains & Automobiles*, in which Steve Martin battles the US transport system to make it home in time for Thanksgiving.

Buses & Trains

There are over 1,000 long-distance and local bus companies in the US, serving

some 15,000 cities and towns, which for many Americans are the only available form of public transport. They carry some 350mn passengers annually on a network covering some 280,000mi (450,000km).

By contrast, the US rail network, although the largest in the world, is mainly devoted to freight. This subsidises the patchy passenger network, which covers just 22,000mi (35,750km) of track, or just 12 per cent of the available railroad – and misses out South Dakota and Wyoming altogether.

> **'Never run after a bus or a man. There will always be another one.'**
> Anon

Long-distance Buses

Cross the US by bus and you'll certainly meet some 'interesting' people. It's a fascinating, if exhausting way to travel – a coast-to-coast trip takes three days, with only a brief chance to grab food and stretch your legs. There are no sleep stops and no showers, but at least there are toilets on board. The main appeal is the availability and price – buses are the cheapest method of travel in the US. Virtually every town has a bus terminal, and if the long-distance service doesn't cover your destination, your ticket will be valid for a local connection.

The most famous long-distance bus company is Greyhound (🖥 www.greyhound.com), recognisable by its iconic running dog (greyhound) logo. It serves over 2,300 destinations, has 13,000 daily departures across the

US, carries some 25mn passengers a year and has a good safety record. On long-distance buses, you buy your ticket before you travel, not on the bus – tickets can be also bought online and collected at bus stations. It may seem to be stating the obvious, but you must ask for the cheapest available fare or you'll be sold a standard ticket.

Bus terminals are busy and sometimes intimidating places, and are often located in less salubrious downtown areas. Keep a careful eye on belongings and don't flash your cash. Allow at least 45 minutes to check in your baggage – longer if you're collecting a ticket, as queues can be lengthy and slow-moving. Keep all your valuables with you inside the bus, and be wary of pickpockets and thieves on long journeys. Occasionally, you may need to board a bus at a 'flag stop', where you wave your arm to get the driver to stop, although if he's full, he will drive on past. It's safer to start evening journeys at a bus terminal.

Long-distance inter-state buses are slow and comparatively cramped, but luxurious (e.g. reclining seats) compared with the bone-shakers of yesteryear. The smoothest ride is in the centre of the bus away from the wheels, while the best views and legroom are at the front. Carry a warm jacket or blanket with you on the bus, for drivers turn up the air-conditioning to help them stay awake at night, and 'central air' (as it's known) can be uncomfortably cold. An inflatable pillow and earplugs are also invaluable.

Local Buses

These are America's least popular method of local transport, although many people have no choice. City (urban) buses are notoriously slow and erratic – in rush hour, it's often quicker to walk. Suburban and rural buses can be infrequent, and during off-peak times (e.g. evenings and weekends) you may wait up to an hour for a bus.

On some buses, you deposit the exact fare in a box; on others you must buy a token or ticket in advance – in New York, tokens are also valid on the subway. Many companies charge a flat-rate fare of one or two dollars, irrespective of the distance travelled. In a few enlightened cities, such as Seattle, some city buses are free.

Bus stops are indicated by signs, shelters or yellow markings on the kerbstone. A few may have timetables and bus routes, but often there's no information at all.

> **'The only way of catching a train I ever discovered, is to miss the train before.'**
>
> G.K. Chesterton (English writer)

Trains

Once the symbol of the new West, America's railroads have been in decline since the second half of the 20th century, as car and air travel became more commonplace. The national network is called Amtrak. Foreigners who are used to fast and efficient rail travel may be shocked at its slowness – trains are four times as slow as high-speed trains in France and Japan. Late trains and infrequent services, along with old rolling stock and poorly maintained tracks, don't encourage people to use the service. Stations are often shabby and unpleasant; New

York's Grand Central is the exception, rather than the rule.

The US rail network links over 500 cities and towns, but don't expect to travel from coast to coast on fast rail transport, which takes over three days! You must change trains (at Chicago or New Orleans), and will travel at an average speed of just 40mph. The busiest and most reliable routes are along the eastern seaboard, from Boston via New York to Washington DC, and west to Chicago, plus southern California. Elsewhere, trains are the preserve of tourists or people with a fear of flying.

Despite all its disadvantages, train travel often costs more than flying, although there are good-value passes available if you have the time to explore, and many tickets allow you to break your journey (stop over) en-route. Carriages are spacious, service is good and you have a window on some of America's most spectacular scenery; the reclining seats are comfortable, and many trains have sleeping car options, while Amtrak's Superliners, which operate in the west, have restaurants, observation cars and even a cinema.

For more information, contact Amtrak (☎ 1-800-USA RAIL, 🖳 www. amtrak.com).

> Buy your ticket before you get on the train. If there's a ticket office open and you fail to use it, the conductor will charge you a surcharge. When you present your ticket, the conductor issues a receipt and puts it in front of your seat or beneath the overhead storage rack. If you leave your seat for any reason, take the receipt with you, as it's your only proof of payment.

Urban Railways & Subways

Many cities have an underground system (referred to as a subway), while others have efficient urban rail systems, which are by far the best way to beat the rush-hour traffic in a big city. Subways do, however, have an image problem, but aren't all like New York City's grimy, graffiti-filled, overcrowded crime zone (at least, that's the impression given by the movies). Many are clean and efficient, including the Atlanta MARTA and the Washington Metrorail systems, which are among the best in the world. A number of systems aren't underground at all, such as the elevated railways in Miami and Chicago (where it's known as the 'El') and the historic tramways (street cars) in San Francisco and New Orleans.

Subway fares are reasonable, and for regular travellers, a selection of passes

HITCHHIKING

Hitchhiking or hitching a lift is legal in most American states, provided you stay off the actual road; however, it isn't the safest way to get around. The increased awareness of personal safety which permeates US society makes people more wary of picking up strangers – and the number of nutcases driving around America's roads means that hitchhikers are always at risk.

But there are still a number of people who thumb a lift across the nation, simply for the experience. If you plan ahead, stay away from the quieter routes and avoid travelling alone, it can be a surprisingly quick way of getting from A to B. Advice on hitchhiking in general and on travelling through the different states can be found on the Digihitch website (www.digihitch.com/usa-map.html).

CYCLING

In America, cycling is a sport, not a means of transportation. The country is too large, distances too great, weather too erratic and traffic too dense for it to be a practical way of getting about, unless you're a cycle courier. If you want to use a bicycle, be aware that most drivers aren't used to sharing the road with cyclists, and this makes you more vulnerable. You also face problems carrying your bike on public transport, although some city buses have room for a few on the front, and finding somewhere to stow it during the day. This may change as America becomes more eco-conscious, but for

is available. Services generally operate between 6am and 2am weekdays, with a reduced service at the weekend and on public holidays.

Although subways have a reputation for being dangerous, millions of people use them every day without incident, although following a few common-sense rules may make travel easier and safer:

● Use the busiest carriages – usually those in the centre of the train – or the one with a guard or conductor. It's best to avoid travelling by subway between 11pm and 7am.

● Platforms are more dangerous than trains. Wait in a well-lit area or close to a manned ticket booth. New York City has 'off hours waiting areas' (marked in yellow) to show you where trains stop outside peak hours.

● Don't stand too close to the edge of the platform – pushing people off the platform isn't unknown.

● Keep a firm hold of your purse, wallet or handbag, especially when near the doors – there are more pickpockets on subway systems than on regular trains.

now, being a cyclist is an uphill slog. However, there are a few exceptions, and some towns (e.g. Madison, WI and Morgan Hill, CA) have a wealth of cycle lanes, while large cities tend to have few.

ACCOMMODATION

If you're travelling long distance across America, you may need overnight accommodation. The choices are varied and depend on your budget, from expensive major hotel chains, such as Marriott and Four Seasons, to cheap motels. Motels and inexpensive chain hotels are usually cheaper if you book ahead. There are also many fleapits, where you'll share your unsanitary sheets with the many-legged residents, therefore it's best to avoid anything very cheap.

American is packed with roadside motels, which are flagged up by neon signs along the side of the highway. Most are comfortable and welcoming – Motel 6 (💻 www.motel6.com) and Super 8 (💻 www.super8.com) are popular chains – while a few resemble Bates Motel in *Psycho*. If a place feels wrong, drive on to the next one.

Some of the nicest accommodation is in bed and breakfast establishments, which are the closest you come to staying in someone's home. Most states have an association of bed and breakfast owners, and there are websites devoted to B&Bs, such as 💻 www.bedandbreakfast.com/usa.html and www.bbonline.com/usa.html. Note, however, that B&Bs aren't a budget option, particularly in cities.

> **'The car has become... an article of dress without which we feel uncertain, unclad, and incomplete.'**
>
> Marshall McLuhan (American writer, *Understanding Media*)

American Football

8.
THE AMERICANS AT PLAY

Americans take their leisure time seriously. However well you think you know them (or not), it's when Americans are at play and at their least formal that you, as a foreigner, are most likely to stand out from the crowd. There are probably more rules attached to rest and relaxation than to any other aspect of US life. Becoming socially adept in a different culture is perhaps the most difficult obstacle to 'fitting in' abroad. It's also the area where you're most likely to make mistakes. To help you avoid social gaffes, this chapter contains information about social customs, dress codes, dining, and social and leisure activities.

> 'A life of leisure and a life of laziness are two things. There will be sleeping enough in the grave.'
>
> Benjamin Franklin (American Founding Father & statesman)

DRESS CODE

As a visitor to American shores, how you look will mark you out as an incomer far more than your accent. The US is a multicultural society, but its inhabitants assume an overall sameness of attire throughout the 50 states, and it may be some time before newcomers adopt the American 'look'.

This conformity of dress is more complicated than it seems. The 'traditional' US outfit of T-shirt and jeans is only one aspect of how people dress. Most have clothes for every occasion, even if they're only likely to wear them once. For a very formal dinner it's an evening dress or tuxedo, then there's sombre clothing for funerals, smart attire for weddings and job interviews, and working clothes appropriate to the job: many blue-collar jobs have a dress code or uniform.

Americans dislike anything overly formal, and this attitude is reflected in their choice of clothing. Away from the celebrity circuit and fashion-conscious cities such as New York, they aren't noted for their fashion sense. Many men dress like larger versions of their children, in vividly coloured shirts and oversized shorts – some of America's most bizarre men's outfits can be seen on the golf course. Older women are seemingly addicted to garish colours and stretch fabrics, while teenagers dress to conform in baseball caps and voluminous trousers. A large proportion of Americans are obese, which may go a long way to explaining their uneasy relationship with clothes.

At the other end of the spectrum is the exaggerated formality displayed by New York bankers in braces and Brooks

Brothers shirts, and by Hollywood actresses who favour top-to-toe designer gear, which even includes an outfit for their dog.

Home

Within the confines of their own homes, Americans dress for comfort and practicality, and will usually have an outfit appropriate to the job. This may be a tracksuit for housework, an apron for cooking or overalls for when they tackle the gardening or wash the car. Bear in mind that friends and neighbours may not want you to see them wearing their house clothes, therefore it's advisable to ring rather than surprising them with a knock on the door!

Many Americans take their shoes off in their homes to protect carpets and wooden floors, therefore it's polite to ask whether you should remove your shoes when you enter someone's home.

Places of Worship

People who attend a service of worship take pride in their appearance, which tends to be conservative. This means a collar and tie for the men, and a smart and often brightly-coloured dress with a hat for the women (older ladies may also wear gloves). This attire can also be worn elsewhere, and the whole ensemble is often referred to as 'Sunday best'.

> If someone compliments you on your outfit, accept their praise with a smile and say thank you. Unlike some cultures, in America it isn't considered polite to protest or to be overly modest.

Social Occasions

Smart casual is the golden rule when invited to a social occasion in America. Most social occasions, that is... You'll feel uncomfortable at a backyard barbecue if you turn up in smart separates to find everyone else wearing shorts and sandals. If you're invited to an event and don't know what to wear, ask the host what they will be wearing, as Americans will bend over backwards to help you fit in.

Work

Blue-collar workers and those in service industries usually have a uniform or a code of dress. People who work in offices may appear conservative and casual (see **Dress** in **Chapter 6**), but this depends very much on the type of business and where it's located. The southern states are more reserved in their attire, as are those on the east coast, while California is more relaxed. Many companies have adopted a 'casual' or 'dress down' Friday code, when employees can wear whatever they like (more or less). In some organisations, the whole week is 'casual' and even in some law offices, employees may wear jeans when they aren't meeting clients or making a court appearance.

Bad Hair Day

Many Americans are obsessed with their looks, especially their hair. There's a seemingly endless range of hair care products in even the smallest drugstore. Then again, this is the country which coined the phrase 'bad hair day' to sum up a day on which your hair's a mess and everything else seems to go wrong. Men live in fear of going bald: it's been estimated that Americans spend over $3.5bn a year on products to treat hair loss. At the other end of the spectrum, women are diligent about removing body hair and nothing will mark you out more clearly as a European than tufts under your armpits.

EATING

In America, food has a culture all of its own. Americans don't eat to live, they live to eat. The US produces a vast amount of food, and prices are cheap in comparison to other countries. As a consequence, it's the fattest nation on earth, with 65 per cent of people overweight and a third clinically obese. Manufacturers produce a vast range of products labelled 'diet', 'slimming' or 'lite', along with reams of information on what is good and bad for you, much of it contradictory. Many people are obsessed by diets, some of which are quite bizarre: these include diets that are low in carbohydrates and high in fibre, or which focus on just one food,

such as grapefruit or eggs. Food is a guilty pleasure for many people who have a love-hate relationship with whatever's on their plate. And there's a lot on the average American's plate. Most portions served up in restaurants and diners are enough to feed two or three 'normal' people, although some restaurants offer smaller portions at lower prices, and it's usually possible to buy one meal and split the food between two people.

It's also considered perfectly acceptable to take unfinished food home with you. The receptacle may be called a 'doggie bag' (although the family dog is unlikely to receive the leftovers). If the 'waitperson' (the politically correct term for whoever brings your order) sees food left on your plate, he or she may ask if you want it boxed up to take away. Saying yes doesn't mean you're greedy, rather it shows that you've enjoyed your meal.

Meals

In the country which invented fast food, it isn't surprising that many Americans eat on the move or while standing at the kitchen counter. As in many western nations, sitting down as a family is reserved for special occasions. It's possible to eat at any time of the day. Many restaurants are open 24 hours a day, and most hotels offer room service no matter what time it is, but there are certain meals which are traditionally eaten at a particular time of day.

Breakfast

Beware the 'breakfast special': a gargantuan meal offered by diners for as little as $5 and consisting of eggs, bacon, sausage, hash browns, grits (a corn-based porridge popular in the south), toast, waffles, pancakes and much more, all washed down with orange juice and a never-ending ('bottomless cup') supply of coffee. It's possible to eat your way through an entire day's calorie allowance, so an American breakfast is a special treat, and many people start the day with coffee, cereal and toast.

Some items on the breakfast menu aren't what they seem, especially to Europeans. Bacon is crisp and often served with maple syrup, while toast or biscuits (like scones, but not as nice) may arrive at your table already buttered. You'll also face one of the strangest aspects of American dining: the bemusing amount of choice, from the type of bread you want for your toast (white, rye, whole-wheat, pumpernickel and English muffins are just a few of the choices) to the almost unlimited ways of frying eggs: 'sunny side up' is fried on one side only, 'over easy' turned but leaving the yolk soft, and 'over hard' turned with a firm yolk.

American name for smoked salmon) served with bagels (soft bread rings) and cream cheese, steak, crepes and a variety of egg dishes.

Lunch

Lunch is something eaten by children every day of the week, and by adults on working days only. Consequently, it's light, simple and quick – and quite probably the only really healthy meal in America.

The contents of a typical lunch box are usually a sandwich (maybe with the ubiquitous peanut butter and jelly filling, known as a PBJ) and an apple. Many working Americans buy their lunch at a delicatessen or 'deli'. These range from plush restaurant-style premises to small counter-service establishments. Most feature a mind-numbing array of foods, especially when it comes to sandwiches. Listening to a seasoned office worker order a range of 'subs' (a submarine, which is a long roll, also called a hero) for his colleagues in a New York deli, and

> **'You can find your way across this country using burger joints, the way a navigator uses stars.'**
>
> Charles Kuralt (American journalist)

Brunch

Americans who miss out on breakfast can always turn to brunch, a meal which fills the gap between breakfast and lunch and is especially popular on Sundays. People invite each other to brunch parties, or a family may go out to a restaurant to graze at an all-you-can-eat buffet. As well as the usual breakfast fare, there may be some more upmarket extras such as lox (the watching how the order is noted and filled with speed and efficiency, offers a fascinating insight into why the US is one of the most efficient countries in the world.

It's as well to rehearse the contents of your sandwich before you get to the front of the queue in a big-city 'deli', so you can recite clearly and concisely exactly what you want, from the filling, such as tuna and mayo (mayonnaise) or a BLT (bacon, lettuce and tomato), to which bread you want it on and which sauces, pickles and relishes should be included. Hesitate for just a moment and you'll have a queue of impatient office workers breathing down your neck – or the server will simply move on to the next person in line.

Dinner

Most Americans dine out at least three times a week. Indeed, around half of the average family's annual food budget is spent on eating outside the home. This might be a visit to a restaurant or just a trip to a fast food joint, where the meal is delivered by staff on roller skates and eaten in the car.

Dinner, more than any other meal, is likely to be a social occasion, with families trying to eat together, and this is especially true at holiday times. What they eat is influenced by their ethnic backgrounds, although it's by no means predictable. Americans are open to trying different cuisines, and the cook of the house will collect innumerable recipes to try out on her long-suffering family – from friends, colleagues, magazines and cookery programmes – and there's always a range of take-away services which offer home delivery. Dinner may be meatloaf one night and sushi the next.

Dinner time is earlier than in Europe, with some small-town restaurants only serving until around 8pm, while an even earlier version of dinner, eaten between 5 and 6.30pm, is referred to as supper.

Bread

Bread doesn't have the same significance that it does on European tables, but it's still a big part of the American diet. Much of the Midwest is given over to growing wheat, and only rice challenges bread as the staple foodstuff. If there's one particularly North American bread, it would have to be cornbread, made from maize flour (maize is commonly known as corn, hence the name), and popular in the southern states.

Barbecues & Potluck Suppers

Real men eat meat and they cook it as well – provided it's outside on the barbecue. Men who don't know a saucepan from a spatula are happy to man the grill, while their womenfolk rustle up salads and sauces. While not as barbecue-crazy as Australians, Americans cook in the backyard whenever they can, and turn some unusual foodstuffs over the charcoal, including marshmallows!

Another typical American invention is the potluck supper, where all the guests bring some food. Potluck means that even the host doesn't know what he or she will be eating. These are usually informal affairs, where the company is as important as the food, although it isn't unheard of for Americans to bring a dish of macaroni cheese to a wedding reception. If you're invited to a potluck supper, it's as well to ask which course you should bring. If you're lucky, it'll be the salad.

> **'The story of the barbecue is the story of America: Settlers arrive on great unspoiled continent, discover wondrous riches, set them on fire and eat them.'**
> Vince Staten (American writer)

Snacks & Desserts

It's hard to resist the temptation to eat between meals when there's food on every corner. Snacks in America can be as large as a meal: a bag of doughnuts, hotdogs at a baseball game, or the remains of last night's Chinese take-away (many Americans are convinced that Chinese food is low fat). There are outlets which focus on cookies (biscuits), milkshakes and, especially, ice cream. The names of calorie-loaded desserts frequently include such words as 'sinful', 'indulgence' or 'devil', further underlining America's guilt trip over fattening food.

Formal & Informal Dining

With their dislike of all things formal, Americans take a relaxed approach to eating, and there are few rules to

follow. You're much more likely to be invited to a casual meal than a black tie dinner, but there are some aspects of etiquette that you should be aware of.

Formal Dining

Even the most upmarket eateries in America are relaxed in comparison to a five-star restaurant in Britain or France: the stuffiest and most expensive restaurants in the US are invariably French. There may be a battery of knives and forks, but the cutlery (or flatware as it's known in the US) is usually arranged in order of use, so that you start by using those items on the outside and work your way inwards. If in doubt, watch what everyone else does. The waiting staff may, in any case, provide the tools you need as each course is served, saving you from making a fool of yourself. Note that it's normal to find the table set with the knife on the left and the fork on the right (the opposite to the way it's set in Europe), as most Americans eat with just a fork.

Informal Dining

Try to adopt the American use of the knife and fork. It's acceptable, if not desirable, to hold the fork in the

right hand and use it to break food into bite-size pieces. If this isn't possible, e.g. with steak, the fork is transferred to the left hand and the knife used to cut the item up. The fork is then returned to the right hand, while the knife is back on the left or leaning against the plate. Holding up the knife may be seen as a sign of aggression, while putting a knife in your mouth is considered bad manners or even foolhardy it's sharp! Food which is too liquid or cannot be stabbed or scooped without falling through the gaps between the prongs, is eaten with a spoon. Only if it's a hamburger, corn on the cob or something else which cannot be tackled with a fork, will Americans pick it up and eat it with their fingers.

> When invited to an informal gathering, such as a barbecue or buffet, you should ask if you can bring something. Even if the answer is negative, take a box of chocolates or a bottle of wine, as some kind of contribution is usually expected.

Seating Arrangements

Prearranged seating usually only applies at a formal sit-down meal, such as a wedding reception or banquet. Usually, friends and acquaintances sort themselves into an acceptable arrangement. If you aren't sure where to sit, ask your host, who will want to make sure that you're comfortable.

Grace

Some religious families say grace before the start of a meal. This won't be a lengthy sermon but rather a few lines thanking the Lord for the food on the table. It's customary to bow your head while grace is being said and to respond at the end with the word 'Amen' before unfolding your napkin. Even if you don't follow your hosts' religion, it's polite to join in; it won't improve your social standing if you refuse to take part. Never start eating before everyone else or you may find yourself with a mouthful of mashed potatoes when it's time to say 'Amen'.

When to Start

Everyone starts eating at the same time when seated at a table, whether in a private home or a restaurant. There will be some signal, such as the end of saying grace, the host or hostess will unfold a napkin, or perhaps it will be a simple request to begin. When the dining arrangement is less formal, such as a barbecue or cold buffet, you can just serve yourself and tuck in.

Conversation

When eating in someone's home, topics of conversation are usually confined to the family, topical news items, sport or local events. The same goes when dining out with friends: forthcoming holiday plans, the achievements of children at school or relatives at work, the dreadful state of the traffic, plus what's on at the cinema and on television are all fairly safe areas. Politics, religion and money are best avoided (see **Conversation** in **Chapter 4** for other taboo subjects). If you're dining with work colleagues, they will probably prefer not to talk shop (unless it's an informal business meal), although this may not prevent them from discussing absent colleagues, particularly those who are the subject of office gossip.

Noises

In some cultures, it's acceptable to burp or make other noises before, during and after eating – in some places, the volume or duration of a belch is considered the greatest compliment to a host. **This isn't the case in the US**, where it should be avoided (even if you hear it from others).

Mobile Phones

Americans are less addicted to these devices than, say, people in southern Europe, and many consider any conversation on a mobile phone, be it verbal or text, to be impolite when dining. If you must deal with a call there and then, leave the table first. Better to switch your phone off when in company or, better still, leave it at home.

Table Manners

When seated at a table, apart from the use of the knife and fork and the other things mentioned above, there are few rules to follow. Always say please and thank you if you need to ask for anything (these are rarely implied when speaking English), try to keep your elbows off the table, and don't reach across to get something but ask someone to pass it to you. In polite society, men will often stand when a lady joins or leaves the table.

> American condiment dispensers rarely have the names written on them. The salt cellar is the one with several holes in the top, while the pepper comes from the one with a single central hole. Just why this should be the reverse of everywhere else in the western world isn't known.

Toasts

When a celebration is arranged to mark someone's birthday, anniversary, marriage or other notable milestone, or even simply to show gratitude to a host or hostess, Americans like to raise their glasses in a toast. The accepted way to gain attention is to tap your own glass with a spoon to gain your fellow diners' attention. Address the group, mention the individual(s) you wish to honour and why, and end with something like 'Please join me in raising your glasses to so and so', at which point everyone will raise their glasses and echo the name(s). Keep it short and simple; it isn't a major speech, just a thank you.

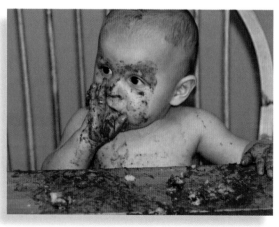

DRINKING

> 'I feel sorry for people who don't drink. When they wake up in the morning, that's as good as they're going to feel all day.'
>
> Frank Sinatra (American singer)

Most Americans drink at some time or other, although regular drinkers only amount to around 60 per cent of the adult population. Attitudes to alcohol are surprisingly strict for such an informal country, with rural Christian communities strongly anti-drink, and there are even 'dry' counties and towns where hooch is banned. Drunkenness is far less acceptable than it is in the UK and many other countries. Although it varies from state to state, you're usually required to be 21 before you can drink alcohol, and those under age aren't allowed in bars.

Licensing laws vary from state to state, with some states limiting the sale of spirits and a few banning the advertisement (though not the consumption) of alcohol. In most places, however, the 24-hour culture means alcohol is readily obtainable, and fairly inexpensive. For $10 it's possible to purchase a bottle of cheap spirits, a bottle of unremarkable wine (wine isn't particularly cheap in the US) or a case of beer. Beer is available virtually everywhere. Some Americans consider beer to be a lesser form of alcohol and many British people would agree, regarding US beer as one step up from tap water (the fact that it's served ice cold further anaesthetises drinkers from any flavour it might have).

Only Bourbon whiskey can truly have a claim to be America's national liquor. In order to qualify as such, it has to be distilled within the nation's borders, and most is produced in the state of Kentucky. Bizarrely, some bourbon is distilled in dry counties where no tastings are allowed.

Bars

America has no equivalent of the British pub (unless it's the fake imported variety) or even the European pavement café, where you can eat, drink and socialise. American bars are for drinkers: beer bars sell beer, cider, wine, and other lower-strength drinks, while liquor bars will sell the strongest spirits.

Local bars, where regulars meet to chat, watch football and bury the problems of the working day, were immortalised by *Cheers*, the Boston bar which was the hub of one of US television's best comedies, but they can, in reality, be rough and ready all-male environments where women may feel uncomfortable. At the other end of the spectrum are slick cocktail lounges with bartenders shaking up a storm of fancy drinks. Cocktails are the most popular drinks in America, and there's a huge range to sample, although a drink in a cocktail bar may cost many times what it would in a working men's bar (assuming the bartender knows how to make cocktails). In between, there are music bars, gay bars, cowboy bars, singles bars – where single people go to meet the opposite sex – and many others.

Unlike in a British pub, Americans don't buy rounds. You either sit at the bar or at a table and order your drinks, and then pay the bill (tab) when you leave. Remember to add a reasonable tip (up to 20 per cent in an upmarket establishment) if you want to be served promptly on your next visit. The price of the drinks will have been calculated to include any bar snacks – suitably salty to keep you drinking – and entertainment, such as performing bar staff. You may also be subsidising the non-drinkers, since many bars offer free soft drinks to 'designated drivers'. Look out for 'happy hour', usually a few hours in the early evening to tempt people leaving work, when many bars cut the price of their drinks (often half price or two drinks for the price of one) and may also provide free food.

Never leave your drink unattended. The habit of 'spiking' (drugging) people's drinks is a problem in the US, where women are especially vulnerable. Your drink may not taste any different, but the results could leave you prey to robbery or worse. The date rape drug Rohypnol may be slipped into victims' drinks, leaving them unconscious or unaware of what is happening. Unless you're in a place where you know and trust everyone implicitly, it's best not to drink anything that has been out of your sight for even a moment.

Smoking

One thing you probably can't do in your local bar is smoke. Ever since California set the standard by banning smoking in public places in 1994, the rest of the US has followed suit to some degree. The west coast state's ban was met initially with a great deal of resistance, but over a period of time smoking in public has become a contentious issue and 'no smoking' signs are quietly effective.

Smoking is now banned in most workplaces, hospitals, government buildings and other public places. Eating establishments have had non-smoking areas for several years, and today it's unlikely that you'll find a smoking area anywhere where food is being served. Casinos may or may not have restrictions, depending upon some unfathomable factor. No form of public transport – planes, trains, buses or taxis – allows smoking. Since the smoking ban was introduced, there have even been reports of cars being stopped because one of the occupants was smoking, the others being asked if they objected.

If you're a smoker and feel the need to light up, your only option may be to go outside (difficult if you're in a car or plane). You should always ask before lighting up in someone's home, and may also find yourself out in the cold around some offices and public buildings, where the ban has been extended to the open air. The only place to enjoy a quiet cigarette may be a purpose-built open shelter sited some distance from the main building.

Individual state laws vary in their attitudes to smoking, and some cities add their own legislation to that of the state – in some states there's a total ban, while in others there are no state laws and only local restrictions. It makes sense to check or ask, although the simplest answer is never to smoke indoors in a public place.

CAFES, RESTAURANTS & DINERS

Quantity rather than quality sums up America's attitude to food. A great deal of it is fast food, from the big-name burgers and pizza joints to Mexican tacos, corn dogs (deep fried hot dogs in batter!) and Kentucky/Tennessee/any other southern state fried chicken. Portions are huge and flavours are often bland. On the upside, the multi-cultural blend of America's population means you can find ethnic restaurants almost everywhere.

In most cities, the diversity of restaurants is amazing. Expect to find food from virtually every ethnic community. In general terms, the most lavish establishments are usually over-priced, while the standard of food isn't overly impressive. When choosing a restaurant of French, Italian, Greek, Mexican, Jewish, Chinese, Polish, Russian, Turkish, Korean, Thai, Indian, Vietnamese, Japanese or any

of the myriad other nations with an outlet somewhere in the US, the best food is to be found at the smaller, family-run establishments. The decor may be a little tacky and the wait for your food a little longer, but overall you get a good meal at a fair price.

Diners are another interesting option. The big-name diners, such as Denny's, are American institutions, offering identical food from North Dakota to the Texas Panhandle, although smaller establishments also offer excellent food in authentic surroundings, from a soda bar to Mom's cherry pie. The least salubrious diners, with the most questionable hygiene, are generally those frequented by truckers along highways in remote areas, and only worth visiting in a food emergency.

American Food

With a larder which stretches around the world, it's difficult to pinpoint true American cuisine. Early settlers ate the same foods as Native Americans, such as turkey, squashes, corn and potatoes, and these foods have retained their popularity today. They've been joined by dishes which were introduced by immigrants but which now seem quintessentially American, such as hamburgers, pizza and fried chicken. In addition, most areas have their regional dishes, from clam chowder in New England to the Creole 'gumbo' stew in Louisiana.

America serves up some of the strangest sounding foods in the world. Where else could you tuck into chitterlings (fried pig's intestines), Hoppin' John (rice and peas) or Hush Puppies (deep fried cornbread)?

Alcohol

Not all US eateries serve alcohol. Many are family-focused and offer only soft drinks and hot beverages. Those that do serve alcohol may try to tempt you in by offering 'free' drinks with your meal, although the price of the food will have been calculated to cover the cost of your cocktail. Alcohol can be expensive, with the cheapest glass of (not very good) wine costing around $10.

Booking & Seating

It's only really necessary to book in top restaurants or at busy times such as weekends. In a smart establishment, where people may wait weeks for a top table, you may have to leave your credit card details as security, and could be charged for the price of a meal if you don't turn up. Wherever you're eating, always wait to be shown to your seat, unless there's a sign saying 'Please seat yourself'.

Slow Service

This is rare in America, where many workers regard the service industry as a vocation rather than a way to pay the bills. You'll find staff ultra-efficient when it comes to seating you at a table, bringing the menu, answering your questions and checking that you're happy throughout the meal. This can become overwhelming, especially for British and French people more used to being ignored by waiting staff. Of course, the tip you're expected to leave at the end of the meal (see below) is a big incentive to good service.

Think before ordering a starter, as the main course is likely to be a meal for two. In fact, many couples order one main course for two, which is acceptable in all but the poshest of establishments. Make the most of any 'freebies', such as the 'eat all you can' salad bars – an irresistible idea in a country which finds it hard to say 'no'– but be aware that vegetables need to be ordered as an extra.

Paying the Bill & Leaving a Tip

In a fast food restaurant you pay when you place your order, in a diner you may pay at a cash desk on the way out, and in most restaurants

you need to ask for the bill (check). The price will include local sales tax but rarely a service change. Service isn't added as a matter of course and, as staff are always near the bottom of the pay scale, most expect a tip – and some turn nasty if they don't get it. Look at leaving at least 15 per cent, although the actual figure could be a little more if you're particularly happy with the service (but rarely less). If you pay by credit card, the total sum may be left blank for you to add a tip – ensure you fill it in or the waiter may add his own tip. If the service is bad, you don't have to tip, although it would be unwise to return to the same restaurant without a disguise!

> **'I'll have a half double decaffeinated half-caf, with a twist of lemon.'**
>
> Steve Martin's character orders a coffee in the film *LA Story*.

Coffee Culture

Americans went off tea around the time of the Boston Tea Party, so if you order a cuppa you can expect to receive a cup of hot water with a teabag on the side. Coffee, however, is king. There are dozens of coffee house chains in the US, the best known of which is Starbucks, which has branches in every city – in 2008, this added up to over 11,000 outlets. Aside from standard coffee, with or without caffeine, which can be prepared in a myriad ways, there are innumerable blends. Starbucks has over 40 blends on offer, from places as diverse as Komodo and Burundi.

If you aren't a coffee expert, the choice can be bewildering, and requires an in-depth knowledge of the choices on offer, the caffeine content, the available milks and creams, and the shorthand for ordering each item. Coffee houses are busy, and service staff want clear and precise instructions, so just as when ordering a deli sandwich, rehearse your order before you take your place in the queue. Coffee is usually served in regular (large), large (enormous) and king (gigantic – enough to bathe in) sizes.

NIGHTLIFE

In major population centres, such as New York City and Los Angeles, the nightlife is extensive and diverse, encompassing cabaret venues featuring international names, rock and piano bars, discotheques (discos) and dance clubs, comedy clubs, and the inevitable sleazy strip joints. You'll find some of the above in most cities and large towns, usually open until around 4am at weekends, although much depends on local licensing laws. In New York, no fashionable club will come alive before midnight, and it'll set you back at least US$20 to get in, before you start paying for drinks… that's if they let you in at all. Nightclub doormen can be choosy, especially when admitting single men. Never argue with them, as they're big, mean and can easily turn nasty.

FAMILY OCCASIONS

Sooner or later, you'll find yourself at an American family gathering, either as a guest or hosting a celebration of your own. The most significant life events for US families are listed below, with some tips on how to enjoy them.

> **'The United States is the only country with a known birthday.'**
>
> James G. Blaine (American statesman)

Birthdays

A lot depends upon the age of the birthday boy or girl and which milestone is being celebrated, but Americans usually celebrate birthdays and expect you to do the same.

Children's Birthdays

American children are indulged, and especially so at birthdays. Young children expect some form of entertainment, such as a clown or magician, and the party will often follow a theme. Older children may prefer to visit a restaurant with their friends, and there are plenty of venues, such as Chuck E Cheese, where children can eat pizza and play on arcade and other games in a safe environment. Cheesy it may be, but it's a lot easier

than planning and arranging something at home. Book early, especially if planning a weekend event.

If you organise a children's party, always provide a little gift or memento (favors) for each child to take away with them, irrespective of their age, or their parents will think you're mean.

The Pinata

The pinata is as essential a part of American birthday celebrations as the cake, cards or gifts. The pinata is a Mexican tradition: a hollow figure filled with small toys and sweets. It's hung just above the reach of the children, who are encouraged to beat it with a stick until it breaks and the treats fall and are gathered by the guests. Often the children are blindfolded to make the game more of a challenge.

Baby Showers & Christenings

An American creation, baby showers are held shortly before the birth of a child, and the idea is to 'shower' the expectant mother with good wishes and gifts for the newborn. Showers are often organised by a close friend, sister or sister-in-law, who will usually have a list of gifts being given by others so the newborn doesn't end up with three car seats and no nappies (diapers). It's a clever idea, in that it allows for a celebration of the new arrival without an actual baby interrupting the event with demands for food or attention.

Although Christian families want to bring their child into their faith, christenings are also seen as naming ceremonies. They usually involve a small informal gathering of close friends and family after the service, but as gifts will have been given at the earlier baby shower, most people won't expect to be invited back to the home. If there's a celebration, it may be held at the home of a friend or neighbour, giving the baby and its mother the chance for much-needed rest, and leaving the substitute host with the job of clearing up afterwards.

When giving a gift of any description for any event, it's usual to enclose a gift card which you should sign, so the recipient knows who sent what and can respond accordingly.

First Communions, Bar Mitzvahs & Other Rites of Passage

The children of families who follow a particular religion will eventually reach a landmark such as their first Holy Communion (Christian) or Bar Mitzvah (Jewish). If you or your children become close friends with someone from a religious family, you could be invited along. Ask the family what to expect: any interest you show will be welcomed, and they will no doubt be pleased to educate you in the ways and rituals of their chosen faith.

A totally secular rite of passage, and one which almost all teenagers anticipate (or dread) is Prom Night. This is a ball which marks the end of students' high school years or graduation, and is an excuse to dress up, ride in a stretch limousine and show off to the rest of the school. Not having a date for Prom Night is social Siberia.

Engagement Parties

Engagement is rarely considered a formal event in a country where around half of all marriages end in divorce. The size and grandeur of an engagement party depends very much on the individuals – and probably also on their social standing. Much as the pomp and ceremony of yesteryear accompanied marriages and liaisons of convenience among noble families, the families of the affluent adore putting on banquets in order to celebrate any milestone in a family member's life, including engagements. Those with less money, or time, are more likely to visit a restaurant to share the announcement, with only immediate family members in attendance. Gifts are optional.

Thanksgiving

The most American of celebrations, as a foreigner you may find Thanksgiving especially alien. It takes place on the fourth Thursday in November, and is a time when families traditionally come together to celebrate good fortune; it has its roots in the harvest festivals of past years, when people would celebrate a good crop. Thanksgiving is just as important as Christmas, and while you won't be expected to host a party, you may well receive an invitation to join one. You should take along a small gift for the host, nothing too ostentatious, much as you would when invited to any other social gathering.

Don't eat before you go as the Thanksgiving meal is a vast and lavish spread of turkey, stuffing, sweet potatoes, cranberry sauce and pumpkin pie. Having consumed so much food, the traditional pastime is to fall asleep in front of the television watching the almost endless football games which are broadcast on this day. Another tradition is watching Macy's Thanksgiving Parade, which takes place in New York. The final float carries Father Christmas, and his appearance signifies the start of the annual Christmas shopping frenzy.

'Happy Holidays' is an acceptable and politically correct way for Americans to greet people of any race or religion on any important holiday. You'll hear it said at Christmas in place of Merry Christmas, and at other times during the year.

Christmas & New Year

Just as you've recovered from the over-indulgence of Thanksgiving, along comes Christmas, which is as big a deal in America as it is in the rest of the western world, only more so. There are a few specifically American yuletide traditions, such as the mystifying eggnog (a sweetened egg drink), but most of the celebrations will be familiar to anyone who has celebrated a western Christmas, or seen any of the many big-screen tributes to Christmas (such as *It's a Wonderful Life*): important ingredients include the tree, gifts from Father Christmas, carol singing and another large turkey dinner.

Unlike Thanksgiving, the guest list isn't restricted to close family, and cards and gifts are exchanged with friends, neighbours and colleagues. Christmas parties can occur anytime in December, and many families hold an 'open house' to which single foreigners may be invited. Follow the same gift rule

as for Thanksgiving. An apt gift is a poinsettia, America's Christmas flower.

New Year's Eve is a night for partying, as it is all over the world, with celebrations focusing on Times Square in New York, where the famous New Year's Eve Ball descends from the flagpole watched by around 1mn people in the square itself and millions more nationwide. In comparison, New Year's Day is a quiet event, as everyone recovers from the excesses of the night before.

Super Bowl Sunday

Only in America can a sporting event take on the significance of a national holiday, and this is certainly the case with Super Bowl, the biggest football game of the year. Super Bowl Sunday takes place in late January or early February, when the winners of the American Football Conference and the National Football Conference battle for the championship. It has become the single biggest party event in American society, and is the second-largest day for food consumption after Thanksgiving. The Super Bowl party feast is typically American: burgers, steaks, hot dogs, popcorn, apple pie, pumpkin pie, ice cream, all washed down with cola or beer – and plenty of it. The television will be on, but you don't have to pay any attention to the game, although it helps to converse with fans if you have some idea of the result.

The Super Bowl isn't just about watching a game of football – many people tune in just to watch the commercials. Companies pay millions of dollars for a few minutes' slot to launch new products or run trailers for upcoming films. The commercials are rated and reviewed, just like any programme.

> Whichever celebration you're invited to, never arrive more than a few minutes late. Only celebrities can get away with turning up fashionably late.

Weddings

In any society, the most ritualistic and lavish celebrations are reserved for marriage, and the US is no exception. Friends and family (many of whom won't have been seen since the last family wedding) are drawn in from far and wide to witness the happy day, and the preparations can take a year or more. America invented the wedding planner, who takes over every aspect of arranging the big day – and charges a premium for the service – but such are the high expectations that organising an American wedding can be a full-time job.

Church weddings are popular, but people are just as likely to tie the knot at the local courthouse or even in their own back yard (albeit, usually a large one). In America, you can get hitched just about anywhere, from the basket of a balloon to several metres underwater.

The amount of notice you have to give varies from state to state. In some states, a couple may wait 30 days to obtain a marriage licence, and have to undergo blood tests before they can tie the knot. One reason Las Vegas is popular as a wedding venue is that it's quick and easy to obtain a marriage licence. This has led to a wedding 'industry' based on turnover rather than taste, with drive-in wedding chapels and officials dressed as Elvis.

As a guest, your main task is to turn up and enjoy yourself, which consists of listening politely to the speeches, admiring the bride and groom, taking umpteen photographs, sending an appropriate gift and tucking into the wedding cake.

Invitations

These are sent out long before the event, and you must respond promptly. Catering, seating arrangements and even the gift list depends on knowing exactly who will attend. Depending on how well you know the couple, you may also be invited to:

- **The Bridal Shower** – this is a party for the bride, held by her maid or matron of honour (see below), which takes place a few weeks before the wedding. As with a baby shower, gifts are expected, and some lucky brides have more than one shower. Your gift should usually be something for the home, and is given in addition to (not instead of) the actual wedding gift. Sometimes, guests bring saucy gifts for use during the honeymoon, but check before presenting the bride with anything risqué.

- **The Bachelor Party** – this is the American equivalent of the British stag party, and an excuse for the groom to have one last wild night before settling down with his bride. Bachelorette (hen) parties are the same idea, but for the girls. If invited to either, your main responsibility is to ensure the groom/bride gets home safely (or not!).

Gifts

Wedding gifts are rarely left to chance. Most couples have a list of suitable items, usually sold by a local department store, which guests can choose from. The earlier you select your purchase, the less likely you are to end up having to make an awkward choice between the colour television and the napkin rings. The store will usually gift wrap, label and deliver all the wedding presents to the venue on the appropriate day, and you can even order online. Guests get gifts too, in the form of sweets or small keepsakes called wedding favours.

Dress

Some formal weddings require men to wear morning dress, but smart suits and 'Sunday best' is usually sufficient. However, most women see a wedding as a good excuse to buy a new outfit and/or hat. The bride is the star, so never wear anything which might upstage her – long white frocks are a definite 'no no'.

Key Players

The bride has her maid or matron of honour (chief bridesmaid), plus other assorted bridesmaids, and maybe a flower girl to hold her bouquet. The groom will have his best man for support; some have extra groomsmen. There may also be a small boy whose job it is to carry a pillow holding the wedding rings. The couple's parents have important roles – the bride's mother is the next most important woman at any wedding – and then there are the ushers who show guests to their seats. A registrar or priest conducts the ceremony.

> **'Marriage is the alliance of two people, one of whom never remembers birthdays and the other who never forgets.'**
>
> Ogden Nash (American poet)

Funerals

Religion has a big influence on how American funerals are conducted, with the timing and ceremony dependent on the deceased's faith. There's usually a service, either at the funeral home or a place of worship, followed by either burial or cremation. Sometimes, the events are preceded by a visitation, in which friends and family are invited to say goodbye to the deceased: the coffin (casket) may be left open with the body on full view.

Almost without exception, funerals take place before midday. It's customary for those mourners closest

to the deceased to attend a luncheon afterwards, and this is often held in a restaurant or at the home of a close friend or family member. Attendance is usually by invitation. In the event that the meal is to be held in a private home, those invited may be expected to bring a dish of food (the meal is usually a cold buffet). These gatherings are sometimes called a wake, and can occasionally take on a party atmosphere, as guests drink and celebrate the life of the deceased.

Displays of grief are usually muted, without the wailing and breast-beating which occurs in some other cultures (although this may depend on the ancestry of the deceased).

Gifts aren't appropriate for funerals. A wreath of flowers may be sent, unless the family have requested otherwise: many prefer to nominate a charity to receive donations in lieu of floral tributes. If you cannot attend a funeral, sending a thoughtful sympathy card or note is the next best thing.

Dress

In the US, as in many western countries, black is the colour for funerals. Most men wear a solid black or dark suit, tie and shoes with a plain white shirt. The amount of black worn by women at a funeral is often dictated by how close they were to the deceased. Normally a black dress, coat and shoes will suffice, although some women like to wear a hat when attending a church service and that, too, should be black. Short skirts or plunging necklines are as inappropriate as wearing scarlet or pink! You should also remember that when there's a burial involved, this will be outside and subject to the weather. If rain is possible, take an umbrella, but ensure it's dark in colour and has no novelty design on it.

> 'I didn't attend the funeral, but I sent a nice letter saying I approved of it.'
>
> Mark Twain (American writer)

CLUBS

Special interest clubs abound in America, where there are group gatherings of every kind. Americans like to 'join in'. Well known clubs, such as the Rotary Club, can be found all over the US, and then there are tennis clubs, golf clubs, gun clubs, children's clubs, dining clubs, slimming clubs, expatriate clubs, political clubs, business clubs, old boys/girls clubs, dog owners' clubs et al. In fact, there's probably nothing so obscure in the US that there isn't at least one group or organisation devoted to it. Joining a club is a good way to meet people, and there should be a list of local clubs at the library.

POPULAR CULTURE

America is often dismissed for having no culture, or at least for having a low-brow popular culture based on television and team sports. However, the nation's diversity has brought together many different ethnic groups, all with their own cultural markers, and there are innumerable events, pastimes and celebrations which are American to the core. Shopping, gardening, DIY, TV and sport do take up a large slice of the average person's leisure time, but there's also ample opportunity to enjoy more highbrow entertainment, such as museums, dance, theatre and art.

Festivals, Fairs & Parades

Americans refer to festivals as 'fests', which are themed gatherings involving the local community. Sometimes the reason is hidden beneath all the razzmatazz, yet the enthusiasm remains undiminished. The festival season takes place during the summer months, when festivals are held around such diverse themes as seafood, popcorn, dragon boats, lemons and Ava Gardner! Your local newspaper will keep you informed of any upcoming 'fests' in your area.

Fairs tend to be larger, less localised affairs, with a commercial vein. Most are regional, ranging from a county fair to the huge state fair. These attract people from all over the area, and feature the local stars of agriculture, technology, music, crafts, and much more. Funfairs, displays and myriad stalls are all part of the attraction, with food (surprise, surprise) taking centre stage.

New England farmer Elkanah Watson is credited with starting the trend for state fairs, when he showed off his sheep under a tree in a Massachusetts square in 1807. An owner of wool mills, his aim was to encourage local farmers to raise Merino sheep for their superior wool.

The US is also the home of the parade, which is often a lavish and colourful display. Closed streets are thronged with people watching processions of colourfully decorated floats, baton-twirling marchers, cheerleaders, musicians, athletes and representatives from local groups and societies. Well-known parades include the St Patrick's Day Parade on 17th March, when all Americans remember their Irish roots (even those who don't have any); the biggest is held in New York. The Big Apple is also famous for its ticker-tape parades, when statesmen, war veterans and, more usually these days, sports champions are welcomed home with a ceremonial march featuring a 'snowstorm' of shredded paper.

Halloween

This festival is celebrated to an extent across the western world, although it has its roots in American culture – to celebrate the day the souls of the dead depart this earth. On the night of 31st October, pumpkins with faces carved into them are placed in windows, and kids in scary costumes go out trick or treating: they knock on neighbours' door to get a treat, usually sweets (candy). It's a good idea to have some candy to hand, as this should stop the little horrors playing a trick on

you! The celebrations can be ghoulish and the height of bad taste, which is probably why Americans love it so.

Gambling

Gambling is a huge business, despite the difference in state betting regulations. Cities such as Las Vegas in Nevada and Atlantic City in New Jersey attract everyone from high rollers at the roulette wheel to blue-rinse ladies lined up at the slot machines. In Vegas, there are even slot machines in public toilets. Mississippi river boats and casinos on Native American reservations provide other avenues for punters.

Americans don't like the word gambling (they prefer to call it 'gaming'), but they're addicted to it, with over $400bn being wagered annually.

Casinos are keen to keep customers inside, and even avoid having clocks in public areas. There's usually no dress

Street Life

Life on the street depends on where you are and what time it is. In many inner-city areas, street gangs are the law, and the police advise you to stay indoors for your own safety. However, by the time you reach suburbia, you may see children playing on the street and be accosted by a six-year-old budding entrepreneur with a lemonade stand. The omnipotence of the car means that many Americans rarely set foot on the streets, and may look askance at people using their feet, unless they are jogging. If you're seeking the cosmopolitan atmosphere found in European cities, where people promenade in the evening, you'll find America's nearest equivalent at the shopping mall.

code, and in a few states at least, they are the only place you can smoke indoors. Provided you look as if you're gambling, you may receive free food and drink, and even low-cost accommodation, so it's worth visiting one of the big gambling centres, if only for the experience.

Aside from casinos, many US states have a lottery, where it's possible (though unlikely) to win enormous prizes of up to $100mn. Despite the huge odds against winning, some individuals spend as much as $100 a day, justifying their expenditure when and if they pick up a $250 prize every fortnight. Americans also gamble on horse racing and other sports events. Punters don't just speculate on the outcome, but also the scorers, the time of the first score, or anything else which has an element of chance.

Although legal gambling is strictly controlled, illegal gambling is widespread, and it's estimated there are around 8mn compulsive gamblers in the US.

Sport

In such a huge country, the glue that holds most people together is sport. Major sporting events on television, like important episodes of soaps and coverage of the presidential election every four years, unite the nation like nothing else. The most popular sports in the US are American football (gridiron), baseball, which is often described as 'the national pastime', basketball and hockey (ice), and fans are usually loyal to their home team. Most prefer to watch their sport on TV – participation comes a long way behind – and many of the main events in the US calendar revolve around sport. The most popular sports are:

● **American football** – also known as gridiron, this tough and often incomprehensible sport is the number one choice for most Americans. It ranges from college teams to the National Football League (NFL) and culminates every winter in the Super Bowl (see **Super Bowl Sunday** above), a showdown between the two top teams and the most-watched sporting event on TV.

> **'Football incorporates the two worst elements of American society. Violence punctuated by committee meetings.'**
>
> George F Will (American journalist & political commentator)

- **Baseball** – this is a traditional American sport which is played by all ages. Children start off in the Little League, where they learn the importance of playing in a team; if they're good enough they may one day progress to Major League Baseball, whose players are as well-loved as soccer stars are in Europe. The World Series, in October, is contested by the top teams from the US baseball leagues. Baseball has penetrated the world to such an extent that even people who have no idea of its rules will have heard of teams such as the New York Yankees and the Boston Red Sox.

- **Basketball** – more Americans play basketball than any other sport, even if they just 'shoot hoops' in the backyard; and even foreigners who scratch their heads at the complexities of gridiron and baseball can comprehend what's happening on the basketball court. America has successfully exported basketball to the world, with players like Michael Jordan becoming household names outside the US, and the Harlem Globetrotters are world famous. The National Basketball Association is the world's top men's basketball league, and the main event is the NBA

Playoffs between the top teams, which takes place in April.

- **Ice hockey** – popular across the northern states, hockey (Americans don't bother with the prefix 'ice') is played by US and Canadian teams, competing for the top prize of the Stanley Cup in early summer.

- **Golf & tennis** – both are popular participation sports, with a certain amount of snobbery attached to belonging to the more prestigious clubs. On a national level, three of golf's most important championships take place in America: the Masters, the US Open and the PGA. Not surprisingly, the best known golfer in the world, Tiger Woods, is an American. The top tennis tournament is the US Open, which takes place at Flushing Meadows in New York in August, and is one of the world's top four Grand Slam tournaments.

Other popular sports include boxing, motor-racing (Indy Car series racing rather

than Formula One), wrestling (the World Wrestling Federation, where sport meets theatre, was born in America) and athletics – the US is a world leader in Olympic track and field. Hunting and fishing are also popular pastimes in rural areas, where they provide some essential male bonding, while town dwellers are more likely to bond at the bowling alley or on a squash court.

Americans have been late to catch on to the appeal of soccer, despite US clubs signing big-name players such as David Beckham. It really is a girl's game: the nation ranks as a world leader in women's soccer, and the women's team far outranks the men.

> There's a ritual that takes place before sporting events called tailgating – not to be confused with driving too close to the vehicle in front. People open up the boots of their cars, or the backs of their vans, and stand around and eat food they've brought along before heading into the game. Sometimes they arrive hours before the game, with their barbecues, and cook hamburgers and steak. Some even bring along TVs so that they can watch other games while eating.

DIY & Gardening

Hiring professionals to do work around the home and garden is expensive, so wherever possible, the average American will try to do it him/herself. Never slow to seize an opportunity, home improvement companies have flooded the market with self-assembly furniture, how-to magazines, and DIY TV programmes, all focused on showing people how to save a few dollars. There are cable TV channels devoted entirely to this subject. The feel-good factor earned by achieving a perfectly laid floor or newly fitted kitchen is also important to the American psyche.

Gardening is nearly always known as yard work, even if the yard includes a couple of acres of lawn. Americans prefer low maintenance gardening, but this doesn't mean that their gardens are unattractive. Many homes have quite glorious floral displays and neatly manicured lawns, kept in order by a fearsome array of mechanical tools and gadgets.

In small-town America, one way to annoy your neighbours is to let your lawn grow long and unkempt. It isn't unusual for towns to fine residents who ignore warnings about keeping their gardens neat and tidy, particularly with regard to mowing front lawns and controlling weeds.

The Arts

Despite its lowbrow image, America is home to some of the world's most important art collections, as well as performing arts of the highest calibre. Most are located in big cities such as Los Angeles and New York, but there are performances throughout the US, and all involved aspire to be the best.

Bookings

There's no shortage of information on entertainment in America. Most major cities have their own 'what's on' guides, such as *Time Out* which is published in nine cities across the US. Local events are publicised at libraries, while national and local newspapers carry a comprehensive list of entertainment options, from the latest movies to exhibitions, sports events and upcoming concerts.

Movie tickets can often be purchased online. Prices vary, depending on the location as well as the age and popularity of a film: tickets for a premiere in New York's Times Square will cost far more than for a classic movie in a regional theatre, but it remains one of the cheapest forms of entertainment. Tickets can be booked up to 30 days in advance (even earlier to catch an early viewing of a new blockbuster) at 💻 www.movietickets.com or in person at cinemas.

Ticket prices for the theatre can be exorbitant for the most sought-after shows, such as those on Broadway. The only way you can see the top shows is by booking in advance, which you can do in person, by telephone or online at 💻 www.telecharge.com or www.ticketmaster.com. There's usually a fee when paying by credit card, which can be avoided by purchasing tickets by (the incredibly old-fashioned method of) writing to the theatre's box office. Enclose a cheque for the required amount, and state as many alternative dates as you can (a minimum of three) in the covering letter.

Cinema

Hollywood is the centre of the world's film industry, and America's premier art form is cinema. Despite strong competition from television and the sale of videos and DVDs, the cinema still draws people in. US film-goers avidly await the release of the latest blockbuster as they leave the auditorium after seeing the last! You can learn a great deal about America by simply watching movies, as it seems the nation has documented its history and culture, its successes and its mistakes, on the silver screen.

Sadly, the iconic single-screen movie houses are rapidly being replaced by multi-screen cinemas in large towns and cities. However, fortunately there are still a few drive-in movie 'theatres' around, where you pay to park your car in front of a huge screen, the sound being provided by speakers clipped to your car's windows. Drive-ins only really work after dark, during dry and warm weather, and few show the latest releases; but a visit to a drive-in movie provides a nostalgic experience of America's cultural heritage.

US Movie Classifications

G – General Audience; all ages admitted.

PG – Parental Guidance Suggested; some material may be unsuitable for children.

PG-13 – Parents Strongly Cautioned; some material may be inappropriate for children under the age of thirteen.

R – Restricted; children under 17 must be accompanied by someone aged over 17.

NC-17 – No one under the age of 17 admitted.

Anyone who looks under 17 will be asked to prove their age by showing some form of ID.

Theatre

From the extravagance of a Broadway spectacular to the enthusiasm of an amateur production, there's a wealth of theatrical entertainment, much of it of a high standard. New York City remains the centre for US theatre (Americans spell it 'theater'), and musicals are the most popular form of the genre. However, there are theatre houses throughout the country, and performing groups and the quality of local productions is remarkably good: slick, well-rehearsed and worth the entrance fee. Americans tend to treat the theatre like the cinema. They don't take it too seriously and they rarely dress up – it's about being entertained rather than being seen.

Music & Dance

America is the birthplace of many modern forms of music. Jazz, gospel and blues have their roots in the African-American communities, as do hip hop and rap. Country provides the soundtrack to life in the Midwest, while the term rock and roll was coined in the '50s by US disc jockey Alan Freed. There are many diverse musical forms, from thrash metal and surf pop on the west coast to the bluegrass of Kentucky. Like cinema, music gives a cultural lesson of life in the US, and the lyrics of Bruce Springsteen or Bob Dylan tell you a great deal about the American psyche.

Music is huge business, with the industry generating about $12bn in America alone, and all the major artists tour the 50 states. Music bars can be found in even small towns, and many cities have their own symphony orchestra (or a number) or even an opera house. Radio remains the best way to stay in touch with America's musical heart, with stations catering to all tastes broadcasting from Seattle to Miami.

Ballet and modern dance are also popular in major cities, but more indigenous dance forms abound. One of the most popular is the square dance, the closest America has to folk dancing, and designated the official dance of 19 US states. Cowboy culture also introduced line dancing, which has now been successfully exported around the world. And, of course, there are discotheques in every city – the most famous of all was Studio 54, which put disco firmly on the map in '70s New York. More old-fashioned dance styles are also enjoying a revival, and you can foxtrot, waltz or salsa in most towns.

The Metropolitan Museum of Art in New York is one of the largest art galleries in the world; known simply as 'the Met', it has over 3mn works of art, and there's only room to display a quarter of the collection at any one time.

Museums & Art Galleries

The US has the largest and best collections of art of any country in the world, including London and Paris. Backed by donations and sponsorship from both corporate and private sources, the buying power of the largest museums and galleries is equal to that of a small country. Even so, Americans are generally relaxed about art, and museums can be informal and welcoming. There isn't a city in America which doesn't have at least one, often dedicated to someone or something of local relevance, and providing an insight into local history. Art galleries are found everywhere; most large shopping malls have a contemporary gallery which is worth a visit.

The cream of America's museums and art galleries include the Metropolitan Museum of Art, The Museum of Modern Art (MoMA) in New York, Boston's Museum of Fine Arts, the Field Museum of Natural History in Chicago, the Museum of Fine Arts in Houston, the Los Angeles County Museum of Art, the Solomon R. Guggenheim Museum in New York City and the National Gallery of Art in Washington DC. The best known of all, the Smithsonian Institution, has 28 different venues across the country (including a zoo), totalling some 136mn exhibits.

At the other end of the spectrum, there are museums dedicated to all manner of strange subjects. How about a visit to the Museum of the American Cocktail in (where else?) Las Vegas, or a trip to the Hippie Museum, which spreads its message of peace and love in Summertown, Alabama? There are even museums dedicated to condiment packets, and to a peculiar musical instrument called the kazoo!

Entrance fees range from $10 or $15 for top museums, to free (maybe only on one day a week or month), although they may 'suggest' a donation from around $5 for adults, and half of that for concessions. Always check opening hours, as they vary considerably: many museums close on Mondays, while there's usually at least one evening per week when they remain open late. Many have disabled access, and there's usually someone on hand to help; although if you have special requirements, it's as well to phone first.

9.
RETAIL THERAPY

America is the biggest shop window in the world, where some stores never close and special offers are promoted by an advertising industry that doesn't understand the word 'no'. Its population is bombarded with commercials, night and day, through the media, by telephone, in the mail, by email, on the street or even at their front doors. In the US, advertising is a billion-dollar business, and it works. Annual retail sales in America top $9 trillion ($9,000,000,000,000) a year, and consumer spending is estimated to account for over two-thirds of the US economy. So if Americans leave their credit cards at home, the country could, theoretically, grind to a halt – not that there's much danger of this happening.

> 'When the going gets tough, the tough go shopping.'
> Anon

Americans' love of shopping is second only to their love of food. Shopping is an addiction, a cure for all ills – not for nothing is it called retail therapy – and it's the number one leisure pursuit in the US. When times are hard, politicians actively encourage people to go out and spend money, as New York's Mayor Rudolph Giuliani did in the wake of the terrorist attacks on the World Trade Centre in September 2001.

The US is seen as the ultimate throwaway society, where prices are low in comparison to services, therefore buying a new toaster is often cheaper than getting the old one fixed – and so much more satisfying.

With retail opportunities at every turn, from the corner deli to your TV screen, it's difficult to resist the urge to buy. But with such a vast choice – even an average supermarket may stock half an aisle of breakfast cereals – it can be difficult for a foreigner to negotiate the American shopping experience. This chapter is designed to help newcomers survive – and enjoy – shopping in the US, and explains the cultural differences you can expect.

CUSTOMER SERVICE

To foreigners used to the slapdash service in some European countries, particularly the UK, shopping in America is a revelation. Customers are routinely greeted with a cheery smile and made to feel important. In most shops, sales assistants will put themselves out to help you find exactly what you want, in the correct size and colour, even if it means going to the stockroom to find it. Many assistants earn commission on their sales, so your purchase is money in their pocket.

There are always exceptions, and service in New York can be blunt to the point of rudeness. Customers can be equally blunt and are usually in a hurry, so shopping transactions are brisk, to the point and often lack social pleasantries.

Customer service extends to help with bagging and packaging your purchases (gift wrapping is included), and many stores offer a home delivery option. Naturally, the helpful boy who loads your bags or carries them up three flights of stairs will be hoping that you'll reward him with a dollar or two – it's the American way.

Unlike half of the world's population, Americans rarely haggle, and goods with no price ticket make them feel uncomfortable. However, they all aspire to being 'smart shoppers', which means never paying the full price for anything if they can possibly avoid it. People spend a lot of time comparing prices and hunting for the best bargains, so there's no shame in asking for a discount, especially when purchasing big-ticket items such

as household appliances or buying goods in bulk. American retailers are realists, and will often give you a discount to secure a sale.

OPENING HOURS

Despite the 24-hour shopping culture, not all America's retail outlets are open every minute of every day. It depends on where you live. Stores in smaller towns may only open from 9 or 10am until 6pm, although supermarkets usually stay open later (until 9pm at least), as do stores in shopping malls. Convenience stores may not shut before midnight. If you live in a city, it's possible to buy anything at virtually any time of the day or night, particularly food and other household items, and many corner shops or delis never seem to close.

It says a lot about America's love of the car that many petrol (gas) stations are open 24 hours a day, 365 days of the year. Most will also sell basic food items – a few are as well stocked as a small supermarket – so you need never run out of milk or gas.

Sundays & Public Holidays

Although there are some strongly religious counties where Sunday trading is prohibited, for the most part, Sunday trading hours aren't much different from the rest of the week. Stores may open an hour later and close an hour earlier, while a few places don't open until the storekeeper has returned from church. It may also be difficult to find certain items on sale on Sundays, such as alcohol. However, in areas with a large ethnic population, Sunday may be one of the busiest trading days

– for example, in Jewish and Chinese districts.

The only public holidays on which shops shut are Christmas Day and Thanksgiving, although you may still find convenience stores open from noon to around 5pm. Other public holidays observe opening hours similar to Sundays.

The Thanksgiving holiday always falls on a Thursday, and few businesses bother to open on the Friday. Indeed, this has become so traditional, that this Friday is widely regarded as the single most profitable day in US retail. The following Monday is known in the retail trade as 'Black Monday', as it's invariably the worst day at the check-outs.

BLACK MARKET

Since the end of prohibition in 1933, when America lifted its ban on the sale of alcohol, the majority of goods have been sold over the counter. The exception is the trade in illegal drugs, which the government spends over £12bn a year trying to combat. Fake goods, such as DVDs and sportswear, aren't as widely available in the US as they are in the Far East. The companies that hold the copyright to widely-copied labels include many American corporations, which don't tolerate black market cowboys ripping off their brands on their own doorstep.

QUEUING

You rarely find much of a queue in an American store. There will be an orderly line at the check-out, but if it gets too long, additional staff will be marshalled to clear any backlog. No manager wants the last impression of his store to be a lengthy and irritating wait to pay. If you come from a country where queuing is an unknown concept, note that it isn't acceptable to push to the front, or try to 'jump' the queue.

America is a popular destination for international shoppers. Cameras, electronic goods, computers, DVDs, sports equipment and clothes are all inexpensive in comparison with other western countries.

SALES & DISCOUNTS

Just like other nations, America has specific sales seasons, with the biggest bargains being offered in January and July/August. Thanksgiving kicks off a pre-Christmas winter sales spree, and sales are also held on other holiday weekends such as Presidents' Day and Veterans' Day (see **Public Holidays** in **Chapter 6** for dates). However, sales aren't limited to certain times of the year; clothing stores offer reductions as the seasons change, and many stores offer discounts and sales during every month of the year.

Discount Shops, Warehouse Clubs & Factory Outlets

These are the cheapest places to shop in America, outside of the sales. Discount shops are basic, no-frills shopping, low on customer service but high on value. Two of the best-known are Kmart and Wal-Mart (the latter is the biggest retailer in the world), and fierce rivalry between the two helps keeps prices down.

Warehouse clubs such as Sam's Club (owned by Wal-Mart) and Costco are the fastest-growing retail sector in America. Shoppers must become members (the fee is around $30 a year), but then gain access to huge discounts on branded goods. If you buy in bulk, you can save a fifth on supermarket prices.

Factory outlets are stores where manufacturers offload out-of-date or overstocked goods (not seconds or damaged stock), which may sell at 50 to 70 per cent below the usual retail price, and includes just about everything, from chocolates to power drills. There are entire shopping malls devoted to factory outlet stores – see 🖳 www.outletbound. com to find a list of outlets across the US.

If you cannot cope with the vast choice, or are just too busy to trawl through the stores, America invented the personal shopper, who will shop for you – or take you on a guided shopping tour – for about $50 an hour.

It may seem strange in such a consumer-oriented society, but getting something for nothing has its own cult following. Thrifties even have their own websites, such as Tightwad Central (🖳 www.tightwad.com), which is packed with money-saving tips and lists of freephone numbers you can call to obtain free samples of everything from coffee to cookbooks.

Black Friday

The biggest shopping day of the year is Black Friday, the day after the Thanksgiving holiday, which many Americans take off work – except those who work in the retail sector. Black Friday is officially the start of the Christmas shopping season, and the term refers to the boost in sales in just one day which is enough to put some companies into profit ('in the black'). Sales in 2007 showed a 22 per cent increase on the previous year. Newspapers delivered on Thanksgiving contain pages of advertisements for sales the following day; some shopping malls even open at 1am in order to catch sales-hungry shoppers, and dedicated sales goers start queuing after they've eaten their Thanksgiving meal!

Another American shopping phenomenon is Cyber Monday – the online version of Black Friday, which follows the post-Thanksgiving weekend.

Discount Coupons

Americans love collecting – and 'spending' – coupons. These are issued by manufacturers, and can often be exchanged at more than one store – some shops will accept another supermarket's coupons, or allow you to use them for a different product, rather than lose your custom. Anyone who associates coupons with thrifty old-age pensioners will be surprised at how popular they are in the US, but when you realise that by clipping coupons, you can cut up to 20 per cent off the weekly shop, they start to make sense. There's even a big fat coupon bible, *Entertainment*, published annually for all regions and cities, which is well worth buying, as it contains hundreds of coupons issued by restaurants, cinemas, hotels, shops and many other local business – see 🖥 www.entertainment. com for information.

TYPES OF SHOP

In America, shops are almost always referred to as stores. A store can be anything from a large department store to a neighbourhood delicatessen, although away from the ethnic quarters of the larger cities, smaller specialist stores such as butchers, bakers and greengrocers are disappearing and being replaced by supermarkets and shopping malls, where everything is offered for sale under one roof. As in many western countries, time is money, and so many Americans do one massive weekly shop, loading up their trolley (American trolleys are known as a caddy or cart, and are, of course, larger than the European version) in just one store.

The terminology used to describe the different types of US stores is shown below:

● **Shopping malls** are vast, covered shopping centres, featuring stores, cafes, restaurants and fast-food outlets, cinemas, bowling alleys and skating rinks, along with car parks big enough for a jumbo jet to land. The largest is the Mall of America in Minneapolis, which sprawls over an area of 4.2mn ft² (390,180m²) and contains over 400 stores – as well as a golf course and a wedding chapel.

More than 40mn customers visit each year.

● **Supermarkets** are food outlets; usually anything else on sale is a sideline. However, the sheer range and choice of food products is overwhelming, with goods from around the world competing for shelf space with American products, well-known brands and cheaper generic varieties. It's reckoned that the US supermarket business is worth in excess of $200bn a year. The biggest players are SuperValu, Kroger and Safeway, although there are numerous smaller chains, both national and regional, as well as those targeting Asian and Hispanic shoppers.

● **Superstores** are enlarged supermarkets, which sell almost everything in just one store, from food and household goods to clothes, electrical items and furnishings.

- **Grocery stores** are the modern-day equivalent of the Wild West trading posts, which sold everything from cattle feed to beans. Nowadays, they are under pressure from supermarkets, and many specialise in the needs of a local area and feature exotic foods from around the globe, such as Mexico, the Middle East, Asia and India. Larger stores often sell clothes and household goods (and may also sell medicines) alongside the provisions, and are sometimes referred to as drug stores.

- **Convenience or corner stores** flourish in cities and suburbs, to keep the local population stocked with beer, cigarettes, milk, soft drinks, gum, sweets (candy), doughnuts and other necessities of modern American life. Many open early and close late – the granddaddy of convenience stores was the 7-Eleven, although those hours (7am-11pm) would be considered inconvenient by today's standards, with many, especially those linked to a petrol station, open 24 hours a day.

- **Department stores & chain stores** are shops selling non-food items, including clothes, electrical items, gifts and household goods. Department stores are often vast, with a wide range of departments spread over a number of floors, each of which may be dedicated to a single department. Most are synonymous with quality, such as Macy's and Bloomingdales in New York, which are among the best-known stores in the world. While many department stores are one-off shops, chain stores have branches in many cities and towns. Many specialise in goods such as clothes,

toys or hardware, while others sell anything and everything. Well-known chain stores include J C Penney and Sears Roebuck.

> The term 'bargain basement' comes from the fact that American department stores used to sell off their cut-price ('off price') goods in the basement or lower ground floor. Some retailers, such as Filene's (Basement) and T K Maxx operate entire stores on this principle.

- **Thrift stores** (charity shops) are run by churches, hospitals and similar charitable organisations, accepting donations of clothing, toys, furniture, books and so forth, and then selling them on to raise money for good causes. If you don't mind second-hand goods, shopping around in thrift stores can produce some remarkable bargains.

MARKETS

Food Markets

The vibrant markets which are the hub of many European and Asian cities aren't a big feature of American life. However, farmers' markets are becoming popular, especially in cosmopolitan cities such as New York, and discerning shoppers will travel some distance to buy fresh produce from local growers. You may pay a little more for the meat, vegetables and fruit on offer at a farmer's market, but it has more flavour than the bland (if good-looking) produce sold in supermarkets.

Other Markets

Flea markets are a good place to pick up household goods, bric-a-brac, clothing, shoes, DIY items, tools – the list is endless. Much of the stock is secondhand (used, pre-owned or even 'pre-loved' as Americans like to put it), and the sheer number of stalls makes browsing a time-consuming activity. If you find something you like, then buy it, as you may be hard-pushed to find the same stall again – but be warned that stall holders are well aware of this, and will try to encourage you to part with your money at the earliest opportunity.

PAYING

In America, prices aren't always what they seem, thanks to a peculiarity known as sales tax. This is the most complex tax in the US, if not in the world, as it's added to only certain items, and at differing rates, according to which state you're in. Sales tax is levied on consumption, so it may (or may not) apply to food, restaurant meals, medicines, general goods and even some second-hand items – it entirely depends on where and what you're buying. This gives rise to some huge anomalies, and prompts many Americans to cross state borders to buy certain items, and is further complicated by the addition of local city and county taxes in some places. For the shopper, it means that whatever price is shown on an item, it's likely to cost more. In 2008, sales tax ranged from zero (in Alaska, Delaware, Montana, New Hampshire and Oregon) to 2.9 per cent in Colorado, and a high of 7.25 per cent in California.

How you pay for goods and services is up to you; the majority of Americans use a credit or charge card (see **Banking** in **Chapter 3**) to pay for goods. They rarely use personal cheques, as many stores don't accept them (cheque fraud is a big problem in the US); and when they do, cheques must usually be drawn on a local bank, and you need at least two forms of ID. Even then you may have to go to a special desk and have the cheque approved before using it. Travellers' cheques, on the other hand, are generally widely accepted – as is cash!

Most stores also offer a store card, which can only be used at that particular outlet (or others in a chain) and which often carries a very high interest rate. The stores compensate for this by also offering loyalty cards, which allow customers to save points towards discounts off their shopping, plane tickets and other incentives.

> 'Food, one assumes, provides nourishment: but Americans eat it fully aware that small amounts of poison have been added to improve its appearance and delay its putrefaction.'
>
> John Cage (American composer)

FOOD & WINE

In spite of the huge choice, American produce rarely tastes as good as it looks – or is as good for you as it should be. Huge shiny vegetables are liberally sprayed with pesticides and preservatives to keep them looking fresh, while meat is often intensively farmed, and bursting with hormones and other drugs.

TV dinners have been an American standby for decades, and ready-to-eat, microwavable, hassle-free meals are a staple of the supermarket aisles. It appears that there's nothing which cannot be frozen, freeze-dried, chilled or otherwise prepared, to save time in a busy household. High levels of fat, sugar, salt, preservatives and other nasties are occupational hazards for eaters of convenience foods, so it's as well to read the labels before you buy.

Anyone used to shopping on a daily basis will be shocked by the size of the portions, which assume that everything will be bought by large families of (very) large people. Milk comes in 2-litre cartons, and breakfast cereals in boxes the size of a small suitcase. If you're shopping for one, it can be difficult to find moderately sized packages.

Meat & Fish

Americans aren't squeamish when it comes to eating meat. Every part of the beast which is edible will be roasted, barbecued, boiled, fried or grilled, and even offal is widely eaten, although it's usually referred to as 'variety meats'. Beef is the most popular red meat, appropriate in a country where cattle herders and a big juicy steak are national icons. Chicken seems to be in every refrigerator in the country – even

Metric/Imperial Conversion			
Weight			
Imperial	**Metric**	**Metric**	**Imperial**
1 UK pint	0.57 litre	1 litre	1.75 UK pints
1 US pint	0.47 litre	1 litre	2.13 US pints
1 UK gallon	4.54 litre	1 litre	0.22 UK gallon
1 US gallon	3.78 litres	1 litre	0.26 US gallon
Capacity			
Imperial	**Metric**	**Metric**	**Imperial**
1 UK pint	0.57 litre	1 litre	1.75 UK pints
1 US pint	0.47 litre	1 litre	2.13 US pints
1 UK gallon	4.54 litres	1 litre	0.22 UK gallon
1 US gallon	3.78 litres	1 litre	0.26 US gallon

Note: An American 'cup' = around 250ml or 0.25 litre.

some so-called vegetarians eat chicken. Fish and shellfish are popular, especially near the coasts where lobster, crab and crayfish are found in abundance, while the major rivers, lakes, bayous and marshes provide an enormous variety of fish.

Milk & Dairy

The main types of milk available in the US are:

> **homogenised vitamin D** – contains about 3.25 per cent fat, and has added vitamin D to compensate for cattle being kept indoors;
>
> **two per cent skim** – the percentage refers to the fat content;
>
> **skim** – also referred to as 'fat free';
>
> **half and half** – a half cream and half milk blend sold in small quantities and used mainly in coffee.

Sour cream, flavoured milks and cottage cheese are popular dairy products in the US. American cheese (usually bland and tasteless – although there are a few exceptions such as 'Wookey Hole' cheddar and imported cheeses, and delis also have to have a reasonable selection) is often sold ready grated, and butter (also tasteless) is sold in sticks. Virtually every dairy product has a diet or 'lite' alternative. Note, however, that words such as diet, lite, fat-free, low-calorie, etc., are invariably euphemisms for bland – it's the 'bad' stuff that gives food flavour!

Organic Food

Organic food is becoming big business in the US. Sales in 2006 increased by 22 per cent over the previous year (and are expected to increase by some 25 per cent a year until 2010 at least), with yogurt and baby foods proving especially popular, according to America's Organic Consumers' Association. Around a third of organic produce is sold through supermarkets, with just over a fifth sold by small specialist stores. Produce which is sold as 'organic' is markedly more expensive, although it's possible to buy cheaper, naturally grown fruit and vegetables from local farmers or co-operatives, in all rural areas – look for roadside stalls, and visit 'pick your own' farms. City dwellers can buy organic produce from farmers' markets (see above).

Alcohol

Although prohibition appears to linger on in some states, such as Utah, alcohol is widely available, provided you're aged over 21 and aren't planning to swig it on the street – 'brown bagging' refers to the practice of drinking from a bottle concealed in a brown paper bag. Note that even carrying an open bottle of alcohol in your car boot is against the law in some states. Don't rely on buying booze at the supermarket, as they don't usually sell alcohol, or may sell wine only. In some states, you may have to purchase it from an official liquor store.

Wine

America is the largest wine-producing country outside Europe, producing more wine than Australia. California is the best-known state for wine, but in fact almost every US state makes wine – and the industry goes back 300 years. Wine exports amount to 5 per cent of the global market, but most of the nation's production is consumed in America.

US wines are usually named after the grape, e.g. chardonnay, zinfandel, pinot noir, etc., although the rules covering the grape content are less strict than in Europe, unless you're buying quality wine. Imported wine is also widely available.

CLOTHES

Blue jeans were first worn in America – by California miners in the 1850s – and they remain one of the best-value buys in US clothing. You can pick up a decent pair of Levi's for around $30. T-shirts, too, are an American stand-by. Sports and casual clothes are the mainstay of the US wardrobe, but you can also find a wide range of good quality clothes almost everywhere, which are often much less expensive than in Europe. The best places to shop for clothes are the factory outlet shops and 'off price' chain stores (see above).

Many Americans tend to dress to conform (see **Dress** on page ??), but if that's not your style, there are high-fashion options at low-fashion prices. You can find designer gear at rock-bottom prices in discount shops in the garment districts of big cities. Meanwhile, the craze for 'vintage' has led to special consignment shops which sell quality second-hand (pre-owned) clothing. Charity (thrift) shops in upmarket areas are also worth a rummage.

> **'It's always the badly-dressed people who are the most interesting.'**
>
> Jean Paul Gaultier (French fashion designer)

Continental to UK/US Size Comparison

Women's Clothes

Continental	34	36	38	40	42	44	46	48	50	52
UK		8	10	12	14	16	18	20	22	24	26
US		6	8	10	12	14	16	18	20	22	24

Men's Shirts

Continental	36	37	38	39	40	41	42	43	44	46
UK/US	14	14	15	15	16	16	17	17	18	-

Shoes (Women's and Men's)

Continental	35	36	37	37	38	39	40	41	42	42	43	44
UK	2	3	3	4	4	5	6	7	7	8	9	9
US	4	5	5	6	6	7	8	9	9	10	10	11

Sizes

America doesn't follow international standards for clothing sizes (not that they ever follow any standards other than their own), which is frustrating if you're used to being a certain size. As a rough guide, women's clothes are about two sizes larger than the UK equivalent, so a UK size 12 is a size 8 in the US. To compare US, UK and European sizes, see the conversion table below.

The trend for 'vanity sizing' has seen clothes sizes slowly increase over a period of time, to match the expansion in Americans' waistlines. This no doubt began as a marketing strategy to help people 'feel good' about themselves, but it now means that every American size number is numerically significantly lower than other countries' sizes, and the inclusion of half sizes (which is almost unique) adds to the confusion. Different clothing companies have created their own size lists, so one manufacturer's 12 is another's 14. **Always try garments on for size.**

> Size zero, which has become synonymous with stick-thin supermodels, is an American invention. It corresponds to a UK size 4 (or even a 6) or a European 30. There are very few American women who can fit into a size zero!

Men's clothing sizes are more standardised, with about 10 different sizes on offer. A lot of clothes are simply sold as extra small through to extra large so, again, it's necessary to try them on.

Americans have some confusing names for items of clothing. Men wear stockings and pants rather than socks and trousers, and hold their trousers up with suspenders rather than braces.

Women wear panties and panty hose (not knickers and tights). A jumper refers to a pinafore dress, while a vest is a waistcoat or sleeveless pullover. If you want a vest, ask for an undershirt.

Shoes

There are many specialist shoe shops selling well-known brands such as Dockside, Selby and Timberland (famous for their boots). American-made shoes are generally good quality, particularly sports shoes and cowboy boots. Shoe repair shops can be found in all towns, and in department stores. As with clothes, there's no standard shoe sizing system; moreover, a shoe with the same physical dimensions is designated a different size for men and women, therefore as with clothes you should always try shoes on (see the conversion chart above). The good news is that Americans generally have big feet, so finding larger than average footwear shouldn't be a problem.

Children's Clothes

There's an infinite choice of clothing for children and babies, and again the quality tends to be good. Much of it is scaled-down versions of adult styles: in America, it isn't unusual to see a whole family wearing identikit outfits. Babies' and children's sizes are calculated according to age, although an American 10-year-old can be far larger than his European counterpart (depending on how many burgers he eats a day), so don't assume the usual size will fit. Good children's shoes are produced by Bass and StrideRite, and many stores offer a foot-measuring service.

COLLECTABLES

Virtually every household in the country includes someone who collects something, from dolls to stamps to tea sets. US manufacturers are wise to this trend, and market special collections, sometimes accompanied by magazines, while serious collectors join groups and attend seminars and discussions. Some collect solely in order to make a profit, and there are many websites and publications advising collectors on which collectables are likely to be the next big money-spinners.

Yard & Garage Sales

The accumulation of so much treasure (or tat) means that space is at a premium in many homes, and even the most sought-after collections may eventually find their way to the other American mania: the yard sale. This is an impromptu sale which takes place in someone's garden or garage, as they clear out the contents of their attic or wardrobe so they can start collecting all over again.

Everyone has a yard sale at some time or other, with most taking place over weekends in spring or summer. They're advertised in local newspapers, on supermarket notice boards or just by word of mouth – drive around the suburbs on a sunny Saturday and you're sure to find one in progress. Americans don't ask much for their cast-offs, and people who are relocating may sell the entire contents of their house, so yard sales can be excellent places to pick up a bargain if you're setting up home.

If you're planning a clear out and want to hold a yard sale, depending on where you live you may need to obtain a permit from City Hall, as well as from your landlord if you live in rented accommodation.

America's longest yard sale takes place along highway 127 in August. It stretches some 630mi (1,010km) from Gadsden, Alabama to West Unity, Ohio, crossing a total of five states and featuring over 5,000 vendors (only in America!). For information, see 🖥 www. 127sale.com.

MAIL-ORDER SHOPPING

For American shopaholics, there's only one thing more attractive than exploring the malls, and that's shopping from the comfort of your own home. Mail-order

shopping has always been popular in the US, and in the days of the early settlers it was the only way people in remote areas could obtain consumer goods. Over half the population shops by mail, and the mail-order business is today worth about $200bn per year.

Around 13bn catalogues are regularly distributed to US homes, with J C Penney and LL Bean among the biggest names. Buyers can order by telephone (the numbers are free), although catalogues are being overtaken by more hi-tech retail methods, such as television shopping channels and the internet – many catalogue companies also have their own website where you can place your order online.

The advantages to mail-order shopping are lower prices – mail-order and internet vendors usually undercut main street – and the fact that goods bought by mail order across a state line are often exempt from sales tax. Buyers must pay for delivery, but companies offer low rates, which keeps prices competitive.

> **'Thank God we're living in a country where the sky's the limit, the stores are open late and you can shop in bed, thanks to television.'**
>
> Joan Rivers (American comedienne)

Television Shopping

Shopping channels are a mainstay of US television, and there are dozens aired by mainstream and cable networks, including America's Store and QVC. They provide a 24-hour salesroom, where presenters demonstrate must-have kitchen gadgets and miracle face creams. Some operate 'auctions' whereby viewers bid for items, in the style of eBay. In addition, many companies buy 30-minute slots on regular TV stations and use them to sell their products (known as infomercials), which may be shown in place of regular shows. Buyers usually order their goods by phone, although they may find that the same items are available cheaper at a local discount store or on the internet.

Unsolicited phone calls by salespeople, known as cold-calling, are a frequent interruption in US homes. Never give your credit card or bank details over the phone to someone who phones you.

Internet

Online shopping (called e-tailing) was slow to take off in the US, but is now one of the fastest-growing retail sectors. Internet World Stats reveal that in 2007, just over 70 per cent of Americans had internet access, and Nielsen reported that 94 per cent of internet users had made online purchases. Increased internet security may be one factor boosting online sales.

Virtually every high-street store now has a website. There are also innumerable internet-only retailers, auction sites and end-of-line outlets – the choice is growing all the time. The biggest drawback is not being able to handle (or try on) the goods firsthand; however, reputable suppliers allow no-quibble returns, and some even refund packing and shipping costs. Many stores also allow shoppers to order online and then pick up the goods from a local store.

Online grocery shopping is increasingly popular, with major supermarkets offering shopping and home deliveries. If your order is large

enough, delivery is free, although the delivery person will expect a tip.

RETURNING GOODS

America has strong laws protecting consumers who have statutory rights. Most retailers offer refunds on goods, or replace them without asking questions, especially if they're defective or not 'merchantable', i.e. they don't perform the function for which they were designed. However, it's important to keep your receipt. Around 10 per cent of all purchases are returned to stores, often for no reason other than buyers changed their minds, so vendors are tightening up their refunds policy. Discount stores can be especially reluctant to offer refunds.

Stores must display their return and refund policy – it's often printed on the reverse of the receipt – but without a receipt, you may have to swap the item for something similar or accept a credit note. Ensure that as well as keeping the receipt, the goods are in the condition

in which you bought them and that you have the original packaging. Refunds are given as cash or by crediting your credit/debit card.

Guarantees

Guarantees (or warranties as they're called in the US) can last from one to five years, depending on the goods. They may offer full or limited protection, and it's possible to extend an item's warranty by paying an extra fee (although they are a waste of money). If you don't return faulty merchandise to the store you bought it from within a certain time period, you may have to pursue the manufacturer to repair it under the warranty. It's advisable to check a store's policy when buying expensive items.

> To save having to complain and/ or return items, it pays to do some research beforehand, particularly for more expensive purchases. One way is via *Consumer Reports* magazine (☐ www.consumerreports.org), an independent consumer magazine that tests and reviews products and services. It's available on subscription and from newsstands, and copies may also be available at your local library.

Complaints

Every large store or organisation has a customer services department, while smaller places have a manager, owner or someone who will do their utmost to redress your complaint – provided it's legitimate – as they all want your return custom. Sometimes, though, you may need to seek help from a third party

There are a number of organisations which champion consumer rights, such as the Consumers Union (☐ www.consumersunion.org) and Better Business Bureaux (☐ www.bbb. org), which are non-profit organisations sponsored by local businesses that can mediate in consumer disputes. You can also take unresolved complaints a stage higher by reporting the retailer to the Federal Trade Commission (☐ www. ftc.gov), which has offices across the US.

Grand Canyon, Arizona

10.
ODDS & ENDS

A country's culture is influenced by many factors and reflected in myriad ways. Among the principal influences are its geography and climate, which are considered here; along with various cultural manifestations, including crime, the national flag and anthem, religion, government and international relations, as well as attitudes to pets, time difference, tipping – and toilets.

> 'We do not inherit the land from our ancestors; we borrow it from our children.'
>
> Native American proverb.

GEOGRAPHY

The 50 United States of America make up the world's third-largest country, both in terms of area and population. Its largest landmass straddles the North American continent, bordered by the Atlantic to the east, the Pacific to the west and the Gulf of Mexico to the south. Its southern land border is shared with Mexico and its northern border with Canada, which separates the US from its 49th and largest state, Alaska. The 50th state is the island group of Hawaii, 1,988mi (3,200km) southwest of the mainland.

In such an immense country, Americans can sample virtually every geographical feature on the planet, from Alaska's Arctic glaciers to Florida's sub-tropical Everglades, with vast forests, arid deserts, soaring mountains and endless rolling plains filling the space in between.

The main geographical features include the Great Lakes, which divide the US from Canada in the country's northeast, and the Appalachian Mountains which divide the states along the Atlantic coast from the Mississippi River basin and the Midwest's agricultural heartland. In the west, the Rocky Mountains rise to over 14,440ft (4,400m) in height, beyond which are the deserts of the west and southwest, home to the spectacular Grand Canyon.

The US is divided into four main areas: east, south, midwest and west. These, in turn, are sub-divided into eight regions:

America is about the same size as China, and two and a half times larger than Western Europe. The UK would fit into its landmass about 39 times.

- **the Northeast** – this is the largest region, stretching from New England (often regarded as a region in its own right) around the

Great Lakes to the coastal plain of Pennsylvania and Washington DC. As far as people in the west are concerned, it also includes many of the Midwest states from the Dakotas down to Kansas and across to Ohio and Tennessee.

● **New England** – this area is made up of several small states along the north-eastern seaboard, including Connecticut, Maine and Massachusetts;

● **the Deep South** – a region comprising many of the south-eastern states, including Alabama, Louisiana and northern Florida (the Panhandle);

● **the Plains or Great Plains** – the heart of the US, this area includes the wide flat central corridor of prairie which sweeps from the Canadian border down to Oklahoma;

● **the Rockies or Mountain West** – this is the region around the Rocky Mountains, which includes such states as Colorado, Montana and Utah;

● **the Southwest** – the home of the dry desert states, including Arizona, New Mexico and much of Texas;

● **the Northwest** – the most temperate region of the US, which includes Oregon, Washington and northern California;

● **the West Coast or Far West** – this region is dominated by the sunshine state of California, and includes Oregon and Washington state.

Many states can theoretically fit into one or more of these regions and not even Americans can agree on which ones belong where.

Vital Statistics

Land area: 3,536,294mi² (9,158,960km²)

Distance from coast to coast: approximately 3,000mi (4,828km)

Highest point: Mount McKinley in Alaska at 20,320ft (6,194m)

Lowest point: Death Valley in California at 282ft (86m) below sea level

Longest river: The Mississippi-Missouri, which links Canada to the Gulf of Mexico and measures 3,902mi (6,275km) in length. It's been immortalised in song on many occasions, including *Ol' Man River* in the musical *Show Boat,* and *Moon River* in the film *Breakfast at Tiffany's.*

Largest lake: Lake Superior, the largest of the Great Lakes. It covers an area of 31,820 mi² (82,400km²) with a volume of 2,904mi³ (12,000km³), and is the largest freshwater lake in the world.

CLIMATE

With such as vast and diverse geography, America's climate cannot help but be one of extremes. The weather in any one state or region is affected not just by its latitude, but by its distance from water: the places with the greatest variation in temperatures are Alaska, the deserts of the south-western states and the landlocked central strip stretching from Canada to the southern Great Plains. More temperate zones (in summer at least) include the north-western Pacific coast and around the Great Lakes.

America's weather can also differ enormously, depending on where you are; in just a single day, there

may be snowdrifts in South Dakota, thunderstorms in Florida and sweltering heat in Arizona. Other weather phenomena include hailstones the size of cricket balls and torrential rain which causes mudslides and flooding, as well as hurricanes and tornados (see below).

Temperatures are especially extreme in the Midwest, where the mercury regularly rises to 104°F (40°C) during summer, and may plummet to -40°F (-40°C) in winter months. Other factors, such as humidity along the coasts and the 'wind chill factor', often exaggerate the temperature. The coldest place is Alaska, where temperatures have been recorded as low as -76°F (-60°C); the hottest is California's Death Valley, where as high as 135°F (57°C) has been recorded.

Despite their diverse and sometimes unpredictable weather, Americans don't talk about it in the way, for example, the British do. There is, however, plenty of media time devoted to it, including frequent forecasts and 24-hour TV weather stations.

Extreme Weather

If you come from a temperate climate like that of Western Europe, you may have trouble adjusting to the extremes of heat and cold which many Americans take for granted. Older people and young children can find it especially hard to cope. Severe cold brings the risk of hypothermia, but sustained daily temperatures of 95°F (35°C) and more can be even more difficult to deal with. The Americans' reliance on air-conditioning and central heating (both are usually turned to the highest setting) can make the transition from indoors to outdoors even more of a shock (which is probably why many Americans never get out of their cars).

Hurricanes

The hurricane season begins in early June and lasts until the end of November, when hurricanes (or tropical cyclones) build up over the Atlantic and the Gulf of Mexico. Those which make landfall can wreak colossal damage. In 1900, a hurricane hit Galveston, Texas, killing up to 12,000 people – the most deadly natural disaster in US history. More recently, in August 2005, the storm surge created by Hurricane Katrina breached the levées (dykes) protecting New Orleans. The resulting floods created huge destruction in which over 1,800 people lost their lives.

Over the last 50 years, records reveal that the number of significant storms each year has risen from six to ten, although the strength of storms has decreased. It's unlikely you would miss a hurricane warning, as these are broadcast on all media and, since Katrina, the government takes no chances, and insists that residents evacuate an area at risk.

Tornadoes

A tornado (or twister) is just one symptom of a violent storm. The word describes the column of rotating air which links the storm cloud with the earth. It's the base of the tornado that causes the most damage, and this is often over 100m (328ft) across, although the largest tornados may spread their destruction in a path more than a mile (1.6km) wide.

Over 1,000 tornadoes are reported in the US each year, although only a small proportion does serious damage. More than half occur in May and June, with the most tornado-prone region being the Great Plains, which extends from central Texas up to the Canadian border (described as 'Tornado Alley'). A growing fascination for this weather phenomenon has led to a craze for 'storm chasing', in which getting as close as possible to a tornado has become a bizarre leisure activity.

An early warning system of radio and television announcements, and even sirens, warns people of approaching tornadoes. The biggest can literally rip a house from its foundations, but you stand a better chance of survival if you shelter in a basement, and many houses in tornado-prone areas have underground storm cellars. Failing that, use a ground floor room with as few windows as possible – some people take refuge in a bathroom or even in the bath! If you're driving when a tornado strikes, you should abandon the vehicle and seek shelter in a roadside ditch. Avoid underpasses and bridges, which, although they may seem like good shelters, act as wind tunnels and actually magnify the force of a tornado.

Earthquakes

During most years in America, thousands of earthquakes take place, of which over 400 measure 4 or higher on the Richter scale. Between 4 and 5, you can expect to feel a shudder as the ground shakes and objects rattle and fall. Only earthquakes measuring above 5 are capable of causing significant damage, and then only over a small area. However, powerful quakes can and do occur. Several have shaken the San Francisco area during the last century, and experts believe that California is due to experience a really big quake in the not too distant future – and when it hits, it could be the biggest-ever natural disaster to affect the US.

Alaska, not California, is the most earthquake-prone place in the US, if not the world. It experiences a magnitude 7 earthquake almost every year. However, its low population and lack of large cities means that the damage to people and property is minimal.

In areas prone to earthquakes, it's as well to be prepared:

● Be aware of danger zones in your home, and avoid placing heavy items in high places, especially above beds.

● Identify the safest place to shelter – for example, under a heavy and sturdy piece of furniture, rather than in a doorway.

● Ensure everyone knows how to shut off the gas and water, and arrange a safe place away from the building as a meeting point.

● Keep shoes, clothes and a torch handy by the bed. A bag packed with bottled water, snacks and a first-aid kit is also a wise precaution.

Fire & Flood

Wildfires scorch their way through California every summer, many begun by arsonists, and fanned by the Santa Ana winds; while flooding is an ever-present danger along the Mississippi-Missouri rivers. The great US floods of 1993 caused $15bn of damage in a huge area of the Midwest, with 75 towns under water and 10,000 homes destroyed, although, amazingly, only 50 people died. If you live in an area prone to forest fires or flooding, this may affect your home insurance.

CRIME

America has a reputation for being one of the most crime-ridden countries in the world, but perhaps 'gun-ridden' is a better way of putting it. Although US crime figures are high, it's the frequency of violent crime and homicides (murders) which drives them up, and the sheer number of Americans carrying guns – over 200mn firearms are thought to be in circulation – fuels these figures.

Statistics invariably show that there are more murders in America than in virtually all other western nations. However, the US murder rate has almost halved from its peak in the early '80s, and the rates of other crimes, such as burglary and vehicle theft, are actually lower than in the UK or Australia.

How you're affected by crime is dependent on who you are and where you live. If you're a young black male, living in eastern Washington DC – the capital is among the most dangerous places in the US – you're many times more likely to be a victim of violence than a middle-aged white woman living in a New England suburb. A great deal of violent crime is gang and/or drugs related, much of it involving blacks and Hispanics, and most Americans are untouched by it.

America has a low tolerance for crime, as illustrated by the high prison population – over 2mn – thanks largely to the 'zero tolerance' policy favoured by many cities, and the existence of the death penalty in the majority of states. Most people are respectful of law and order and of the police who enforce it, and take care to protect their property – and not just because their insurers insist on it.

Common sense is your best defence. Always be aware of your surroundings, and avoid inner city and other 'no go' areas – ask your friends and neighbours which areas are safe and which to avoid – such as deserted car parks and badly-lit and unpopulated areas, especially after dark. Keep your valuables hidden out of sight, and ensure that your home

is well secured; many city apartments have several locks and bolts, and residents use them all, even if they're only popping out for a few minutes. Guard against car-jacking by driving with your windows shut and doors locked, and don't stop for anyone unless it's a policeman (but be wary of bogus cops) or someone you know.

It's a good idea to carry a small amount of cash, between $20 and $50, in case you're a victim of street robbery. There's a school of thought that you're more likely to escape unharmed if you can hand over some 'mugger's money'. If you're attacked, it's advisable not to resist, as your assailant is likely to be armed.

FLAG & ANTHEM

Americans are the most patriotic of people. Their passion for their homeland is infectious, and will soon rub off on you. Even if it doesn't, remember that while it's perfectly OK for an American to criticise their country and people, they often react badly to outsiders making derogatory remarks. Their nationalistic fervour is summed up by two of the most enduring symbols of the US: their flag and their national anthem.

Flag

Variously known as the Stars and Stripes, the Star-Spangled Banner or even Old Glory, the American flag is one of the most immediate symbols of the 21st century. You'll see it everywhere: flying above government buildings, schools and universities, as well as car dealerships and fast-food joints – and frequently

outside private homes. It famously even flutters on the surface of the Moon. The 13 stripes represent the original states which rebelled against the British Empire during the American Revolution; the stars stand for today's 50 states (originally there were 13).

There are many rituals and traditions connected with the flag, including a specific way of folding it. It should never be allowed to touch the ground, and if too tattered to be flown, must be disposed of 'respectfully'. The Flag Code vetoes displaying the flag in advertising or on disposable goods such as handkerchiefs, although these rules are rarely adhered to in the commercially-minded US (however, clothes, such as shirts, made from the stars and stripes, are prohibited). However, showing outright disrespect for the flag won't win you any friends. Should you wish to exhibit a little patriotism of your own, and fly your country's flag alongside that of the US, make sure that Old Glory flies above the other flag.

Anthem

America's national anthem is *The Star-Spangled Banner*. It was written

as a poem in 1814 by Francis Scott Key, a 35-year-old amateur poet, and is set to the tune of a popular British drinking song, *The Anacreontic Song*, written by John Stafford Smith. It was only officially adopted as the anthem of the US by congress in 1931, and has since been translated into several languages, including Hebrew, French and Samoan.

The Star Spangled Banner

O! say can you see by the dawn's early light
What so proudly we hailed at the twilight's last gleaming.
Whose broad stripes and bright stars through the perilous fight,
O'er the ramparts we watched were so gallantly streaming.
And the rockets' red glare, the bombs bursting in air,
Gave proof through the night that our flag was still there.
O! say does that star-spangled banner yet wave
O'er the land of the free and the home of the brave?

On the shore, dimly seen through the mists of the deep,
Where the foe's haughty host in dread silence reposes,
What is that which the breeze, o'er the towering steep,
As it fitfully blows, half conceals, half discloses?
Now it catches the gleam of the morning's first beam,
In full glory reflected now shines in the stream:
'Tis the star-spangled banner! Oh long may it wave
O'er the land of the free and the home of the brave!

And where is that band who so vauntingly swore
That the havoc of war and the battle's confusion,
A home and a country should leave us no more!
Their blood has washed out their foul footsteps' pollution.
No refuge could save the hireling and slave
From the terror of flight, or the gloom of the grave:
And the star-spangled banner in triumph doth wave
O'er the land of the free and the home of the brave!

O! thus be it ever, when freemen shall stand
Between their loved home and the war's desolation!
Blest with victory and peace, may the heav'n rescued land
Praise the Power that hath made and preserved us a nation.
Then conquer we must, when our cause it is just,
And this be our motto: 'In God is our trust.'
And the star-spangled banner in triumph shall wave
O'er the land of the free and the home of the brave!

The anthem is always sung before a sporting event, and the occasion is deeply respectful. People stand to attention, their right hand placed over their heart, facing the flag. Gentlemen are expected to remove their hats. Poking fun at this pillar of US tradition is always risky: comedienne Roseanne Barr alienated many fans with her tasteless rendition at a baseball game in 1990.

The song has a range stretching over an octave, making it notoriously difficult to sing. Fortunately, only one stanza (verse) – the first – is usually sung.

GOVERNMENT

America is the world's oldest surviving federal republic. Its system of government is based on the Constitution of 1787, which ensures that power is shared by the executive, legislative and judicial (legal) branches of government, so that no single body can achieve total control. The first two are elected by the people and function as separate entities. In addition, power is split between national, state and local governments. State governments are headed by a governor, elected every four years, while local government is administered by the mayor and city hall.

Washington, District of Columbia (or DC), America's capital, is the only US city that isn't part of a state. Although it's physically situated in the state of Maryland, it's a separate autonomous (self-governing) area.

The Constitution

The US Constitution is America's supreme law. As the first written constitution, it stands alongside the Magna Carta as one of the most famous non-religious documents in history. It isn't a book of rules, but rather a contract between the government and the people. Since its original inception, it's been amended and added to many times, but still manages to reflect the values of most Americans.

The Constitution consists of a statement of purpose, followed by seven Articles which define where the power of government lies, as well as its limitations. After these come the Amendments. The first ten are known as the Bill of Rights, and were ratified collectively; the remaining 17 were added and ratified separately. The best-known amendments in the Bill of Rights are the Second Amendment, which allows Americans to carry firearms, and the Fifth Amendment, which protects the rights of people accused of committing a crime to remain silent.

Executive Government

This comprises the President, together with his cabinet and other officers, such as ambassadors and federal judges, who are nominated by the President and appointed with the approval of the Senate. The Executive has the power to administer and enforce federal law, and can veto bills passed by Congress; but it cannot make laws, and generally chooses to work with rather than against Congress. Problems can occur when the President and the majority in Congress come from opposing political parties.

As Commander-in-Chief of the military, the holder of the office of President is generally regarded as the most powerful individual on earth. He (or she… one day!) serves a four-year term, with a maximum of two terms, and is elected directly by the people. Each political party nominates a person to run as their presidential candidate, who then selects a running mate who, if elected, becomes the Vice-President.

Legislative Government

Known as Congress, this is the section of government which is responsible for making the laws. It comprises the House of Representatives and the Senate, both of which are voted into power by the public. Their tasks include approving (or not) presidential appointments to senior positions such as Supreme Court judges, ratifying treaties, raising revenue and running a seemingly endless number of powerful committees and decision-making groups.

- The House of Representatives consists of 435 members (congressmen and women), each serving a two-year term. Every ten years, the seats are apportioned among the states according to their population; therefore while the seven smallest states have just a few representatives, California has over 50.

- The Senate is the senior house of Congress. It consists of two senators from each state, each elected for a six-year term, although around a third of seats are contested every two years.

Lobbyists

A role that's peculiar to US politics is that of the lobbyists, members of professional pressure groups which are employed by big business and other organisations to distribute 'funds' and other financial support among Congress, in the hope that new legislation will favour their employers. It usually does, and this method of 'buying votes' (legal bribery) is seen as perfectly acceptable and democratic in the US.

The Judiciary

The Supreme Court is the highest in the land, consisting of the Chief Justice and eight Associate Justices, who effectively serve for life and can only be removed by impeachment or resignation. They are appointed by the President, and are responsible for interpreting and validating laws passed by the executive and legislative. They have the power to overturn any laws deemed not to be in accordance with the Constitution, and their powers have come to the fore when the US government and/or president has been hit by scandals, such as Nixon was during Watergate, or other contentious issues such as abortion. The Chief Justice is the third most powerful person in the US after the President and Vice-President.

44th US President, Barack Obama

The main drawback of the Supreme Court is that its members are political appointees, appointed by the president, and an Administration can pack the court with its own conservative or liberal supporters, which can determine the Court's decisions for decades.

State & Local Government

Although power has been steadily flowing into the hands of central government over the last few decades, the individual states still control much of their own affairs, from setting taxes to drafting laws. State government is organised along the same lines as national government, with the governor taking the presidential role. The next rung down the ladder is occupied by the local government, which consists of more than half a million elected officials across the US. These may govern counties, cities and municipalities, and their responsibilities are similar to those of local councils or authorities, and include administering education, emergency services, highways, trading laws and other local matters.

> 'Apparently, Arnold [Schwarzenegger] was inspired by President Bush, who proved you can be a successful politician in this country, even if English is your second language.'
>
> Conan O'Brien (American comedian, on the action-hero actor's more recent role as Governor of California)

Political Parties

The success of the federal government system probably owes as much to its two-party make up and its electoral system as to anything else. Elections are decided on a system of 'winner takes all', which means that minor parties rarely gain many votes – Americans dislike the concept of losers, and don't 'waste' their votes on someone who stands little chance of winning. This leaves only two plausible parties to vote for, and every election is a contest between the Democrats and the Republicans.

A strange aspect of the presidential elections is the 'electoral college' system of voting, whereby voters cast their votes for electors (rather than the candidate) that are aligned to one party and candidate. There are a total of 538 electors, and the party which gains the majority (270) is the one which puts its leader in the White House. Due to this system, some recent elections have been uncomfortably close. The election process is long and complex, taking around a year from the selection of candidates to the inauguration of the president.

Republican Party – founded in 1854, the Republican party is the champion of the middle classes; conservative, religious, pro big business and anti welfare state. The southern states and the so-called Bible belt are predominantly Republican. After the 2008 elections, the Republicans had 174 seats (out of 435) in the House of Representatives, and 43 seats (out of 100) in the Senate.

Democratic Party – the oldest political party in the world, founded in 1792 by Thomas Jefferson. Democrats are further to the left than Republicans (but not very far), favouring higher taxes to tackle social needs; and are thus more popular

Capitol building, Washington DC

with workers and ethnic minorities. The northern states, with their strong manufacturing traditions, tend to favour the Democrats. After the 2008 elections, the Democrats had control of both the House of Representatives (255 seats out of 435) and the Senate (55 seats out of 100), plus the presidency.

Other parties include the Libertarian Party and the Green Party, both of which have no representatives in government. Independent candidates have done slightly better: they had two Senate seats in 2008, but lost their only voice in the House of Representatives in 2006. None pose any threat to the two main players.

America has its share of frivolous political parties, which stand no chance of election but at least put a smile on people's faces. These include the OWL Party – OWL stands for 'Out With Logic, On With Lunacy' – which has the motto 'We don't give a hoot!' The Guns and Dope Party, meanwhile, campaigns for wacky ideas such as replacing one third of Congress with ostriches… although some Americans may feel that there are plenty of ostriches in residence already.

INTERNATIONAL RELATIONS

> '**America is a large friendly dog in a small room. Every time it wags its tail, it knocks over a chair.**'
> Arnold Joseph Toynbee (British historian)

Since the end of the Cold War and the disintegration of the Soviet Union, America has been the only world superpower. It was a founder member of the United Nations (UN) and the North Atlantic Treaty Organisation (NATO) and is also a permanent member of the UN Security Council. The intervention of the US in the two world wars was hailed as a turning point in both conflicts, resulting in the eventual victory of the Allies, and America's stand against the Soviet Union helped to maintain world peace.

However, the US has faced increased criticism from the rest of the world in the last decade or so, during which its authority has been undermined by its ill-advised and often aggressive foreign policy, particularly its interventions in Afghanistan and Iraq, and its detention of 'political' prisoners in Guantánamo Bay, Cuba.

The World

America's gung-ho foreign policy has damaged its relationship with many nations, especially those in the Arab world. Many are suspicious of the reasons behind its military intervention in the Middle East in response to the attacks on the World Trade Centre, when the US declared war on Saddam Hussein's Iraq. The fact that the ensuing battle to stabilise Iraq has caused the deaths of a great many US soldiers and Iraqi civilians, has further damaged America's reputation.

US foreign policy is often influenced by the potential threat posed by other nations, whether as a source of illicit drugs or, more recently, terrorism. This attitude dates back to the late-19th century, when the US made an agreement with China to ban opium shipments, and

it also explains the lack of any significant trade agreements with Latin American countries.

Arab and Islamic nations have never had strong bonds with America, which have been stretched to breaking point by events in Iraq and Afghanistan since September 11 (9/11), and by its stand off with other Muslim countries, such as Iran and Syria, as well as its close cooperation with Israel. Further east, with the Soviet bloc dismantled and Russia 'neutered', China is now seen as the nation most likely to challenge the supremacy of the US. Meanwhile, the credit crunch of 2008 revealed America's financial vulnerability, and the disastrous effects that debts 'made in America' have had on the economies of other western countries.

In the aftermath of the World Trade Centre attacks, the man in the street has become suspicious of foreigners in general and Muslims in particular. However, the events of September 11 have also made the average American more aware of his nation's image and its standing on the world stage. As a result, privately if not publicly, many Americans are uncomfortable with their leaders' strong-arm tactics, and favour a less aggressive and more diplomatic approach.

However, it isn't all negative. America's role in nuclear disarmament, the Middle East peace negotiations, and as mediator in many other disputes must not be overlooked. It's significant that only eight nations don't have an embassy in Washington DC or a US ambassador on their soil.

Europe

The US has a long and solid alliance with Western Europe. Many Americans have their ancestral roots in European countries, and the relationship between the US and Europe strengthened as the Communist threat diminished. The European Union (EU) and United States share many common goals and problems.

Britain has long been a particularly close ally of the US, especially during the '80s when British Prime Minister Margaret Thatcher and US President Ronald Reagan forged a close friendship – one which lead some dissenters to dismiss the UK as America's 51st state. Not all European countries are as cosy with the US: France's former president, Jacques Chirac, was especially critical of America's conduct in Iraq, although most Europeans (including France) would rather work with the US than against it.

RELIGION

Brash and commercialised, at first glance America appears to be a Godless society, although religion is surprisingly significant. Some 60 per cent of the population say that religion plays a 'very important' role in their lives, while eight out of ten claim to have specific religious beliefs.

There are some 80 separate religions in the US with over 60,000 followers. Christianity is by far the most popular, from happy-clappy, born-again believers to strict fundamentalists. According to the CIA World Factbook, around 50 per cent of Americans are Protestant, 25 per cent Roman Catholic and almost 2 per cent Mormons (officially the Church of Jesus Christ of Latter-Day Saints). Other Christian beliefs account for 1.5 per cent, 1.7 per cent follows the Jewish faith, 0.7 per cent are Buddhists and a surprisingly small 0.6 per cent are Muslims. Of the remainder, just over

12 per cent aren't affiliated with any particular faith, and 4 per cent have no religion.

> **'When fascism comes to America, it will be wrapped in the flag and carrying the cross.'**
> Sinclair Lewis (American writer & wit)

The First Amendment of the US Constitution guarantees everyone the right to freedom of religion. The government remains neutral on the subject, neither rejecting nor endorsing any religion. It isn't taught in schools, unless the school promotes and advertises itself as a religious school. However, at the same time, there's easy access to information about every religion. Satellite and cable TV has enabled certain faiths to be beamed directly into the home, and while this has led to a greater understanding and tolerance of other faiths, in general terms, many people still believe that the only God who matters is male, white and indisputably American.

Many individuals want to be seen to be attending church, even if they don't go. The number of citizens who regularly attend church services is given as about 40 per cent in a number of polls, yet church statistics reveal that the true figure is half that amount.

MILITARY SERVICE

There's no draft in the US. However, all male permanent residents and US citizens aged 18 to 25 must register for military service with their local board of the Selective Service System or online (💻 www.sss.gov). Residents must register within 30 days of their 18th birthday. All male immigrants are required to register within six months of entering the US, but may be exempted if they've served at least one year in the armed forces of another country. Failure to register can result in a fine of up to $25,000 and/or a five-year prison sentence.

PETS

Pet ownership in the US is at an all-time high. Two-thirds of American households have at least one pet, according to a survey by the American Pet Products Manufacturers' Association, and 45 per cent of pet owners have more than one pet. If you come from a country where animals generally live outside or where they're considered unclean, you may well find the attitude of American pet-lovers perverse. Cats and dogs are considered part of the family, and usually live in the house, sleep on their owners' beds, eat gourmet foods and even wear designer clothes. In more extreme cases, pampered pets are treated to spa trips, birthday parties and can even get 'married' to other pampered pets or have formal burials. Unsurprisingly, in 2007 the US Pet industry was worth around $41bn.

If you want to take a pet to the US, it will be subjected to a number of health, customs and quarantine regulations, and will need to be vaccinated, have a health certificate and, in some states, a licence. Rabies is a problem is some parts of the US. Depending on where you live, you may need to keep a dog on a leash at all times in public places, and you must clear up after it. Rented accommodation often forbids the keeping of pets, therefore you should check before you sign a lease.

TIME DIFFERENCE

The sheer size of the US means that someone can sitting down to lunch in

New York while his Californian cousin is eating breakfast. The 48 contiguous states are divided into four time zones, while Alaska and Hawaii are even further behind the clock. A few states, such as Tennessee, straddle two time zones, with the clock changing at the county line. The main time zones are:

- Eastern Standard Time (EST) – cities include New York, Washington DC and Miami. This region is five hours behind Greenwich Mean Time (GMT) or Coordinated Universal Time (UTC) as it's now more correctly known.

- Central Standard Time (CST) – includes Chicago and New Orleans. This region is six hours behind GMT.

- Mountain Standard Time (MST) – includes Denver and Phoenix. This region is seven hours behind GMT.

- Pacific Standard Time (PST) – includes San Francisco, Los Angeles and Las Vegas. This region is eight hours behind GMT.

- Alaskan Standard Time (AKST) – this state is nine hours behind GMT.

- Hawaii Standard Time (HST) – the Hawaiian Islands are ten hours behind GMT.

During winter, clocks are altered to account for the seasonal hours of daylight, which is referred to as Daylight Saving Time (DST). This begins at 2am local time on the first Sunday in November, and ends at 2am on the second Sunday in March. Arizona and Hawaii don't observe Daylight Saving Time.

To remember whether the clock goes forward or back, the phrase 'spring forward, fall back' may help.

TIPPING

Americans are known to be big tippers, and American workers expect big tips. If this seems greedy, remember that the service industry pays very low wages, and many workers depend on their tips (gratuities) to survive. That said, some people take tipping to ludicrous extremes, and in America you may well feel pressurised to pay for service which doesn't warrant your gratitude. **Americans tip everyone!**

As a rough guide, you should tip the following:

- **In a restaurant** – 15 to 20 per cent, depending on the quality of the establishment. If it's an upmarket restaurant where it's difficult to get a table, it's wise slip the *maitre d'hotel* at least $10 if you want to visit again.

- **In a bar** – 15 to 20 per cent at the end of the evening, although you may get better service if you leave money on the bar **before** you start drinking.

- **At the hairdressers or barbers** – 10 to 20 per cent, and remember to give at least $1 to everyone who has even touched your hair.

- **For having your luggage carried by an airport or hotel porter** – $1 per bag.

- **To the chambermaid who cleans your room** – $1 to $1.50 a day.

> If you live in an apartment, keep the doorman or superintendent sweet by tipping $1 to $5 for extra services, such as carrying bags. The same applies to the block's handyman, otherwise you won't find him very handy.

- **To nightclub doormen and bouncers** – from $1 to $10, assuming you want to guarantee they'll let you in again.

- **Hotel concierge** – $2 to $10, depending on how much of his time you've taken up, and how helpful he has been.

- **To toilet and cloakroom attendants** – 50 cents to $1.

- **To the valet who parks your car** – up to $5, depending on the establishment and the value of your car.

- **Delivery people** – at least $1, although they'll expect more when delivering a heavy item of furniture.

- **Taxi drivers** – 15 per cent, unless they're exceptionally rude and you're exceptionally brave.

Petrol station attendants and cinema ushers are among the few American workers who don't expect a tip.

TOILETS

Americans dislike the term 'toilet'. In polite society, they use euphemisms such as restroom, bathroom or even comfort station. In someone's house, you should always ask if you can use the bathroom. Out and about, you'll need the men's or ladies' room. Further down the social ladder, you may hear people say 'I have to go potty' or 'I'm going to the can'. Can and john are popular US slang for toilet, but are not words you should use in public.

Public toilets are always free, although they can be scarce and are often difficult to find (shopping malls always have restrooms, as do major stores). Even signs can be coy. Always double-check that you're entering the right one, as the difference between men's and women's toilets isn't always clear.

Public buildings have adequate toilets which are usually maintained to a reasonable standard. Restaurants and stores have 'restrooms'. You'd have to be caught very short to use one at a railway or bus station, as they're notorious for being less than hygienic. Inner-city public toilets after dark are not the safest places to be.

APPENDICES

In the USA

L isted below are the contact details for the embassies and high commissions (Commonwealth countries) of the main English-speaking countries in The US. A full list of embassies and consulates in America is available from the US Department of State's website (🖳 www.state.gov/misc/list/index. htm). A list is also available at the Electronic Embassy website (🖳 www. embassy.org).

Australia: Australian Embassy, 1601 Massachusetts Ave, NW, Washington DC 20036, USA (☎ 202-797 3000, 🖳 www.usa.embassy.gov.au).

Canada: The Embassy of Canada, 501 Pennsylvania Ave, NW, Washington DC 20001, USA (☎ 202-682 1740, 🖳 www.canadianembassy.org).

Ireland: Embassy of Ireland, 2234 Massachusetts Ave, NW, Washington DC 20008, USA (☎ 202-462 3939, 🖳 www.embassyofireland.org).

New Zealand: Embassy of New Zealand, 37 Observatory Circle, NW, Washington DC 20008, USA (☎ 202-328 4800, 🖳 www.nzembassy.com).

South Africa: Embassy of the Republic of South Africa, 3051 Massachusetts Ave, NW, Washington DC 20008, USA (☎ 202-232 4400, 🖳 www.saembassy.org).

United Kingdom: The British Embassy, 3100 Massachusetts Ave, NW, Washington DC 20008, USA (☎ 202-558 6500, 🖳 www.britainusa.com).

Abroad

L isted below are contact details for America's embassies in the main English-speaking countries. A comprehensive list of US embassies and consulates worldwide can be found at the US Department of State website (⌨ www.usembassy.gov).

Australia: The American Embassy, Moonah Place, Yarralumla, Canberra ACT 2600, Australia (☎ 2-6214 5600, ⌨ www.canberra.usembassy.gov).

Canada: The Embassy of the United States of America, PO Box 866, Station B, Ottawa, Ontario K1P 5T1, Canada (☎ 613-688 5335, ⌨ www.canada. usembassy.gov).

Ireland: U.S. Embassy Dublin, 42 Elgin Road, Ballsbridge, Dublin 4, Republic of Ireland (☎ 1-668 8777, ⌨ www.dublin.usembassy.gov).

New Zealand: Embassy of the United States of America, P O Box 1190, Wellington, New Zealand (☎ 4-462 6000, ⌨ www.newzealand.usembassy. gov).

South Africa: US Embassy, PO Box 9536, Pretoria 0001, South Africa (☎ 12-431 4000, ⌨ www.southafrica.usembassy.gov).

United Kingdom: US Embassy, 24 Grosvenor Square, London W1A 1AE, United Kingdom (☎ 20-7499 9000, ⌨ http://london.usembassy.gov).

> **The business hours of embassies vary and they close on their own country's holidays as well as on American public holidays. Always telephone to confirm opening hours before visiting.**

APPENDIX B: FURTHER READING

There are numerous publications written about America. The following is just a brief selection. Books are listed under subject in alphabetical order, with the title followed by the author's name and the publisher (in brackets).

Business

American Business Values, A Global Perspective, Gerald F Cavanagh (Prentice Hall)

Business Protocol: Contemporary American Practice, David Robinson (Atomic Dog)

Business Travel Guide to United States of America: East Coast (Mercury Business Books)

Speak Business English like an American: Learn the Idioms and Expressions You Need to Succeed on the Job!, Amy Gillett (Language Success PR)

Culture

101 American Customs: Understanding Language and Culture through Common Practices, Harry Collis & Joe Kohl (McGraw-Hill)

American Ways: A Guide for Foreigners in the United States, Gary Althen (Intercultural Press)

American Ways: An Introduction to American Culture, Maryanne Kearny Datesman, JoAnn Crandall & Edward N Kearny (Pearson Education)

Brit-think, Ameri-think: A Transatlantic Survival Guide, Jane Walmsley (Penguin)

Made in America, From Levis to Barbie to Google, Nick Freeth (Motor Books)

Oxford Guide to British and American Culture (Oxford University Press)

Xenophobe's Guide to the Americans, Stephanie Faul (Oval Books)

History

A History of the American People, Paul Johnson (Weidenfeld & Nicolson)

American Colonies: The Settling of North America, Alan Taylor (Penguin)

A People's History of the United States: 1492 – Present, Howard Zinn (Harper Perennial)

Bury My Heart at Wounded Knee: An Indian History of the American West, Dee Brown (Vintage)

Letter from America, Alistair Cooke (Penguin)

The American Civil War, Stephen D Engle, Gary W Gallagher, Joseph T Glatthaar & Robert Krick (Osprey)

The American Future: A History, Simon Schama (Bodley Head)

The Limits of Liberty: American History 1607-1992, Maldwyn A Jones (Oxford University Press)

The Penguin History of the United States of America, Hugh Brogan (Penguin)

Language

American-English, English-American: A Two-way Glossary of Words in Daily Use on Both Sides of the Atlantic, Anthea Bickerton (Abson Books London)

Bum Bags and Fanny Packs: A British-American American-British Dictionary, Jeremy Smith (Carroll & Graf)

Divided by a Common Language: A Guide to British and American English, Christopher Davies (Houghton Mifflin Company)

Made in America: An Informal History of the English Language in the United States, Bill Bryson (Black Swan)

Speak American, Dileri Borunda Johnston (Random House)

Webster's American English Dictionary, Merriam-Webster (Federal Street Press)

Literature

An American Dream, Norman Mailer (Harper Perennial)

Breakfast of Champions, Kurt Vonnegut (Vintage)

Gone with the Wind, Margaret Mitchell (Pan)

Invisible Man, Ralph Ellison (Essential Penguin)

To Kill a Mockingbird, Harper Lee (Arrow)

The Adventures of Huckleberry Finn, Mark Twain (Penguin Classics)

The Grapes of Wrath, John Steinbeck (Penguin Classics)

The Great Gatsby, F Scott Fitzgerald (Penguin Modern Classics)

The Red Badge of Courage, Stephen Crane (Wordsworth Classics)

The Sound and the Fury, William Faulkner (Vintage Classics)

Uncle Tom's Cabin, Harriet Beecher Stowe (Wordsworth Classics)

Living & Working in America

Buying a Home in America, Graeme Chesters (Survival Books)

Buying or Renting a Home in New York, Graeme Chesters and Bev Laflamme (Survival Books)

Immigration Made Simple, Barbara Brooks Kimmel & Alan M Lubiner (Next Decade)

Living & Working in America, David Hampshire (Survival Books)

US Immigration Made Easy, G Scott Thomas (Prometheus Books)

Tourist Guides

Discover America (Reader's Digest)

Lonely Planet USA (Lonely Planet Country Guide)

National Parks – The Family Guide: A Complete Family Travel Guide to All America's National Parks, Monuments, Memorials, Battlefields, Seashores, Dave Robertson & June Francis (On Site)

The Comprehensive Guide to Train Travel in North America, Jack Swanson & Jeff Karsh (Rail Ventures)

The Rough Guide to USA (Rough Guides)

Unauthorized America: A Travel Guide to the Places the Chamber of Commerce Won't Tell You About, Vince Staten (Harper Perennial)

United States of America (Berlitz Pocket Travel Guides)

USA (Eyewitness Travel Guides)

Where to Stay in the United States of America (Frommer's Family Travel Guides)

Wild West: A Traveler's Guide, Michael McCoy (Globe Pequot Press)

Travel Literature

A Walk in the Woods: Rediscovering America on the Appalachian Trail, Bill Bryson (Black Swan)

Blue Highways: A Journey into America, William Least Heat-Moon (Fawcett)

Drive thru America, Sean Condon (Lonely Planet Journeys)

Notes from a Big Country, Bill Bryson (Black Swan)

On the Road, Jack Kerouac (Penguin Modern Classics)

River Horse: The Logbook of a Boat across America, William Least Heat-Moon (Houghton Mifflin)

Stephen Fry in America, Stephen Fry (Harper Collins)

The Lost Continent: Travels in Small-Town America, Bill Bryson, (Abacus)

Travels with Charley: In Search of America, John Steinbeck (Penguin)

Miscellaneous

American Mania: When More is Not Enough, Peter Whybrow (Norton)

American Popular Music: From Minstrelsy to MTV, Lawrence Starr & Christopher Waterman (OUP USA)

Beyond Light: American Landscapes, Robert Werling (Merrell)

Eccentric America: The Bradt Guide to All That's Weird and Wacky in the USA, Jan Friedman (Bradt Travel Guide)

Fast Food Nation: What the All-American Meal is Doing to the World, Eric Schlosser (Penguin)

Get Up and Go: The History of American Road Travel, Sylvia Whitman (Lerner)

Hollywood Babylon, Kenneth Anger (Bantam Doubleday Dell)

Only in America, Matt Frei (Fourth Estate)

The American Diner Cookbook: More Than 450 Recipes and Nostalgia Galore, Linda Everett & Elizabeth McKeon (Cumberland House)

The Everything American Presidents Book: All You Need to Know about the Leaders Who Shaped U.S. History, Martin Kelly and Melissa Kelly (Adams Media Corporation)

The Oxford Companion to American Food and Drink, Andrew F. Smith (OUP USA)

The Wind is My Mother: The Life and Teachings of a Native American Shaman, Bear Heart and Molly Larkin (Berkley Publishing)

USA Cookbook, Sheila Lukins (Workman)

What's Cooking? The History of American Food, Sylvia Whitman (Lerner)

APPENDIX C: USEFUL WEBSITES

The following pages contain just a few of the thousands of websites dedicated to America and the Americans.

Business

Better Business Bureaux (💻 www.bbb.org) – Links to local better business bureaux around the US.

Employment Law (💻 www.dol.gov/compliance/guide) – Useful guide from the US Department of Labor.

National Association of Self-Employed (💻 www.nase.org) – Excellent information source for those who want to work for themselves.

US Chambers of Commerce (💻 www.uschamber.com) – Provides links to each state and city's chamber of commerce

Women Connect (💻 www.uswc.org) – An online networking website with connections to women's organisations across the US.

Culture & Entertainment

American Family Traditions (💻 www.americanfamilytraditions.com) – Cheesy, Waltons-style website; heavy on promoting family values but with some interesting cultural information.

American Jokes & Humour (💻 www.thejokes.co.uk/american-humor.php) – A broad selection of the type of jokes which allegedly make Americans laugh.

Culture & Ethnic Groups (💻 www.usa.gov/citizen/topics/history_culture. shtml) – Part of the vast www.usa.com website, with sections devoted to cultures and ethnic groups including African Americans and Hispanics.

Festivals & Events (💻 www.2camels.com/festivals/usa.php) – Articles and reports on the more unusual US festivals.

Native American Culture (💻 www.greatdreams.com/native.htm) – Huge resource with many links providing information about indigenous Americans, their languages and beliefs and culture, from Cherokee to Inuit.

Movie Tickets (💻 www.movietickets.com) – Lets you purchase tickets for the latest films in advance.

Popular Culture (⌨ www.wsu.edu/~amerstu/pop) – Washington State University provides links to sites on various forms of popular culture, including music, film, television, advertising, sports, fashion, toys, magazines and comic books.

Theatre (⌨ www.telecharge.com) – Online box office with theatre news, ticket prices and a facility for booking tickets across the US.

Ticket Master (⌨ www.ticketmaster.com) – Use this website to locate and purchase tickets for concerts, sports, arts, theatre and many other events.

Education

High Schools (⌨ www.high-schools.com) – Lists every high school in the US, both private and public, with contact details.

National Center for Education Statistics (⌨ www.nces.ed.gov) – Statistical information on the American education system, presented in many different ways.

US Department of Education (⌨ www.ed.gov) – The official website of the US Department of Education, with tips for parents and students.

US Study Guide (⌨ www.usastudyguide.com) – An international guide to education and study in the US, including schools, colleges, universities and even cooking schools

Government & Immigration

Federal Trade Commission (⌨ www.ftc.gov) – The premier consumer protection website, with information covering every possible issue you might encounter, from unhelpful store assistants to identity fraud.

Green Card Lottery (⌨ www.dvlottery.state.gov) – Take your chance in the US Diversity Lottery online.

Immigration Support (⌨ www.usimmigrationsupport.org) – This independent agency's website contains exhaustive details about visas, green cards, social security and citizenship, as well as downloadable instructions and application forms.

Internal Revenue Service (⌨ www.irs.gov) – Everything you ever wanted to know about US taxes.

US Census Bureau (⌨ www.census.gov) – Government statistics on every aspect of life in the US; the next census is not until 2010 but many of the 2001 stats have been updated.

US Citizen and Immigration Services (⌨ www.uscis.gov) – The official line on visas, green cards, work permits and more

US Department of Health & Human Rights (💻 www.hhs.gov/ocr/index.html) – State information on civil rights, health information privacy and health service users' rights.

US Department of State (💻 www.state.gov) – News on all aspects of government, including embassies and consulates, travel, education, careers, current issues and more.

US Government (💻 www.usa.gov) – Everything from taxes to healthcare is included on the official website of the US government.

US Social Security Administration (💻 www.ssa.gov) – This government website includes contact details and application forms, and covers every aspect of social security in the US.

The White House (💻 www.whitehouse.gov) – The official site of the US President's residence, providing information on current US policies and proposals, proclamations and press briefings.

Language

American-British and British-American Dictionaries (💻 www.travelfurther.net/dictionaries) – Discover the differences between the American and British uses of the English language, in a fun way.

American English A-Z (💻 www.americanaccent.com) – Guide to American pronunciation with audio tips.

American Slang (💻 www.spraakservice.net/slangportal/american.htm) – Surf for 57 varieties of slang, including local argot from Boston to New Orleans and from gangland slang to police terminology.

America Study Guide (💻 www.americastudyguide.com/dir/esl/index) – State-by-state directory of English as a Second Language (ESL) programs across the US.

English Language Schools (💻 www.englishinusa.com) – Comprehensive directory of American English language schools and internet tutoring programs.

Learn American English Online (💻 www.learnamericanenglishonline.com) – Useful resource for speakers of languages other than English.

Slang (💻 www.englishdaily626.com/slang.php) – A dictionary of commonly used American slang and sayings.

Spelling (💻 www.2.gsu.edu/~wwwesl/egw/jones/differences.htm) A handy set of tables illustrating the basic differences between English and American spelling.

Living & Working

Au Pairs (🖳 www.aupairusa.org) – Everything the would-be au pair might need to know.

Bureau of Labour Statistics (🖳 www.bls.gov) – All the facts and figures about employment (and unemployment), inflation, pay and benefits, including salaries for over 800 occupations and over 400 industries.

Blue Collar Jobs (🖳 www.bluecollarjobs.com) – A resource for finding skilled and unskilled jobs in the US.

Career Builder (🖳 www.careerbuilder.com) – Vacancies in a variety of sectors, plus advice on careers and a place to upload your CV.

Consumer Reports (🖳 www.consumerreports.org/cro/index.htm) – Product reviews, consumer rights and more.

Find A Lawyer (🖳 www.lawyers.com) – Search facility for legal eagles in every state.

Franchise Finder (🖳 www.ftc.gov) – A resource to check out all the franchise opportunities available in the US.

HomeGain (🖳 www.homegain.com) – Find a real estate agent, obtain a valuation and search homes for sale online.

Insurance Information Institute (🖳 www.iii.org) – Independent advice on insuring your home, car and health.

My Money (🖳 www.mymoney.gov) – The US government's website dedicated to teaching Americans the basics about financial education. Contains important information from 20 federal agencies.

US Law (🖳 www.uslaw.com) – Collection of legal articles on all points of law, plus a find-a-lawyer resource and the chance to put your questions to a legal team.

Media

Google News (🖳 www.news.google.com) – Constantly updated national and international news items from the world's favourite search engine.

National Climatic Data Center (🖳 www.ncdc.noaa.gov) – Links to every kind of weather forecast across the 50 states.

Radio Locator (🖳 www.radio-locator.com) – Search US stations by zip code or call letters or find an internet feed from your favourite radio channel.

TV Guide (🖳 www.tvguide.com) – Listings for all the US television channels, plus articles, previews, DVD picks and more.

USA Today (🖥 www.usatoday.com) – An online version of the nation's most popular daily newspaper.

World Newspapers (🖥 www.newspapers24.com) – Catch up with news from your hometown with this website linking to over 12,000 newspapers around the globe.

Travel & Tourism

American Automobile Association (🖥 www.aaa.com) – The umbrella website for America's automobile clubs with tips and advice for drivers and travellers.

Amtrack (🖥 www.amtrak.com) – Fares, routes and timetables for train travel across the US with America's national railway company.

Cars.com (🖥 www.cars.com) – Online dealer for trade and private care sales, plus research into different models and shopping advice.

Department of Motor Vehicles (🖥 www.dmv.org) – Not an official government site but one which gives all the information you need to know about driving legally in the US, presented state by state.

Greyhound (🖥 www.greyhound.com) – All the information on timetables and fares on the numerous routes of America's famous long-distance bus service.

Travel Channel (🖥 www.travelchannel.com) – The website of the television channel of the same name.

US Department of Transport (🖥 www.dot.gov) – The official transportation website, giving details on travel documentation requirements, the latest security measures, car safety, legislation, and much more.

USA Tourist (🖥 www.usatourist.com) – Tips, links, photos, maps, events and lists, designed to make your journey easier, cheaper and trouble free.

World Travel Guide (🖥 www.wtgonline.com) – General website for travellers and expatriates with a wealth of information on destinations in America.

Miscellaneous

AARP (🖥 www.aarp.org) – The website of the American Association of Retired Persons contains useful information for retirees, baby boomers and older (and not so old) US residents, with tips on health, money and much more.

American Pet Association (🖥 www.apapets.org) – Fun facts and bizarre stats about America's relationship with its four-legged friends.

Bloomingdales (🖥 www.bloomingdales.com) – Online link to one of the world's best department stores.

Dating Diversions (🖥 www.datingdiversions.com) – Humorous site with tips on the dating behaviour of prospective partners from Connecticut to California.

ESPN: Sports (🖥 www.espn.go.com) – All the sports news across the US from gridiron to basketball.

Foodies (🖥 www.foodies.com) – Celebrating American cuisine with recipes, tips and more.

Junk Food Mecca (🖥 www.junkfoodmecca.com) – Feast on links to the websites of every purveyor of junk food across the 50 states.

Life in the USA (🖥 www.lifeintheusa.com) – The complete web guide to American life for immigrants and Americans, written by Americans, with subjects ranging from sympathy cards to soccer mums.

Mall of America (🖥 www.mallofamerica.com) – Visit the biggest shopping mall in the US from comfort of your armchair.

Smithsonian American Art Museum (🖥 http://americanart.si.edu/index3.cfm) – An online ticket to view the world's largest art collection.

Symbols of the United States (🖥 http://govdocs.evergreen.edu/symbols.html) – A resource with links to sites covering America's most enduring symbols, including the flag, anthem and others. Also lists the nicknames, flags, birds and flowers adopted by each state.

The USA Online (🖥 www.theusaonline.com) – Comprehensive interactive website containing details on just about every aspect of American life including the 50 states, national parks, US history, the presidents, society, population and the economy.

Tightwad Central (🖥 www.tightwad.com) – Credit crunch-friendly website dedicated to saving you cash, full of frugal tips and freebies.

US Geological Survey (🖥 http://earthquake.usgs.gov/eqcenter/eqarchives) – The latest earthquake statistics; worth a read before you decide where to put down roots.

World Health Organisation (🖥 www.who.int/countries/usa/en) – Direct link to health advice and statistics across the US.

Seattle, WA

Ouray Ice Park, Colorado

APPENDIX D: AMERICAN IDIOMS

There are a number of words in American English which are different from English in the UK and elsewhere. The following list is of words and phrases that you're likely to hear, but is by no means comprehensive.

American	British
Acclimate	Acclimatise
All-purpose flour	Plain flour
Aluminum	Aluminium
Armoire	Wardrobe
Baking soda	Bicarbonate of soda
Baseboard	Skirting board
Bathroom	Toilet
Bill (money)	Banknote
Billfold	Purse or wallet
Bouillon cube	Stock cube
Bowling	Ten pin bowling
Broil (cooking term)	Grill
Burlap	Hessian
Busboy	Waiter
Caboose (train)	Guard's van
Call collect (phone)	Reverse the charges
Caramel	Toffee
Check (dining)	Bill
Checkers	Draughts
Checking account (banking)	Current account
Cheesecloth	Muslin
Chew out	Tell off, reprimand
Chips	Crisps
Cleats (boots)	Studs
Comforter	Duvet
Confectioner's sugar	Icing sugar
Cookie	Biscuit
Cop	Police
Corn	Maize or sweetcorn
Cornstarch	Cornflour
Cot	Camp bed
Cotton candy	Candy floss
Crosswalk	Zebra crossing

Cuffs (trousers)	Turn-ups
Cursive writing	Joined up writing
Cut in line	Jump the queue
Decorating tip	Icing nozzle
Denatured alcohol	Methylated spirit
Diaper	Nappy
Directory assistance	Directory inquiries
Divided highway	Dual carriageway
Drapes	Curtains
Dry goods store	Draper's shop
Dumpster	Skip
Duplex	Semi-detached house
Dust ruffle	Valance
Eggplant	Aubergine
Elevator	Lift
Endive	Chicory
Fall	Autumn
Fanny (slang)	Buttocks
Far lane (driving)	Offside (passing) lane
Faucet	Tap
Fava bean	Broad bean
Field (sport)	Pitch
Field hockey	Hockey
First floor	Ground floor
Fish stick	Fish finger
Flashlight	Torch
Football	American football
Formula	Baby milk
Freeway	Motorway
Fries (potato)	Chips
Frosting	Icing
Garters	Suspenders
Gas	Petrol
Given name	Christian name
Glider	Garden seat
Grab bag	Lucky dip
Grade (school)	Form
Hardware seller	Ironmonger
Heavy cream	Double cream
Hockey	Ice hockey
Hood (car)	Bonnet
Jumper	Pinafore dress
Kitty corner	Diagonally opposite

Knock up	Get pregnant
Latex paint	Emulsion
Mail slot	Letter box
Mezzanine (theatre)	Dress circle
Mineral oil	Liquid paraffin
Muffler	Exhaust silencer
Nightstick	Truncheon
Nipple (baby's bottle)	Teat
Orchestra (theatre)	Stalls
Pacifier	Dummy
Parakeet	Budgerigar
Parentheses	Brackets
Parka	Anorak
Pants	Trousers
Panties	Knickers
Poncho	Cagoule
Popsicle	Ice lolly
Produce stand	Greengrocer
Pushpin	Drawing pin
Realtor	Estate agent
Relish	Pickle
Roast (meat)	Joint
Roadster	Convertible
Rubber	Condom
Rutabaga (vegetable)	Swede
Saltine	Cream cracker
Scallion/Green onion	Spring onion
Sedan car	Saloon car
Sheers	Net curtains
Sidewalk	Pavement
Sneakers	Plimsolls
Snow peas	Mangetout
Soccer	Association football
Station wagon	Estate car
Stick shift	Manual gearbox
Stroller	Baby buggy or pushchair
Suspenders	Braces
Tag	Label
Tennis shoe	Trainer
Tic-tac-toe (game)	Noughts and crosses
Transmission	Gearbox
Trunk (car)	Boot
Turn signal (car)	Indicator

Turtle neck (clothes)	Polo neck
Undershirt	Vest
Vest	Waistcoat
Vet	Ex-serviceman
Walker	Zimmer frame
Walking shoe	Lace-up shoe
Wash up	Wash hands/face
Wrench	Spanner
Zucchini	Courgette

The two languages cross over in such a way that there are also a number of words and terms which make sense in English but will leave Americans confused. For example:

British	**American**
Book (a ticket or seat)	Reserve
Bangers	Sausages
Barmy	Crazy
Bloke	Man
Car park	Parking lot
Chock a block	Crowded
Cotton wool ball	Cotton ball
Cot	Crib (this is also slang for someone's home)
Court shoes	Pumps
Drawing pin	Thumb tack
Flatmate	Roommate
Fortnight	Two weeks
Fringe	Bangs
Hire	Rent
Hoover	Vacuum cleaner
Jiffy	Short period of time
Kerb	Curb
Off-licence	Liquor store
Pips	Seeds
Puncture	Flat (tyre)
Sellotape	Scotch tape
Serviette	Napkin
Whip round (collection)	Passing the hat
Zed	Z (zee)

American Sayings/Slang

There are enough sayings and slang phrases in the American language to fill a book, but here are some of the more commonly used, along with what they actually mean.

- **antsy** – restless, e.g. She's been real antsy since she got back from her vacation.

- **armpit** – an undesirable place, e.g. Don't go to that bar, it's a real armpit.

- **Average Joe** – a normal or regular person. Bruce may be famous but he acts like your average Joe.

- **awesome** – great, e.g. What an awesome view.

- **ball park figure** – a rough estimate, e.g. Could you give me a ball park figure for fixing my car?

- **beat** – exhausted, e.g. After working two jobs, I'm really beat.

- **big guns** – powerful people, e.g. The boss brought two big guns to the meeting.

- **bomb** – awful/really bad, e.g. His new movie bombed at the box office. This shouldn't be confused with 'Da Bomb' (see below).

- **bummed** – depressed, e.g. I was really bummed after I read that letter. Also, 'a bummer' is a bad experience.

- **cheesy** – cheap and tacky, e.g. That's a cheesy looking suit. It can also mean hackneyed or old hat, as in: The singer at the club was really cheesy.

- **chow down** – tuck in or eat up, e.g. I'm hungry so let's chow down.

- **cold fish** – dull/boring person or (more often) someone who doesn't show their feelings, e.g. She's going out with a cold fish.

- **couch potato** – lazy person, someone who watches a lot of TV e.g. At weekends my husband turns into a coach potato.

- **crash** – sleep, e.g. Is it Ok if I crash at your apartment tonight?

- **crib** – home, e.g. When are you going to show me around your crib?

- **croak** – die, e.g. Grandad finally croaked at the age of 97.

- **Da Bomb** – the best, e.g. Did you try the new pizza place? The food's Da Bomb.

- **damage** – cost or expense, e.g. Ask for the bill so we know what the damage is?

- **dork** – dull or stupid person, e.g. Hal only got 30 out of 100 in his test; he's a real dork.

- **downer** – sad, e.g. Failing my driver's test was a real downer.

- **fat cat** – person with great wealth and power, e.g. the credit crunch is the fault of the fat cat bankers.

- **flip out** – lose control with anger or excitement, e.g. He flipped when I told him I'd damaged his car.

- **gourd** – head, e.g. If you want to learn then use your gourd.

- **have a prayer** – have a realistic chance e.g. He doesn't have a prayer of getting into college.

- **in someone's hair** – constantly annoy someone, e.g. The boss is always in my hair.

- **jerk someone around** – waste someone's time, e.g. They didn't want to buy the house, they were just jerking us around.

- **klutz** – clumsy person, e.g. Keep Ann out of the kitchen, she's a total klutz. Klutz has its roots in the Jewish language, as does a lot of US slang, such as 'chutzpah' meaning nerve or cheek, and 'schmuck' (see below).

- **La La Land** – an unreal place or fantasy land, often used to describe Hollywood, e.g. She's living in La La Land if she thinks she's going to be an actress.

- **mellow out** – calm down and relax, e.g. You're so stressed, you need to mellow out.

- **mosey along** – walk slowly, e.g. Shall we just mosey along the river?

- **no brainer** – something that requires little or no brain power, e.g. If you use frozen pastry, making apple pie is a real no brainer.

- **nuke** – heat up in a microwave oven, e.g. Just nuke it for a couple of minutes and it's ready to eat.

- **psyched up** – mentally ready, e.g. The team is psyched up for Saturday's game.

- **put your John Hancock here** – sign, e.g. Here's the contract, just put your John Hancock on the dotted line.

- **rug rat** – toddler, e.g. Is it OK if we bring the rug rats to your house?

- **schmuck** – idiot, e.g. He locked himself out of his car, what a schmuck!

- **screw up** – make a mistake, e.g. If you screw up one more time, you're fired.

- **wheels** – personal transport, usually a car, e.g. I need some milk, can I borrow your wheels?

- **wuss** – weak person, e.g. Sally can't stand the sight of blood, she's such a wuss.

- **zone out** – lose concentration, e.g. I zoned out during the chemistry lecture.

lava flowing into the sea, Kilauea volcano, Hawaii

APPENDIX E: MAP OF STATES

The map opposite shows the 50 states which constitute the United States of America, listed in alphabetical order below (official abbreviations are shown in brackets). The District of Columbia (DC), the nation's capital and seat of government, is geographically situated in Maryland (MD).

Alabama (AL)	Montana (MT)
Alaska (AK)	Nebraska (NE)
Arizona (AZ)	Nevada (NV)
Arkansas (AR)	New Hampshire (NH)
California (CA)	New Jersey (NJ)
Colorado (CO)	New Mexico (NM)
Connecticut (CT)	New York (NY)
Delaware (DE)	North Carolina (NC)
Florida (FL)	North Dakota (ND)
Georgia (GA)	Ohio (OH)
Hawaiian Islands (HI)	Oklahoma (OK)
Idaho (ID)	Oregon (OR)
Illinois (IL)	Pennysylvania (PA)
Indiana (IN)	Rhode Island (RI)
Iowa (IA)	South Carolina (SC)
Kansas (KS)	South Dakota (SD)
Kentucky (KY)	Tennessee (TN)
Louisiana (LA)	Texas (TX)
Maine (ME)	Utah (UT)
Maryland (MD)	Vermont (VT)
Massachusetts (MA)	Virginia (VA)
Michigan (MI)	Washington (WA)
Minnesota (MN)	West Virginia (WV)
Mississippi (MS)	Wisconsin (WI)
Missouri (MO)	Wyoming (WY)

Golden Gate Bridge, San Francisco, CA

INDEX

A

Accommodation 68, 169
    Buying a home 70
    Rented property 68
Alcohol 182, 207
Americans at play 171
    Cafes, restaurants &
    diners 181
    Clubs 190
    Dress code 171
    Drinking 179
    Eating 173
    Family occasions 184
    Nightlife 183
    Popular culture 190
Americans at work 133
    Black economy 144
    Business etiquette 145
    Contracts 140
    Employing people 148
    Finding a job 135
    Permits &
    paperwork 134
    Starting or buying a
    business 140
    Trade unions 149
    Work ethic 133
    Working week 149
    Working women 144
Anthem 220
Appendices 233
    A: Embassies 233
    B: Further
    Reading 235
    C: Useful
    Websites 239
    D: American
    Idioms 247
    E: Map of
    America 254
Arts 194
Attitudes to foreigners 42
    Race relations 42
    State patriotism &
    civic pride 43

B

Baby showers &
christenings 184
Banking 90
    Choosing a bank 90
    US money 90
Bars 179
Birthdays 184
Black
    Economy 144
    Market 201
Body & sign language 124
    Gestures 124
    Personal space 126
Breaking the ice 97
    Community life 97
    Confrontation 111
    Dealing with
    officials 112
    Expat community 110
    Invitations 105
    Meeting people 101
    Respecting
    privacy 107
    Sexual attitudes 98
    Taboos 108

Bureaucracy 67
    Civil servants 68
    Getting round it 68
Buses & trains 165
Business
    Buying 141
        Gifts 145
        Hours 145
        Lunches 146
        Premises 143
        Visas 142
Business etiquette 145
    Business cards 145
    Dress 146
    Meetings 146
    Negotiating 147
    Regional
    differences 147
    Timekeeping 148
Buying a home 70
Buying or hiring (renting)
a car 71

C

Cafes, restaurants &
diners 181
    Alcohol 182
    American food 181
    Booking &
    seating 182
    Coffee culture 183
    Paying the bill &
    leaving a tip 182
    Slow service 182
Car hire (rental) 72
Car insurance 78

Change of culture 13, 22
  America is
  different 13
  Culture shock 15
  Multicultural
  society 23
  New life 23
Charity & good works 37
Childbirth 77
Children 40, 117, 127
Christmas & New Year 186
Cinema 195
Citizenship 67
Civil servants 68, 112
Class system 41
Climate 216
  Earthquakes 218
  Extreme weather 217
  Fires & floods 219
  Hurricanes 217
  Tornadoes 218
Clothes 208
  Children's 210
  Shoes 210
  Sizes 209
Clubs 190
Coffee culture 183
Collectables 210
  Yard & garage
  sales 210
Community life 97
  Community
  regulations 97
Confrontation 111
  Gun culture 112
Constitution 222
Contracts 140, 148
  Collective
  agreements 140
Conversation 108, 177
Cost of living 93

Council services 83
Crime 219
Culture shock 15
  Reducing the
  effects 19
  Stages of culture
  shock 16
Customer service 199
Cycling 168

D

Dating 103
Dealing with officials 112
  Civil servants 112
  Police 112
  Teachers 112
  Workers 112
Dialects & accents 122
Dining out 107
Discount
  Coupons 202
  Shops, warehouse
  clubs & factory
  outlets 201
Discrimination 139
DIY & gardening 194
Dress 146
  & Behaviour 110
Dress code 105, 171
  Home 172
  Places of worship 172
  Social occasions 172
  Work 172
Drinking 179
  Bars 179
  Smoking 180
Driving 155
  American roads 156
  Drivers 155
  Drive safe 159

Finding your way 159
  Licence 71
  Licence points
  system 158
  Motorcyclists &
  pedestrians 160
  Parking 161
  Parking illegally 161
  Petrol stations 162
  Road rules 157
  Roundabouts 160
  Traffic jams 161

E

Earthquakes 218
Eating 173
  Conversation 177
  Grace 177
  Meals 173
  Mobile phones 178
  Noises 178
  Seating
  arrangements 177
  Table manners 178
  Toasts 178
  When to start 177
Education 79
  American education
  system 81
  American or
  international
  school? 80
  in Bi-lingual
  regions 122
  University 82
Electricity 84
Emails & texts 130
Embassies &
consulates 233
Emergency
  Services 73

Treatment 75
Employment agencies 137
Engagement parties 185
English language 117
Executive government 222
Expat community 110
  Advantages &
  disadvantages 111
Extending invitations 107
Extreme weather 217

F

Families 22
  Values 36
Family occasions 184
  Baby showers &
  christenings 184
  Birthdays 184
  Christmas & new
  year 186
  Engagement
  parties 185
  First communion, bar
  mitzvah & other rites
  of passage 185
  Funerals 189
  Super bowl
  Sunday 187
  Thanksgiving 186
  Weddings 187
Festivals, fairs &
parades 190
Finding a job 135
  Discrimination 139
  Employment
  agencies 137
  Job hunting 137
  Job market 135
  Pensions &
  retirement 139
  Qualifications 136

Salary 138
Selection process 138
Speaking English 136
Fire & flood 219
Flag & anthem 220
Food & wine 206
  Alcohol 207
  Markets 204
  Meat & fish 206
  Milk & dairy 207
  Organic food 207
Forms of address 126
  Children 127
  Formal &
  informal 126
  Surnames & titles 127
Franchising 142
Friendship 102
Funerals 189
Further Reading 235

G

Gambling 191
Gas 84
Geography 215
Gestures 124
Getting started 65
  Accommodation 68
  Banking 90
  Bureaucracy 67
  Buying or hiring a
  car 71
  Cost of living 93
  Council services 83
  Education 79
  Emergency
  services 73
  Health services 74
  Immigration 65
  Insurance 78

Staying informed 87
  Taxes 92
  Utilities 84
Gifts 106
Government 222
  Constitution 222
  Executive 222
  Judiciary 223
  Legislative 223
  Political parties 224
  State & local 224
Greetings 128
  Good manners 128
Guarantees 213
Gun culture 112

H

Halloween 191
Health services 74
  Childbirth 77
  Emergency
  treatment 75
  Hospitals 76
  Insurance 78
  Medicines 76
  Plastic surgery 77
  Private healthcare 75
  Registering with a
  doctor 75
  State healthcare 74
  Visiting the doctor 75
History 28
Hitchhiking 168
Holidays 150
Homosexuals 101
Hospitals 76
Household insurance 79
Hurricanes 217

I

Icons 43
  Flora & fauna 59
  Food & drink 60
  People 43
  Places & structures 55
  Symbols 58
Immigration 65
  Citizenship 67
Income tax 92
Indigenous
  Languages 120
  People 28
Insurance 78
  Car 78
  Health 78
  Household 79
  Liability & legal 79
International relations 225
  Europe 226
  World 226
the Internet 87, 212
Invitations 105
  Dining out 107
  Dress code 105
  Extending
  invitations 107
  Gifts 106
  the Meal 106
  Parties 106
  Receiving 105

J/L

Job
  Hunting 137
  Market 135
Judiciary 223
Language barrier 115
  See also 'Other
  Languages' 119

American Idioms 247
Body & sign
language 124
English language 117
Forms of address 126
Greetings 128
Learning American
English 115
Other languages 119
Telephone, letters &
email 129
Learning American
English 115
  Children 117
  Know before
  you go 116
  Once in America 116
Leave 151
Legislative
government 223
Letters 129
Loans 142

M

Mail-order shopping 211
  Internet 212
  Television 211
Maps 6, 254
Marketing 144
Markets 204
  Food 204
  Others 205
Meals 173
Meat & fish 206
Medicines 76
Meeting people 101
  Dating 103
  Friendship 102
Meetings 146
Me, myself & I 36
Men 99

Military service 227
Milk & dairy foods 207
Minority languages 121
Mobile phones 178
Money 90
Moral majority 37
Motorcyclists &
pedestrians 160
Multicultural society 23
Museums & art galleries
197
Music & dance 196

N/O

Negotiating 147
Nightlife 183
On the move 155
  Accommodation 169
  Cycling 168
  Driving 155
  Hitchhiking 168
  Public transport 162
Opening hours 200
  Sundays & public
  holidays 200
Organic food 207
Other languages 119
  Chinese 120
  Dialects &
  accents 122
  Education in bi-lingual
  regions 122
  French 120
  Indigenous
  languages 120
  Minority
  languages 121
  'New' languages 121
  Other European
  languages 120
  Spanish 119

P

Parking 161
  Illegally 161
Parties 106
Patriotism & pride 36
Paying the bill & leaving a tip 182
Pensions & retirement 139
the People 35
  Charity & good works 37
  Eternal optimists & great achievers 38
  Family values 36
  Fears & insecurity 37
  Have a nice day! 38
  Me, myself & I 36
  Moral majority 37
  Patriotism & pride 36
Permits & paperwork 134
Personal space 126
Petrol stations 162
Pets 228
Planes 163
Plastic surgery 77
Police 112
Political parties 224
Popular culture 190
  Arts 194
  Bookings 194
  Cinema 195
  DIY & gardening 194
  Festivals, fairs & parades 190
  Gambling 191
  Halloween 191
  Museums & art galleries 197
  Music & dance 196
  Sport 192
  Street life 192

Theatre 196
Potted history 28
  20th century 31
  21st century 33
  From early settlers to the birth of the United States 29
  Indigenous people 28
  Slavery 29
the Press 89
Private healthcare 75
Public holidays 151
Public transport 162
  Buses & trains 165
  Planes 163
  Taxis 163

Q/R

Qualifications 136
Queuing 201
Race relations 42
Radio 89
Receiving invitations 105
Refuse collection 83
Religion 227
Rented property 68
Respecting privacy 107
Retail therapy 199
  Black market 201
  Clothes 208
  Collectables 210
  Customer service 199
  Food & wine 206
  Mail-order shopping 211
  Markets 204
  Opening hours 200
  Paying 205
  Queuing 201
  Returning goods 212
  Sales & discounts 201

Types of shop 203
Road rules 157
Role of men & women 99

S

Salary 138
Sales & discounts 201
  Discount coupons 202
  Discount shops, warehouse clubs & factory outlets 201
Sales tax 93
Sense of humour 38
Sexual attitudes 98
  Homosexuals 101
  Men 99
  Roles of men & women 99
  Women 100
Shoes 210
Slavery 29
Smoking 180
Social
  Occasions 172
  Security 92, 148
Sport 192
Starting or buying a business 140, 141
  Business premises 143
  Business visas 142
  Franchising 142
  Grants 142
  Loans 142
  Marketing 144
  Starting a business 141
State
  Healthcare 74
  & Local government 224

Patriotism & civic
pride 43
Staying informed 87
the Internet 87
the Press 89
Radio 89
Television 87
Street life 192
Surnames & titles 127

T

Table manners 178
Taboos 108
Conversation 108
Dress &
behaviour 110
Taxes 92, 149
Income tax 92
Sales tax 93
Social security 92
Tax fraud 93
Taxis 163
Teachers 112
Telephone, letters &
email 129
Email & texts 130
Internet 87
Letters 129
Telephone 129
Television 87
Shopping 211
Thanksgiving 186
Theatre 196
Time difference 228
Timekeeping 148
Tipping 229
Toasts 178
Toilets 230
Tornadoes 218
Trade unions 149

Joining a union 149
Traffic jams 161
Types of shop 203

U

University 82
Useful Websites 239
Utilities 84
Electricity 84
Gas 84
Supply problems 85
Telephone &
internet 86
Water 85

V/W/Y

Visiting the doctor 75
Water 85
Websites 239
Weddings 187
Who are the
Americans? 27
Attitudes to
foreigners 42
Children 40
Class system 41
Icons 43
People 35
Potted history 28
Sense of humour 38
Women 100
Workers 112
Work ethic 133
Working week 149
Holidays 150
Leave 151
Working women 144
Yard & garage sales 210

Survival Books

Essential reading for anyone planning to live, work, retire or buy a home abroad

Survival Books was established in 1987 and by the mid-'90s was the leading publisher of books for people planning to live, work, buy property or retire abroad.

From the outset, our philosophy has been to provide the most comprehensive and up-to-date information available. Our titles routinely contain up to twice as much information as other books and are updated frequently. All our books contain colour photographs and some are printed in two colours or full colour throughout. They also contain original cartoons, illustrations and maps.

Survival Books are written by people with first-hand experience of the countries and the people they describe, and therefore provide invaluable insights that cannot be obtained from official publications or websites, and information that is more reliable and objective than that provided by the majority of unofficial sites.

Survival Books are designed to be easy – and interesting – to read. They contain a comprehensive list of contents and index and extensive appendices, including useful addresses, further reading, useful websites and glossaries to help you obtain additional information as well as metric conversion tables and other useful reference material.

Our primary goal is to provide you with the essential information necessary for a trouble-free life or property purchase and to save you time, trouble and money.

We believe our books are the best – they are certainly the best-selling. But don't take our word for it – read what reviewers and readers have said about Survival Books at the front of this book.

Buying a Home Series

Buying a home abroad is not only a major financial transaction but also a potentially life-changing experience; it's therefore essential to get it right. Our Buying a Home guides are required reading for anyone planning to purchase property abroad and are packed with vital information to guide you through the property jungle and help you avoid disasters that can turn a dream home into a nightmare.

The purpose of our Buying a Home guides is to enable you to choose the most favourable location and the most appropriate property for your requirements, and to reduce your risk of making an expensive mistake by making informed decisions and calculated judgements rather than uneducated and hopeful guesses. Most importantly, they will help you save money and will repay your investment many times over.

Buying a Home guides are the most comprehensive and up-to-date source of information available about buying property abroad – whether you're seeking a detached house or an apartment, a holiday or a permanent home (or an investment property), these books will prove invaluable.

Living and Working Series

Our Living and Working guides are essential reading for anyone planning to spend a period abroad – whether it's an extended holiday or permanent migration – and are packed with priceless information designed to help you avoid costly mistakes and save both time and money.

Living and Working guides are the most comprehensive and up-to-date source of practical information available about everyday life abroad. They aren't, however, simply a catalogue of dry facts and figures, but are written in a highly readable style – entertaining, practical and occasionally humorous.

Our aim is to provide you with the comprehensive practical information necessary for a trouble-free life. You may have visited a country as a tourist, but living and working there is a different matter altogether; adjusting to a new environment and culture and making a home in any foreign country can be a traumatic and stressful experience. You need to adapt to new customs and traditions, discover the local way of doing things (such as finding a home, paying bills and obtaining insurance) and learn all over again how to overcome the everyday obstacles of life.

All these subjects and many, many more are covered in depth in our Living and Working guides – don't leave home without them.

The Expats' Best Friend!

Culture Wise Series

Our **Culture Wise** series of guides is essential reading for anyone who wants to understand how a country really 'works'. Whether you're planning to stay for a few days or a lifetime, these guides will help you quickly find your feet and settle into your new surroundings.

Culture Wise guides:

- Reduce the anxiety factor in adapting to a foreign culture
- Explain how to behave in everyday situations in order to avoid cultural and social gaffes
- Help you get along with your neighbours
- Make friends and establish lasting business relationships
- Enhance your understanding of a country and its people.

People often underestimate the extent of cultural isolation they can face abroad, particularly in a country with a different language. At first glance, many countries seem an 'easy' option, often with millions of visitors from all corners of the globe and well-established expatriate communities. But, sooner or later, newcomers find that most countries are indeed 'foreign' and many come unstuck as a result. **Culture Wise** guides will enable you to quickly adapt to the local way of life and feel at home, and – just as importantly – avoid the worst effects of culture shock.

Culture Wise – The Wise Way to Travel

The essential guides to Culture, Customs & Business Etiquette

Other Survival Books

The Best Places to Buy a Home in France/Spain: Unique guides to where to buy property in Spain and France, containing detailed regional profiles and market reports.

Buying, Selling and Letting Property: The best source of information about buying, selling and letting property in the UK.

Earning Money From Your French Home: Income from property in France, including short- and long-term letting.

Investing in Property Abroad: Everything you need to know and more about buying property abroad for investment and pleasure.

Life in the UK - Test & Study Guide: essential reading for anyone planning to take the 'Life in the UK' test in order to become a permanent resident (settled) in the UK.

Making a Living: Comprehensive guides to self-employment and starting a business in France and Spain.

Renovating & Maintaining Your French Home: The ultimate guide to renovating and maintaining your dream home in France.

Retiring in France/Spain: Everything a prospective retiree needs to know about the two most popular international retirement destinations.

Running Gîtes and B&Bs in France: An essential book for anyone planning to invest in a gîte or bed & breakfast business.

Rural Living in France: An invaluable book for anyone seekingthe 'good life', containing a wealth of practical information about all aspects of French country life.

Shooting Caterpillars in Spain: The hilarious and compelling story of two innocents abroad in the depths of Andalusia in thelate '80s.

**For a full list of our current titles, visit our website at
www.survivalbooks.net**

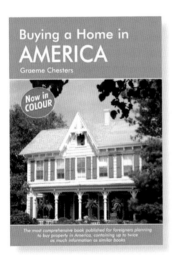

LIVING & WORKING IN
AMERICA

Living & Working in America is the most comprehensive and up-to-date source of practical information available about every-day life in the USA. It's packed with over 400 pages of important and useful data, designed to help you avoid costly mistakes and save both time and money.

Vital topics include:

♦ How to find a job with a good salary and conditions

♦ How to obtain a visa

♦ How to avoid and overcome problems on arrival

♦ How to find suitable accommodation

♦ How to make the most of post office and telephone services

♦ How to endure American TV and radio

♦ How to survive motoring in America

♦ How to obtain the best health treatment

♦ How to stretch your dollars further

♦ And much, much more.

This book is guaranteed to hasten your introduction to the American way of life. Regardless of whether you're planning to stay for a few weeks or indefinitely, *Living and Working in America* has been written for you!

Buy your copy today at www.survivalbooks.net

Survival Books – The Expats Best Friend

PHOTO

CREDITS

205 © Ginasanders, 207 © Perrush, 208 © Olgalis, 210 © Alexkalina, 211 © Micropix, 212 © Dayzeedayzee, 213 © Sebast1an, 214 © Cphoto, 219 © Alptraum, 220 © Hixnhix, 223 © Mistydawnphoto, 225 © Blakely, 226 © Kmitu, 229 © Slidezero, 231 © Dmitryp, 232 © Sergeibach, 246 © Mavrick, 253 © Garyhartz, 256 © Lbg, 268 © Awcnz62, 268 © Pxlar8, 268 © Erickn, 269 © Nsilcock, 269 © Elkeflorida

www.shutterstock.com

Pages 16 © EML, 19 © Chad McDermott, 45 © James Steidl, 55 © Kaspars Grinvalds, 63 © Victorian Traditions, 84 © Eray Haciosmanoglu, 89 © Stephen Firmender, 100 © EML, 105 © Luis Louro, 118 © gary718, 121 © Victoria Graca, 123 © EML, 125 © Supri Suharjoto, 126 © EML, 128 © Alexander Raths, 134 © Stanislav Perov, 143 © Chad McDermott, 148 © Tihis, 154 © Kenneth C. Zirkel, 160 © EML, 174 © Denis Miraniuk, 217 © Trutta, 238 © Artifan, 245 © Natalia Bratslavsky, 268 © Dmitry Pichugin, 269 © Yury Zaporozhchenko

Culture Wise Series

Current Titles:

America
Australia
Canada
England
France
Germany
India
Japan
New Zealand
Spain
Turkey

Coming soon:

Cyprus
Dubai
Greece
Holland
Hong Kong
Ireland
Italy
Switzerland

Culture Wise - The Wisest Way to Travel